Praise for *Becoming Magnetic*

'Erika Cramer's work challenges, empowers and inspires – equipping women to live fully, fiercely and without limits.'
Melissa Ambrosini, bestselling author

'Erika Cramer does not mince words. She lives her truth and is committed to women falling in love with themselves. I fell in love with her the first time we met.'
Kemi Nekvapil, bestselling author of *POWER*

'With *Becoming Magnetic*, Erika doesn't just inspire, she ignites a journey towards deep self-confidence, powerful self-acceptance and lasting transformation. She has taught me the value of self-mastery, which is so aligned with the power of self-reliance. Run, don't walk, to get this book and put it to work for you!'
Maha Abouelenein, author of *7 Rules of Self-Reliance*

'Erika Cramer is a woman who walks her talk. She teaches from first-hand experience, empowering her audience to back themselves in ways they don't yet know they are capable of. Her no-nonsense approach is delivered as both loving support and perpetual wisdom. Erika is a fabulous teacher, highly successful and definitely magnetic. This book will change lives.'
Bronnie Ware, author of international bestseller *The Top Five Regrets of the Dying*

'*Becoming Magnetic* is Erika Cramer at her best: no BS, just real talk on how to stop holding back and start showing up confident and magnetic. If you're ready to own it, this book's got the goods.'
Taki Moore, author and founder of Million Dollar Coach

'In *Becoming Magnetic*, Erika takes you on a journey of self-discovery, showing that authentic power lies in owning every facet of who you are.'
Chris Do, Emmy award-winning designer, director, CEO and Chief Strategist of Blind and the founder of The Futur

'Raw, real and relentlessly powerful, Erika Cramer's *Becoming Magnetic* is the ultimate guide to owning your confidence and radiating unapologetic magnetism. It's a game changer.'
Mel H. Abraham CPA CVA ASA, *USA Today* bestselling author of *Building Your Money Machine* and *The Entrepreneur's Solution*

becoming MAGNETIC

Erika Cramer, known as The Queen of Confidence, is a globally recognised confidence and mindset coach, TEDx speaker and best-selling author. From overcoming a life marked by trauma, foster care and early widowhood, Erika has dedicated her career to empowering women worldwide to step into their confidence and take ownership of their lives. As the award-winning host of *The Confidence Chronicles* podcast, which has amassed millions of downloads, Erika continues to inspire and guide women to break through limitations and embrace their full potential. Her no-nonsense, compassionate coaching approach equips women with the tools and mindset to stand tall in their authenticity, become magnetic in all areas of life, and lead with confidence. In addition to her coaching, Erika is pursuing a degree in psychotherapy, expanding her expertise to better serve her global audience of confident women ready to make their mark.

thequeenofconfidence.com
@thequeenofconfidence

becoming MAGNETIC

ERIKA CRAMER

PENGUIN BOOKS

UK | USA | Canada | Ireland | Australia
India | New Zealand | South Africa | China

Penguin Books is part of the Penguin Random House group of companies whose addresses can be found at global.penguinrandomhouse.com.

First published by Penguin Books, 2025

Cover design by Adam Laszczuk, Erika Cramer, Hamish Cramer, Jacqui Naunton and Vanessa Chng © Penguin Random House Australia Pty Ltd
Author photograph by Mary Miller | Smile Darling Photography
Typeset in Bembo Std by Midland Typesetters, Australia

Every effort has been made to trace creators and copyright holders of quoted material included in this book. The publisher welcomes hearing from anyone not correctly acknowledged.

Printed and bound in Australia by Griffin Press, an accredited ISO AS/NZ 14001 Environmental Management Systems printer.

A catalogue record for this book is available from the National Library of Australia

ISBN 978 1 76134 889 1

penguin.com.au

We at Penguin Random House Australia acknowledge that Aboriginal and Torres Strait Islander peoples are the first storytellers and Traditional Custodians of the land on which we live and work. We honour Aboriginal and Torres Strait Islander peoples' continuous connection to Country, waters, skies and communities. We celebrate Aboriginal and Torres Strait Islander stories, traditions and living cultures; and we pay our respects to Elders past and present.

To the future version of *you*.
The one who has always been waiting, just within reach.
May *she* recognise herself in these pages,
and feel invited to step forward, boldly,
to meet you right here, in the now.

To Hamish, thank you for everything, truly . . . *everything*.

CONTENTS

Prologue xiii
Introduction xvii

MAGNETISM 101: UNDERSTANDING THE WORK

1 From rock bottom to radiant 2
2 The choice to change 24
3 Radical shifts require radical responsibility 44
4 Unveiling your magnetic potential 62
The 10 Myths about Magnetism 90

THE FIVE PHASES OF MAGNETISM: DOING THE WORK

5 Phase 1: Self-mastery 96
6 Phase 2: Your true north 126
7 Phase 3: Your alter she-go 148
8 Phase 4: Your evolution 176
9 Phase 5: Your magnetic aura 202
Micro-skills to embody the work 219

BEING MAGNETIC: LIVING THE WORK

10 Magnetism in your personal life 226
11 Magnetism in your career and business 264
12 Signs that you're on the right track 292
The Magnetic Manifesto: words to live by 319

BONUS SECTION: PRACTISING MAGNETISM

Eleven secrets to alignment, energy and more magnetism 326

Resources and next steps 335
Acknowledgements 345

PROLOGUE

In our fast-paced world, where it seems as though everybody's hustling for their place in the spotlight, looking to be validated and accepted, where many of us seem so worried about perfectionism, how many likes we get on social media or the opinion of others – there's this cool, almost mystical vibe some women effortlessly exude.

It's as if they've tapped into a secret rhythm or found some kind of magic elixir that the rest of us missed out on while we were too busy trying to keep up. It's like they glide through life with this effortless grace, turning heads and drawing in opportunities as if they're following some invisible beat that's just for them; like they're dancing and grooving through life's chaos with the kind of confidence and swag that makes you think *damn, what's she got going on?*

When a woman steps into her power, radiating this kind of energy, she doesn't just walk into a room. No. She absolutely OWNS it. It's as if she's the conductor and the whole place, everyone in it, suddenly tunes itself to HER frequency. She exudes warmth, self-assurance and a sense of grounded safety. People want to listen to her speak, talk to her or just be around her. They feel more settled in their own skin after interacting with her, and want her to be part of their lives. It's not just charisma; it's deeper, more primal. She seems to draw good fortune and great people toward her – like a magnet. And those who don't have good intentions seem to instinctively keep their distance, sensing they can't disrupt her energy.

The crazy thing is that she's not even trying to be the centre of attention – it's just that attention naturally gravitates toward her.

She doesn't just navigate the world, she captivates it.

She steps into the room, and it's as if the universe itself rolls out the red carpet. She seems to operate in 'solutions only' mode. Challenges appear to shrink in her presence, not because they don't exist but because she exudes this confidence, this absolutely unshakable self-belief that everything will not only be alright, but it will 100 per cent turn out in her favour.

And the wild part? It almost always does.

This is the power of being magnetic.

INTRODUCTION

Becoming magnetic: intentionally creating the life you want by cultivating the energy, presence and mindset that pulls it in.

Am I cursed? Or just messed up? What is wrong with me? Why do bad things always happen to me? Am I unlucky or just damaged goods? Who will ever want me . . . an uneducated, broken, Latina from the 'hood?

For years, I carried these words like a weight, letting them dictate my life. Every time I repeated them, it was like I was tearing myself down, all while pretending nothing was wrong. I slapped on a smile, cracked a few jokes and hid behind some make-up, thinking that would be enough to fool everyone – including myself. But deep down, I knew the truth.

I had zero confidence, no sense of self-worth and absolutely no idea how to turn things around. Let's be real – I wasn't even sure if I was the problem or if anything could be fixed at all.

I wasn't just lacking magnetism; I was actively repelling the very things I needed to thrive – things like strong boundaries, real confidence, meaningful relationships and belief in who I am. I was stuck in a cycle of self-doubt and self-sabotage, unable to see that the power to change was within me all along.

I never felt good enough, smart enough, pretty enough, educated enough, skinny enough – I felt just plain not enough. I questioned everything I did and couldn't seem to be comfortable 'being myself' no matter how many times people told me to do just that. I simply didn't know who that 'self' really was. I didn't know myself without the opinion of others, without comparison and criticism. I constantly second-guessed myself, while desperately seeking validation from everyone around me. Deep down, I just wanted to be told that I was good enough, yet it never happened.

I learnt how to evaluate how 'good' I was based on the way other people felt about me. I didn't have a sense of self, never mind something as alluring as 'magnetism'. Back then, I wouldn't even have known what the hell that word meant. To be honest, it was something I knew nothing about. I would NEVER in a million years have believed that I'd write a book teaching women how to become magnetic . . . yet here we are.

It all started in 2017: my life began to transform in ways I could hardly believe, let alone describe. Every aspect of my existence expanded beyond anything I had ever experienced. Love, health, success and opportunities seemed to arrive as if the universe itself was kissing me on the forehead. Blessing after blessing unfolded, sometimes in the form of challenges (of course) but even when there were bumps in the road, it was exciting to be travelling down it. And it wasn't just my life that was shifting; my clients, friends and the incredible online community I had built were also reporting these life-altering changes. It felt as if we had cracked a code, uncovering the answers to questions that had lingered for years: *Who am I? How can I build more confidence? When will I feel enough? How can I stop letting the opinions of others hold me back?*

I was able to teach my amazing clients and the women in my community how to tap into their inner power and attract what they wanted from a place of abundance rather than lack.

We stopped hiding from our past and faced it head on. We made peace with the parts of ourselves we once buried deep, transforming old wounds into the wisdom we'd needed to build the future we truly desired. This wasn't about glossing over the hard stuff; there was nothing 'love and light' about the difficult things we had to work through. It was about doing the deep, uncomfortable work, owning it, using it and taking back control. We didn't just reclaim our stories – we rewrote them, on our terms.

The more we confronted our pasts and embraced who we were, the more we unlocked the doors to what we truly wanted. Self-acceptance wasn't just a trending term; it was the key to everything. And as we leaned into this work, something remarkable happened – we found each other. We weren't just a group of women on a self-improvement journey; we became a powerful force, bound together by shared experiences and a hunger for something more.

In doing so, we decided how we'd show up in the world, shifting our frequency and becoming more than we ever thought possible. This wasn't about staying comfortable; it was about challenging ourselves, stepping up and living the work every single day. And as we did, the changes came – powerful shifts that couldn't be ignored.

It wasn't luck or chance. It was conscious magnetism. The more we lived in alignment with our true selves, the more we started to attract what we deserved. This wasn't just about healing – it was about stepping into our power, claiming our space and watching the world respond. And in that moment, I understood: this is what becoming magnetic was really about.

When I began discussing this concept in my programs, with my clients and through social media, the response was overwhelming. It made me reflect deeply on how I moved through the world and how I supported my clients to do so as well: **magnetism** was at the heart of it all. After releasing a podcast on the subject and seeing the huge response of private messages, emails and endless questions come through, I knew I had to write this book.

I'M DIRECT, SOMETIMES TOUGH, AND I SAY THE THINGS OTHERS WON'T, AND I DO IT IN SERVICE OF YOU.

MAGNETISM AND YOU

So, what exactly is magnetism? In simple terms, it's the invisible energy you radiate – your essence, presence and confidence. It's that powerful force, rooted in authenticity, that not only attracts the right people and opportunities into your life but also repels the ones that don't serve you. Beyond just drawing things in, it's also about setting boundaries and creating space for what's meant for you.

When you're truly magnetic, people can feel your energy before you even say a word. It's not just charm or charisma – it's the alignment of your being, what you believe and how you show up. It's the courage to be unapologetically you. When you embrace your full magnetism, your presence becomes undeniable. You speak with conviction, live with intention and you stop seeking validation because you know who the hell you are.

Forget simply putting on a confident front – the journey to magnetism means tapping into the core of your being, stripping away the layers that have kept you small and allowing your true self to shine. I see it all the time in the women I work with. They come to me thinking something's missing, only to realise that their magnetic potential was there all along. It just needed to be unlocked.

That's why this book is called *becoming* magnetic – because this is a process. It's about stepping into the version of yourself that's been waiting beneath the surface, the version that captivates and commands the room without even trying.

NO FLUFF

I get it. You might be reading this and thinking, *This magnetism stuff sounds like some new-age, buzzword nonsense. Something people throw around to sound profound, but in reality, it's just fluff.* Believe me, I was right there with you once. I used to side-eye terms like 'energy' and 'vibration', thinking they were just feel-good words with no real substance. But let me tell you something – I've lived this. I've seen it happen in my own life, and in the lives of the women I coach every day.

Magnetism is real, and it's not some mystical woo-woo thing that only the spiritually enlightened can tap into. It's practical, it's tangible and it's something every single one of us already has.

I wasn't born into this knowledge. I too used to think success and attraction were just luck or natural charisma that some special people had, and the rest of us didn't. But once I started paying attention, I realised something bigger was happening: my energy was shifting, and so were the results in my life. Opportunities that seemed impossible were suddenly within reach. The things I once only dreamt of? They started finding their way to me – not just only because I wished for them, but also because I actively became the person who could attract them.

And that's what this book is about – becoming magnetic, *intentionally creating the life you want by cultivating the energy, presence and mindset that pulls it in.*

Now, don't get me wrong – this isn't some superficial feel-good story where you can think happy thoughts, recite a few affirmations and the universe will serve up your dreams on a silver platter. Real magnetism doesn't work that way, and I'm not here to sell you on that BS.

What I'm talking about is deeper. It's the gritty, uncomfortable work of getting real with yourself – digging into your past, understanding your patterns and actively transforming your behaviours and how you show up.

That's where magnetism goes beyond the surface-level concepts we've all heard before. You can't fake this. The universe responds to who you are, not who you pretend to be. If you're showing up inauthentically, if you're still hiding behind masks, all the positive affirmations in the world won't help.

In all honesty, magnetism is **not** for the faint of heart. It's not a case of sitting back and hoping for good vibes. It's about stepping into your power, taking radical responsibility for your energy and making the necessary changes to become the woman you want to be. It's work – but it's the kind of work that pays off.

I'm not here to fill your head with vague ideas or empty promises. *Becoming Magnetic* is packed with real steps that will challenge you to dig deep and transform. But at the end of the day, **you** have to show up and do the work.

So if you've ever felt sceptical or cynical about concepts like *magnetism* or *energy*, I get it. But I challenge you to stay open. Try the exercises, see how it feels when you begin to shift your energy and start living in alignment with your true self. You might just be surprised at how much your life begins to change.

WHAT TO EXPECT

Before we get into the thick of *Becoming Magnetic*, I have to tell you straight up: none of this is going to work if you keep hiding from yourself. There is no magic wand here. There's no quick-fix pill or instant magnetism success button. Like anything worth having, magnetism takes time, commitment and a lot of real, honest work.

But, if you're ready to get uncomfortable, to look at the parts of yourself you've been avoiding and do the work that's required, *Becoming Magnetic* has the power to change everything – the power to help you step into the woman you've always wanted to be.

The woman who takes up space without asking permission.
The woman who shows up for herself, stands by her values and speaks her truth with conviction.
The woman who no longer waits for the world to tell her she's enough because she already knows, believes and behaves like she is.

That's what this journey is about. And let me tell you right now, taking your space in this world is both your right and your responsibility.

Becoming magnetic doesn't mean overshadowing others or being louder than the next person. It means fully embodying who you are and walking in that power.

However, let me warn you: this isn't for everyone.

It's not for the people who want to play small, hide in the shadows or keep telling themselves the same tired stories about why life isn't working out for them. If that's where you're at, *Becoming Magnetic* will only be another collection of words that you'll toss to the side after a few chapters. Honestly, that's fine if you're not ready.

But if you're here – I mean really here – and if you're ready to go deep, push yourself and become the woman you've always been capable of being, then you've picked up the right book.

This process will challenge you. It will invite you to confront the patterns, habits and beliefs that have kept you stuck. But you already know that version of you isn't cutting it anymore. You know you're capable of more, and *Becoming Magnetic* is here to help you claim it.

Magnetism is real, and it's powerful. It's about shifting your energy, your mindset and your actions. It's about taking charge of the energy you put out into the world and watching how it transforms what comes back to you. It's about being so damn real and grounded in who you are that people can't help but be drawn to you.

You don't have to chase, beg for or plead for attention – it naturally gravitates toward you because you've become an undeniable force. Far more than just attracting people and opportunities, magnetism is also about repelling the things that are no longer aligned with you. When you step into your magnetic power, you'll find the things that don't serve you will start falling away. It can feel uncomfortable at first – after all, many of us have been conditioned to think we need

Forget transforming into someone else – you're going to reveal the person you've always been.

to make everyone happy, fit into everyone's expectations and be liked by everyone.

That's not what being magnetic is about.

It's not enough to simply read *Becoming Magnetic*, nod along, and think positive thoughts. You've got to get in the trenches, face your fears and start taking action. No amount of vision boarding or feel-good mantras will make you magnetic if you're not willing to show up and put in the effort.

Becoming magnetic requires determination and a willingness to do the uncomfortable work that most of us avoid doing.

The good news is – you don't have to do it alone. In the pages of *Becoming Magnetic*, I'm going to walk you through every step. Forget transforming into someone else – you're going to reveal the person you've always been: the confident, powerful, magnetic woman who's been hiding beneath the layers of self-doubt and external expectations.

WILL *BECOMING MAGNETIC* WORK FOR YOU?

After working with thousands of women across the globe and coaching for more than a decade, I've noticed that so many of us love to binge podcasts, devour audiobooks and consume endless amounts of self-growth content online. We call ourselves personal development junkies – I'm guilty of it too – but here's the thing: what will actually make *Becoming Magnetic* work for you? What will make this particular experience different? Why won't it be just another inspirational book you leave on your shelf after a week or two?

The difference will be **you.**

That's it.

It all comes down to you deciding to action what you learn from these pages. *Becoming Magnetic* is packed with practical steps, deep coaching questions and powerful exercises – all designed to support you in stepping into your most magnetic self.

But wait, doesn't every self-development book promise that?

They do.

So what makes this one *'the one'*?

You do.

You deciding that this is the moment you stop buying a bunch of self-help books that collect dust – the ones you don't finish or, worse, the ones you don't act on.

This is the book that will transform your life because **you will choose** to let it be.

I know the potential of the content in *Becoming Magnetic* – it's life-changing. But its power is only unleashed when you decide to show up for yourself.

I'm known by my clients as the ass-kicking coach who doesn't let them play small or hide behind clever words and feel-good statements. I've lived the struggle; I've been through hell and back, and because of that, I'm here to give it to you straight. I'm direct, sometimes tough, and I say the things others won't. And I do it in service of you.

Because you deserve nothing less than being held to your greatest and highest potential.

I'm also a nurturer and a mother, a widow, a wife, a sister and a daughter. And I truly love this work. I am honoured I get to do *this* for a living. I care deeply about seeing women step into their full power and attract the life they dream of and deserve.

If anything I say here challenges you, good. That's a signal there's something worth digging into, something important to uncover. That discomfort? It's calling you to lean in, reflect and grow. *Becoming Magnetic* is going to push you, challenge you, but most importantly, it's going to invite you to do the work (more on what that *actually* means later).

I can guide you, but I can't make the choice for you. That part is up to you.

So, I hope you're ready to step up and to take action, because everything you desire is on the other side of that choice.

Let's make *this* the book that transforms you, the one you actually use to become magnetic.

Because damn do I know that it can.

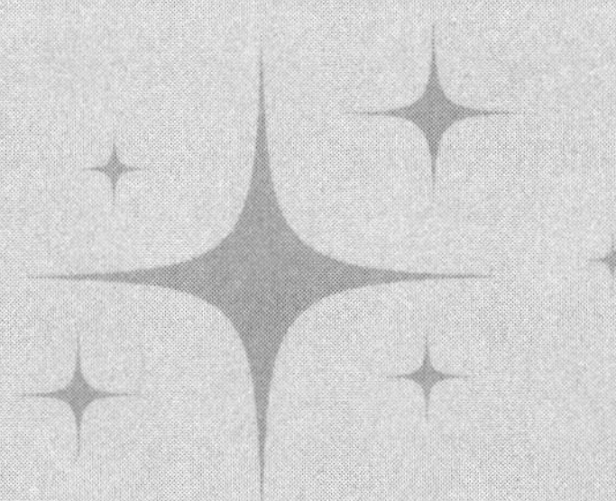

MAGNETISM 101: UNDERSTANDING THE WORK

1

FROM ROCK BOTTOM TO RADIANT RADIANT RADIANT

I wrote *Becoming Magnetic* because we need it. Damn it, I need it! Having spent over a decade working alongside women, helping them step into their confidence, heal their past and create lives they genuinely love, I realised something vital. We need support, we need real and raw, no-nonsense, tangible steps for **actual** change. We need a guide that can not only invite us into what's possible but also share a practical process of HOW to do this. *Becoming Magnetic* is that guide.

I want you to feel like I'm right there with you every step of the way, supporting you, pushing you and reminding you of who you **truly** are. My mission is simple: to support women like you in stepping into your most magnetic selves, unapologetically claiming your space and attracting everything you truly desire.

I've laid out a clear, actionable process that will not only transform how the world sees you but, more importantly, how you see yourself. There's nothing I'd love to see more than a world full of amplified, empowered women radiating magnetism – lighting the way not just for ourselves, but for all women who walk this path with us and those who come after. I want *Becoming Magnetic* to be a bold invitation to harness your power and expand your potentiality.

You may be wondering why I am so obsessed with change. Well . . .

TRANSFORMING YOURSELF IS ABOUT CONTINUOUS IMPROVEMENT; IT'S NOT A SUMMIT YOU REACH.

- It's because I know what it's like to live as a broken woman.
- I know what it's like to hustle and grind for worth, love and self-acceptance.
- I know what it's like to feel lost, uninspired and in complete lack.

Truth is, I really shouldn't be where I am right now. I technically 'shouldn't' be living the amazing life I currently am. I truly thought I'd end up on the streets, struggling with an addiction, in prison or dead.

I never imagined that my most painful experiences and darkest moments would become the very lessons I now share to inspire and guide others. It's all a dream come true and it's because I BECAME the woman who created it. I built her up, I educated her, I healed (and continue to heal) her. My life is expansive, joyful, adventurous and I've been able to achieve most of the lifelong dreams I desired by the age of forty. Sometimes I truly can't believe that I get to live and lead this life but then I remember how hard I work to magnetise it all.

Because the truth is, your past doesn't get to define who you become. When you can stand in your story, find the gifts in your hardships, the lessons in your suffering and draw on your inner strength – those hardships form part of you. They don't have to break you; in fact, they shape you into who you are meant to be. These experiences teach you resilience, courage and the power of overcoming adversity. Because you faced them and rose above, you become stronger, wiser and more grounded. Each challenge you overcome adds another layer to your character, contributing to the powerful, resilient human being you are today. And yes, sometimes I'm still a hot-mess-express, of course, but the tough cards life dealt me MADE me – they didn't break me. And the cards you were dealt don't have to break you either.

Today, when people meet me at events or see my business brand online – 'The Queen of Confidence' – they assume that my confidence and magnetism come from my success. Many people think with a business name like that, I must be confident all the time, but that couldn't be further from the truth. It wasn't (and it still isn't) 'easy' for me. Confidence has been the hardest, most excruciating thing I've ever had to fight for. I had to face my inner critic and confront my inner demons. I had to radically shift my perspective and take wild emotional leaps to make amends with the person I once hated – me. I had to learn forgiveness and reclaim the parts I had lost to trauma, abuse, grief and pain. Magnetism was not bestowed on me; it was self-generated. And if I could do it, anyone can.

So as confident and powerful as 'The Queen of Confidence' may sound, don't get it twisted. There were (and still are) dark times where I have to dig deep and excavate my shadows. Transforming yourself is about continuous improvement; it's not a summit you reach.

THE GIRL WHO LOST HER SPARKLE

As a little girl, I was vibrant, energetic, very friendly and outgoing. I was naturally magnetic: I talked to strangers, danced unapologetically and had so much energy. Like most free-spirited kids, I was brimming with an enthusiastic zest for life. Sadly, by the age of five, that little girl's light began to dim.

I was born and raised in a small city just outside Boston, Massachusetts. My dad left when I was only two, leaving my mom to raise me on her own. She had been diagnosed with bipolar disorder in her teens and frequently experienced manic episodes, especially when she would stop taking her medication, which happened often.

During her manic periods, she would become physically and verbally abusive. Throughout my childhood and teen years, Mom was in and out of mental hospitals and I was in and out of the foster-care system, changing schools and living with different foster families. When Mom had stabilised I would be back with her, but then, out of nowhere, she would have one of her episodes and start hitting me nonstop until the neighbours called the police. Once, she beat me so badly that the cops came to take her. I tried to defend her and got a bit out of control, and we were both arrested and cuffed on our wrists and ankles. As we were thrown into the back of a police car together, I yelled and swore at the cops (I was hot-headed, sure, but on the other hand, who cuffs a five-year-old?).

Being in the foster-care system was tough. As you may know, these systems need work in most countries. I was constantly changing homes and being placed with different families, and although I loved living with other kids, this is where my experience of sexual abuse began. I learnt that I didn't matter, that I was shameful and bad and that no one was going to save me from my circumstances.

The sexual abuse was one thing, but not having anyone from my family come and claim me? That really hurt. As a child I believed that meant all kinds of things about my worthiness. I told myself *No one wants you. You're not worth fighting for. You're not good enough to be chosen.* And having my dad walk out at such a young age: this was just more 'evidence' for me. I became a very angry child. I was angry at the social worker for taking me away, angry at the doctors who experimented with my mother's medication like she was a lab rat, angry at my dad for leaving me, angry at the system, the foster home people, my mom, my teachers – I was angry at the whole world.

The accumulation of abuse, being placed in foster care and Mom's illness slowly ate away at my light and my love for connecting with others. I had a massive chip on my shoulder and was constantly in fights at school. I doubted myself in every class and my grades always suffered. I struggled with feeling like I wasn't good enough or smart enough. I was convinced people didn't like me, and I practically lived in the detention centre of every school I went to.

When I was seven years old, Mom took us on a family vacation to Puerto Rico with her boyfriend at the time (one of the only men in my childhood who was kind and safe to be around). Unfortunately, she didn't take enough medication on the trip, and within three days of being unmedicated, she had a really bad fight with her boyfriend. All I remember is being pushed into the front seat of the rental car grasping my pink teddy bear, Lisa, as Mom drove away furiously into the rain that night.

She screamed as the rain pelted down on the car, and night-time made it hard to see. In her psychotic state, Mom smashed into a huge tree, flipping the car three times before landing upside down. She ripped me out of the wreckage, and we tried to get help from people who lived in a house nearby. Mom was paranoid and believed the men in the house were going to hurt her (she'd had her own fair share of experiences with abuse) so we left the crash scene and started to walk. We walked day and night, sleeping on patios, in bushes and breaking into people's cars. My sneakers broke into pieces from all the walking. Three days later we were found by family, albeit exhausted and confused.

My father, who had left for Puerto Rico when I was two years old, found out about the accident. He came to find me and took me away from my mom for a year. When I was finally reunited with her the following year, we jumped back into the same cycle: Mom getting sick, another foster home, sexual abuse, and visiting Mom in mental hospitals.

When I was nine years old, my mother met a new boyfriend and he moved in. I never felt comfortable around him. I didn't know why, but his vibe made me uneasy. Seeing Mom happy made me reluctant to say anything as I didn't want to mess things up for her. Until I started getting late-night visits in my bedroom from him. He manipulated Mom to believe he was a nice guy who loved her, but he had other motives. He'd chosen us because we were vulnerable – he was drawn to people he could take advantage of. He would sneak into my room late at night, sit by my bedside and molest me. When Mom realised he wasn't in their bed, she'd wake up and come and find him in my room. When she asked what he was doing, he pretended he was checking on me.

One day, I decided to tell my mother what he was doing. She always spoke to me about my body and autonomy – I am sure that her own experience with sexual abuse made her want to prevent it from happening to me. She told me to speak to her if anyone ever touched me 'down there'. She told me that it was not okay for anyone to touch me in my private area and that I should always tell her about it. I figured Mom would want to know what he was doing, so I told her. She looked angry and called him into the room. He started crying and telling her he would 'never do that'. I felt terrible. I told her 'never mind' and left the room. Puzzled and confused, I questioned if I'd made the whole thing up. But that night he was back in my room. It was real.

The following day, I sat Mom down and told her everything. She confronted him and kicked him out. We never saw him again. After decades of deep healing, therapy and coaching work, I have been able to recognise that although that was a terrible experience, it was the thing that at nine years old helped me find my voice, and in turn has led me to become the outspoken, justice-seeking woman I am today.

OFF TO BOOT CAMP

Although my abuser was out of our lives, I was still traumatised, and school was hell. If someone tried to check in on me or see how I was coping I would tell them: 'I'm good, it's all good, I am fine. I don't need to get emotional or talk about my feelings.' I had been in therapy for years, but I never felt understood. I had no idea what a safe space looked or even felt like.

At sixteen years old, I met Jeovanni, my first real love. We got on so well and vibed on the dreams we shared of moving to Los Angeles.

We both decided to join the military as our ticket out of Boston and onto the west coast. Because my grades were horrendous and my Mom was poor, it seemed like my best option for an education and to make something of myself was to join the military. In his senior year of high school, Jeovanni joined the Marine Corps, and I followed in his footsteps, joining the US army in my senior year.

Halfway through my military boot camp training, the attacks of 9/11 happened. It was such a hectic time to join. No one saw that coming. I served in the US army for ten years (eight years active; my last two years inactive) and moved across the country. My first couple of years in the army were exciting. I learned so much about discipline and structure, something I'd missed out on in my adolescence. It was a huge moment of independence for me. I married Jeo in secret before he went off to fight the war in Iraq. I was only nineteen years old. It was a long and scary two years waiting for Jeo to come back home to me.

The year he got back from war, I decided to put my dreams on hold so he could chase his. I felt so guilty that he'd missed so much life being deployed in the Marine Corps and going to war, so I felt it was his time to live. He loved music and always wanted to step into that field, so since I could easily get a transfer, I suggested we move from California to Florida so he could study at his dream college and pursue his lifelong desires of being a music producer and DJ. I was twenty-one when we moved to Florida.

THE VOID

At twenty-three-years-old I woke up in the emergency room of the Orlando Regional Medical Center to cold scissors sliding against my thighs. A group of medical professionals hovered around me, and someone was cutting my $80 jeans off my legs. That really woke me up – they were my most expensive piece of clothing. Why was someone cutting them to shreds?!

I packed up my entire life and moved to the other side of the world. And do you know what? All my skeletons, traumas, doubts, fears and unresolved pain followed me.

In the background, I could hear Jeovanni screaming and yelling. He was arguing with the hospital staff, but I didn't know why; it seemed as if they were holding him down. Immediately, I began apologising: 'I'm so sorry, he's not usually like this, please! I am so sorry.' My mind was so messed up back then that even when I was lying in a hospital bed, bloodied, broken and bruised with no idea what was wrong with me, I still cared more about upsetting the nice hospital staff than I cared about what I was doing in the hospital in the first place.

A few seconds passed, and I blacked out again.

When I woke up the next morning, hazy and still unaware of what was going on, I slowly realised I was in a very bad way. I had barely made it out alive from a horrific drink-driving accident. The doctor told me I had fractured my back in two places and that the bone was damaged so badly they needed to fuse it with titanium. My left ankle had been crushed and needed hardware as well. 'You're very lucky,' he told me. 'If you had been in any other position when you crashed, you could have been paralysed permanently.'

'Accident? What accident?! Surgery – what are you talking about? What happened to me?' I was in shock, still with no idea why I was in hospital. Memories started flooding back in snippets and bursts.

Oh my God.

Jeo had been driving. Earlier that night, we'd been invited to a nightclub with some friends who had a VIP booth. We had no money to spend on drinks or gas, but there was just enough in the tank to get us there and home. Besides, they had a VIP booth, so that meant free drinks.

At the end of the night, we got into the car to drive home. Jeo sat in the driver's seat and his friend got in the front passenger seat, and I drunkenly demanded that they both put their seatbelts on. I climbed into the back seat, right in the middle – which is where I planned to hover over them so I could make sure 'we were all safe'. . . yet I never put a seatbelt on myself.

Sounds like something a drunk person would do, huh? Yup, I was wasted. So were Jeo and his friend. The car we were driving was a red Mitsubishi Lancer Evolution – you know, the car from *2 Fast 2 Furious*? Jeo's parents had bought it for him when he returned from Iraq as a 'welcome home' gift. These cars don't have a safety chip, which usually limits the speed a driver can reach before it prevents the car from going any faster. This car could go 152 miles per hour (or 244 kilometres per hour) with no chip. You can imagine what happened next. We took off and then we all fell asleep – at what point I am not sure. What I *do* know is that we fell asleep in fifth gear, going the maximum speed that car could go. I woke up seconds before we crashed but it was too late. Our car was headed straight into a ditch. My vision went black.

The jaws of life were needed to break the car open. Paramedics took us via helicopter to the nearest emergency room. Jeo went into a coma for twelve hours, due to severe head trauma. Thankfully, when he came to, he was cleared to go home. His friend walked out with only a fractured rib, which was a miracle. I was broken and battered beyond belief. I had broken my back, but even worse, I had broken my spirit.

MY SECOND CHANCE

The recovery was brutal. I'll spare you all the gory details, but I was in the hospital for almost a month, permanently attached to a morphine pump to numb the excruciating pain. Learning to walk again was a nightmare, and trying to pee without a catheter was agony.

The three months that followed, however, did change my life. In many ways, I was literally starting again: I had to develop the mental resilience to learn to walk on my own, to be able to shower with no assistance. Being able to walk to the front door unassisted was one of my goals. I knew I didn't want my old life back. I wanted a new one. A new start. I had dreams, goals, wants and desires, but it never seemed like there was a chance in hell they were within my reach. I worried that I had wasted my life. *What was I here for?*

Since childhood, I'd always wanted to be an actress and performer. So, I started imagining a life where I stepped toward that direction. If I wanted to be J-Lo, what was my first step going to be? Getting rid of my ratty-ass regrowth, for one. I asked Jeo to take me to a hair salon. I was blonde at the time with two-inch regrowth. I was swollen and broken and couldn't walk, but damn it, I was determined to look better than I felt. So, I went to the hair salon. Afterwards, I felt like a million bucks. I figured if I looked better, I would feel better about myself. Sometimes you need the boost of a physical pick-me-up to get you in the right frame of mind.

That little trip to work on my outer self gave me the confidence to start working on a new goal. I knew I couldn't expect to walk on set and book a movie star role; I had to start small. I thought modelling could be a gateway into performing. I slowly put myself out there, showing up, taking risks and making moves toward the life I wanted. I began emailing photographers from my bed and booking jobs. As I recovered and got stronger, I started doing more and more magazine shoots and eventually ended up in music videos with famous rappers. Eventually, I was back working full-time in the army as my day job, I had started hairdressing school at night (to help me transition out of the military) and on weekends I was modelling and doing music videos in Miami. It was a crazy time!

It took a near-death experience to give me the push to go after my dreams. My life did change, and I was more excited about my future. But it was only at the surface level: looking good and feeling good.

I hadn't processed any trauma or taken an honest look at why we drank so much that fateful night – or any night for that matter.

DEAFENING SILENCE

It was a Sunday afternoon. The night before, Jeo and I had decided to have a house party to celebrate Cinco de Mayo. There was a big boxing match happening between Oscar De La Hoya and Floyd Mayweather, so we invited our closest friends for some drinks. We had an awesome time, in the safety of our own home, drinking, eating and having great conversations. I had to work at my unit the next morning, so I decided to slow down the drinking around midnight and went to bed.

On Sunday morning, I jolted awake, thinking I'd overslept. I noticed Jeo wasn't in bed next to me. My phone showed he had called me at 1.20 am. No text, no voicemail. I quickly got up to check if he had passed out in the living room, but he wasn't there. His two friends were sleeping on the couch, but where was Jeo?

I woke them up. One said Jeo had left late last night to give one of our friends a key he had left at our house. I was confused because we'd had a house party – we weren't going anywhere. After the accident, we'd promised to never drink and drive again. It didn't make sense – why did he leave our house to return a key to someone? I was worried that maybe he'd fallen asleep in his car outside in the parking lot, but I was running late, so I told his friends to look for him and that I'd check back in later.

On my way in, I couldn't stop wondering where he could have been. When we finished our morning formation, I went to find my staff sergeant. I told her we had had a party last night and Jeo wasn't home when I woke up. She told me not to stress, and to keep calling his phone and maybe try calling some hospitals or police stations, just in case. His phone kept ringing, which gave me hope. And his friends were looking for him too.

At quarter to twelve, it started raining. I looked out the window: *where is my husband?* By this point I was panicking. I told my staff sergeant I was scared. She let me leave work and I drove back home to meet his friends. I prayed the entire drive home that I would walk in the door and see him sitting on the sofa, looking sheepish, with some crazy story that he'd fallen asleep at a friend's house . . . but no luck.

At home, I checked the house phone and noticed the hospital had called at seven o'clock in the morning. That was weird. The hospital calling wasn't the weird part – when I broke my back, the surgery had set me back over $120,000 that I didn't have, as we'd naively declined to purchase the army's health insurance, so they were constantly calling to chase for money. They never called that early, though. I called back and asked if they had anyone by the name of Jeovanni Lopez there.

The male voice said: 'Ma'am, we're sorry, we can't give you information like this over the phone, it's probably best that you come in if you think he may be here.' I was worried, but he sounded so casual that I figured it was a good sign. Even so, I asked Jeo's good friend Ryan to come with me – he had been looking for Jeo all day and was also worried.

I'll never forget the moment I walked into the emergency room lobby. My eyes locked with the young man at the front desk: the same kid I had spoken with twenty minutes earlier. 'Hi, I'm the woman who called looking for my husband, Jeovanni?' He looked at me, then quickly looked down. He pointed at the private room near the ER entry doors and asked me to please wait there.

These are the rooms where they tell you the 'news'. I instantly felt sick. Inside the room, I was pacing. They kept me there for what felt like hours, and I had to keep prodding for answers. 'Can anyone tell me anything?' I was getting fed up with waiting, but worse, I began to get really scared. It was torture.

Finally, the double doors to the ER swung open as if in slow motion. I locked eyes with a nurse in bright blue scrubs, and then a doctor in a tan suit jacket with a clipboard in his hand. As soon as our eyes met, their gazes dropped.

The nurse spoke first. 'I'm so sorry. He didn't make it.' Time stood still. I heard the words, but I couldn't comprehend what she was saying.

The nurse spoke again. 'I am so very sorry. We did everything we could.'

An eternity passed while my brain tried to catch up.

'What do you mean? He didn't make it? I don't understand.'

'Jeovanni Lopez, your husband, he didn't make it. I am so sorry, we tried everything,' she repeated.

In the background, I could hear Ryan wailing as he fell to the floor. But I had no words. No feeling. Nothing. A void. Nothing made sense. Nothing felt real. It was deafening silence in between words, in between breaths. Stillness consumed me. I was frozen and numb.

When my brain caught up, I snapped. I ripped off my army jacket and threw it across the room, screaming at the top of my lungs. I grabbed a lamp and smashed it against the wall.

The nurse and doctor tried to console me. Instantly, I went back to that blank state, eerily calm and frozen. I kept repeating, 'What do I do? What am I supposed to do now?'

The nurse said, 'Oh honey, you don't have to do anything. We're so sorry for your loss.'

On Sunday 6 May 2007, at 4.35 am, my husband Jeovanni Lopez died from internal bleeding from a drink-driving accident. He had veered off the road, hitting a ditch and flipping his car. He hadn't been wearing a seatbelt.

That moment was the hardest, most excruciating thing I've ever had to live through. Nothing compared to this unfathomable loss.

I walked into the hallway and lay on the floor, sobbing and wailing at a reality I couldn't accept or understand.

YOU CAN RUN BUT YOU CAN'T HIDE

Rock bottom hit. Grief and insanity worked in tandem and tortured me. The next three to five years were a blur. I got into bad relationship after bad relationship so I didn't feel alone. I took on modelling jobs so I could feel desired, pretty and worthy. I numbed myself out of my life, trying to 'control-alt-delete' my past. And I hate to admit it, but I kept drinking and driving. I was desensitised to the extreme. I didn't want to deal with it, because I had an unconscious belief that if I let myself cry too much or deal with his death, then I would become bipolar like my mother. So I just blocked my deepest traumas and kept soldiering on.

In 2009, I met an Australian man at a hairdressing conference in Las Vegas. He was completely different from anyone I had ever dated before: different accent, different style, different upbringing. Australia had never been on my radar to be honest; I didn't even know where it was!

I fell in (what I thought was) love with this guy and decided that he was my ticket to a new life and clean slate. It was irrational how fast I decided to leave my old life behind. I figured I could start again and leave my past in America.

I packed up my entire life and moved to the other side of the world. And do you know what? All my skeletons, traumas, doubts, fears and unresolved pain followed me across the South Pacific Ocean. Who would have thought!

I had moved continents to start a new life with a man who ended up being no good for me. Instead, he confirmed what I felt about myself at the time. That I was not worthy. Not good enough. Fundamentally flawed. Yes, he was a match to my internal belief system. I put up with ridiculous amounts of pain in that relationship. I was homesick and unhappy, but I was determined to make Australia work.

I refused to go back home. I was scared that if I did, every time I saw a kangaroo or heard about the land down under, I would cringe and feel like a failure. I didn't want to leave Australia on those terms. I knew there was more to this magical and beautiful country. I could feel it.

I was at another rock bottom, but this time living as a single widow in a foreign country. At the time, the only two people I had in my life were my nail technician and my personal trainer, Hamish. Seriously? My service providers were my only friends.

I dedicated myself to working full-time and going to the gym to help me out of my 'eat pray love and tubs of ice-cream' cycle. Hamish and I developed the most incredible friendship. He was on a journey of self-development and was like no man I'd known before. He was soft and gentle, but strong and masculine – so kind and very self-aware.

He had coaches and mentors and he believed in the universe, manifestation and positivity. I had no idea about any of this stuff back then. I was troubled and struggled to accept myself. I had serious work to do, but Hamish led the way. He cared for me and listened to me. He was the first person I told my life story to – ALL of it. He loved me and accepted me for who I was, and everything I had been through.

In the summer of 2014, Hamish and I were married. It was the happiest day of my life.

He introduced me to his coaches and mentors. And I was ready for it. I went deep into ALL the pain, suffering and trauma I had swept under the rug over the years. I invested time and energy into unravelling all the wounds that were not healed, and finally began to challenge the negative beliefs I held about myself. It was a bumpy

NO ONE IS COMING . . . TO FIX, SAVE, REPAIR, CHANGE OR RESCUE YOU.

ride, but over the course of twelve months, I was transformed. I began to magnetically attract healthy people and better opportunities. My new life was unrecognisable. I had built it from the ground up, with grit and courage. I was so damn proud of myself.

This transformation didn't stop at twelve months. It kept going. And it's still going today. You see, the inner work doesn't stop, but it does get easier.

I've shared my story with you because I want you to know that I get it.

I get what it's like to grieve, to be abandoned, abused and neglected.

I get what it's like to struggle, lack confidence, feel lost, be depressed and overwhelmed by life.

I get it.

However, I also know that you **can** create the most beautiful and magnetic life no matter what has happened in your past, IF you are willing to work for it.

And I'd like to remind you that often, those traumatic experiences are not your fault. It's not your fault if you were abused, neglected or rejected.

But it does become your problem to deal with. It does become your responsibility to heal.

So I am here to tell you that if you've had your joy, happiness, innocence – or your magnetism – eroded or stolen, then I promise you, YOU can reclaim it. In fact, you MUST.

You really are the one you've been waiting for. It's you.

Because the hard truth is – **no one is coming to save you.**

NO ONE IS COMING . . . to fix, save, repair, change or rescue you.

Other people can inspire and support you, as Hamish did for me, and it's great to do this work in a community of like-minded people, but it's still YOU who has to do the work for yourself.

No one is going to grant you the space, the voice, the recognition, the validation, the money, or the acknowledgement you think you deserve. YOU have to be willing to claim it yourself.

Because I truly believe the first step to real magnetism is claiming it. Knowing it belongs to you, just as much as it does anyone else. We can't sit back and wait for 'some day'. That day when you'll magically be healed, happy and powerful. That day when everything perfectly falls into place. That day when you finally lose your fear of taking up space, when you earn that raise, put yourself out there and voice your honest opinion.

Why wait for 'some day'? Why not today? Why not now?

Many of us will wait years, even decades, for permission to step into our fullest power and potential. I don't know about you, but I'm tired of waiting. Every day you wait for someone else – some system, some institution – to solve your problems, you're giving away your power. And let's be real, it's not just your potential on the line. It's the future of every woman who follows. We can't afford to stay stuck, silenced or sidelined.

It's time to stop waiting. We are the change. This isn't about playing small or waiting for the right moment. This is about stepping up – right now. You've got the strength, the smarts and the fire to push forward the change you want to see. Why wait for someone to grant you permission when the power's been in your hands all along?

We're more connected, more resourceful and more informed than any generation before us. This is our moment to show up, claim our space and show the world what we're made of.

In the next two chapters we're going to cover some much needed groundwork before stepping into the depth of becoming magnetic. There's real work to be done if we're serious about claiming our most magnetic selves.

Each one of us carries the seeds of greatness – the potential to make a real impact that goes far beyond our immediate circles. We've got the tools, the knowledge and the determination. The question is not: *Can* you do it?

It's ***WILL*** you?

2

THE CHOICE TO CHANGE CHANGE CHANGE

From the moment I met Hamish, he was a catalyst for change in my life. He's been like a lighthouse, guiding me through some of the darkest times. He was the first person I'd ever met who was seriously doing the work – no fluff, no bullsh★t. He wasn't afraid to dig deep, confront his own demons, and throw himself into therapy, coaching and personal growth.

Meanwhile, I was in a completely different place. I didn't have a clue about healing or what 'doing the work' even meant. I thought life just dealt you a hand, and you had to play it as it was. I figured I was just one of those unlucky people. I didn't see any way out. On a deep, unconscious level, I was convinced I was unlovable. So when Hamish showed up with his rock-steady presence, I tried to tear it all down. I tried to sabotage the only real love I'd ever known because, deep down, I didn't believe I deserved it. My beliefs about myself didn't match the kind of love he was offering.

What I didn't realise back then was that I was making sure my life lined up with my own low opinions of myself. My self-loathing was reflected in toxic relationships, predators, drama and chaos. By keeping my self-esteem in the gutter, I was making sure everything else stayed there too.

However, something about Hamish's self-transformation work got through to me. I could really *see* him BEING who he said he was. He wasn't just talk, he was walking the talk. Hamish embodied the change he wanted to see, just like Mahatma Gandhi, the leader who championed non-violent resistance and inspired millions with his belief in being the change you wish to see in the world. That's why I always tell my clients to 'be Gandhi' when they're starting their path to self-development. It's a reminder that even when it's hard, you don't have to preach or tell – you just live it. Hamish saw something in me I was only just starting to see in myself: that we attract what we are, that we draw in who we're being, and that's a lesson I carry with me and share with others every single day.

After he shared the impact self-development had had on his life, I felt as though he was gently inviting me to consider and initiate my own path for healing. I said then and there that I was ready to be the one and to do the work (whatever that meant!). And I didn't just SAY it – I actually did it. I was committed to doing the necessary work of evolving and getting myself out of pain. I had not only made a decision, I was taking the action.

And here's the crazy thing – when you start doing the inner work on yourself, everything around you starts to shift. Your experiences change. The people you attract change. The opportunities that come your way, even the way you think about your past, change. But back then, I was too caught up in my old ways to notice that all this internal work was actually paying off in my relationships, my work, my friend groups and my overall happiness and wellbeing. All I could feel was the contrast. And let me tell you, that contrast scared the hell out of me. It was so far from what I was used to that I didn't know how to handle it.

THE MESSY MIDDLE

Watching Hamish live his truth pushed me to take the plunge, to go all in on my own journey of healing and growth. And that's what we all need to do. We have to be willing. We have to risk stepping outside our comfort zones if we want to create the lives we've been dreaming of.

It's like jumping off a cliff and trusting that you'll figure out how to fly on the way down. Or like a trapeze artist letting go of one bar to grab onto the next. In that split second between letting go and catching what's next, there's risk – real risk. You could fall, you could fail, you could make mistakes. But if you don't risk it, you don't grow. You don't *become*. And that's both simple and incredibly challenging.

Living the life you want and becoming the person you're capable of isn't some pipe dream or social media fantasy. It's real, and it's possible – but only if you're willing to take the risk. It's about daring to make a move, knowing it's going to be messy, knowing it's going to challenge you, but doing it anyway.

This is where most people pull back – the phase I call 'the messy middle'. This is that space where you're not who you used to be, but you're also not yet who you're becoming. It's the middle of transformation – where you've stepped out of the old, but the new hasn't fully taken shape yet.

This in-between stage feels wobbly, uncertain and straight-up uncomfortable. You're standing on ground that doesn't feel solid, and that's when the doubts creep in. You start questioning whether you should've made the leap in the first place. It's that space where the safety of the familiar starts calling you back, and the anxiety of the unknown makes you second-guess your decisions.

Let me paint you a picture. Imagine you're leaving an island of pain and isolation where you've been stranded for what feels like forever – think *Castaway* vibes, without Wilson. You've decided to sail away from that island. Sure, it's a place that sucked, but it's the devil you know. Every rock, every hardship, it's all familiar. But now you're out in the open ocean, where the waves are relentless, and you're all alone.

You could fall, you could fail, you could make mistakes. But here's the truth: if you don't risk it, you don't grow.

The compass you're relying on might be half broken, and the GPS seems to be sending you in circles. It's terrifying because, even though the island was a nightmare, it was *your* nightmare.

But that island isn't where you're meant to stay. There's another island – a paradise – waiting for you, but you can't see it from where you are. The journey there is rough. You'll be tested. The waves will knock you around, and you might question if you're even heading in the right direction. But that's the nature of growth. You can't know what's on the other side until you get there, and that requires trust – trust in yourself, trust in the process and trust in the fact that this discomfort is 100 per cent part of the journey. I mean, as if this HUGE shift in your life isn't going to require complete (temporary) discomfort?

That messy middle is the transition. It's where the old you is fading, and the new you is coming into being. It's like you're in the middle of the ocean, not quite on paradise island, but far away enough from the island of pain that turning back isn't an option. I hate to break it to you, but you and I both know that you can't reach new places without leaving the old ones behind. You can't see the opportunities and blessings of paradise island from the lonely ocean. But once you've made that transition, everything you've been working toward will start to come into view. You start to see something on the horizon. It's faint at first – just a small line where the sky meets the ocean – but it's there, and it's real. As you get closer, that line grows, starts to take shape, and suddenly, you can make out the silhouette of the land.

This isn't just any land – it's the place you've been dreaming of, the place where everything you've been working toward is finally within reach. The friends who truly get you, the career that lights you up, the love that fills you with joy, the abundance that allows you to live fully – it's all there, waiting for you on that shore. The closer you sail, the clearer it becomes. You start to see the details – the lush greenery, the vibrant colours, the bustling life, the sounds of laughter and music, the warmth of the sun hitting your skin. You realise that this is the place where you belong, the place where you're meant to thrive.

Here's the wild part – it's been there all along. It's not that this place suddenly appeared, it's that you've finally moved toward it. It was hidden from view because you were stuck on pain island, too far away to see it. But now, because you dared to sail through the unknown, to push past your fears, to keep going even when the waters were rough, you can see it clearly. With every moment, you're getting closer to stepping onto that land, to living that life you've always known was possible. This is the moment when everything starts to come into focus, when all the effort, the struggle, the growth suddenly makes sense because you can finally see what's been waiting for you all along.

You're becoming someone new, someone you haven't met yet, and that process is challenging, but it's also what makes it worth it.

A WORD ON FEAR

This absolute mission across the ocean is obviously not for the faint-hearted. If you think you're going to magnetise your way through this without fear knocking at your door, let me be clear – you're mistaken.

Fear is part of the deal. It's always going to be there, riding shotgun on this journey with you. But remember – you're the one driving. Fear might be in the car, hanging out in the back seat with two seatbelts and a helmet on, but it doesn't get to touch the wheel. It's allowed to come along for the ride, but ultimately, only you decide where you're going. And fear isn't just going to politely and quietly sit there, minding its own business. No, it's going to scream, yell and try to convince you to slam on the brakes and stay right where you are. Staying where you are? Allowing fear to take the wheel yet again? *That's* the danger. That's where dreams die.

Becoming magnetic isn't about waking up one day and magically having all the confidence and charisma in the world. It's about having the courage to get up, face your fear and take action anyway. It's about learning how to trust yourself, knowing that even if you fall you'll get back up and go again. It's about pushing through the discomfort, leaning into the uncertainty and showing up as the bravest version of yourself, even when it feels impossible.

If you're really serious about stepping into who you're meant to be, then courage isn't optional – it's essential. It's the foundation, the bedrock, the non-negotiable piece of the puzzle.

> **courage** *(noun) The feeling of pee dripping down your leg and/or skid marks in your undergarments while you are doing something you are super scared to do.*

This is courage! It's butterflies having a dance party in your stomach and trips to the toilet to do a spiritual poo. You're nervous. You're scared. You are absolutely freaking out. But you move forward despite it. Because real courage is about taking steps and making progress while you are simultaneously sh★tting yourself. So much fun, right?!

Most of the time when we're doing something that makes us really scared or nervous, our natural instinct is to reject the unknown – that magical place where great things happen, but where we don't always control how these things unfold.

I want to share a visual exercise with you to help you imagine what courage looks like. Imagine you're walking across a field through a thick fog. It's hard to see anything below your ankles and you can barely see two steps ahead of you. You really want to get to the other side of the field, but to do so, you have to surrender to the unknown – you literally have no idea what lies in front of you. Poisonous snakes? Maybe. Fallen logs and tree branches? Possibly. A clear, flat path free of any tripping hazards? Could be! You're freaked out, because you literally can't see a thing. I can already hear the control freak in you saying, 'No, no, no,

Erika! You've got to be kidding. How will I walk if I can't see my next steps? What if I trip on something? What if I get hurt?'

I know. It's scary. But it can also be magical, exhilarating and life-changing. This is the unknown – and courage is all about embracing and surrendering fully to that which we don't always know. Here's the thing: you can't know what lies ten steps ahead. Or even two steps ahead. You actually don't get the privilege of knowing any of that until you actually start walking. When you commit to walking with courage, you can't know *exactly* what's going to happen. All you know is that you made a choice, a decision to move away from the pain island – and now you've got to muster up the courage to go forward into the thick fog without seeing the whole picture. Sure, you try to pre-plan or work it out in advance as much as you can, but with courage, there comes a time when you actually need to surrender. There is no secure and safe path that guarantees you won't trip over in the fog. You have to walk. You need to do this scary, unknown thing. You can't intellectualise it anymore. You just have to move.

How?

You put one foot in front of the other. Once you take the first step, you start to notice that a few more steps become visible. How much? A little bit, that's all. That's all you can see at first, just a few steps in front of you. But the more you walk, the more the fog opens up and shows you what lies ahead. Then, all of a sudden, you come across a path. And now you have more options: you can go left or right, or straight ahead. These paths seem so much clearer as the fog begins to lift, but now you have more choices to make. You get more options and more clarity as you walk. As you take more steps, you build more courage. Your path becomes clearer and clearer, your route starts to become more familiar, and now you can see so much more, the fog becomes a mist. As you start gaining more trust in yourself, sooner or later, you're not worried about falling over or tripping, as you've gained some great momentum and now the fog has cleared completely. You're no longer as scared because now you know that if you trip and fall, you can pick yourself back up again and take the next step.

Let's be real – courage doesn't come from wishing you had it. It's earned by walking straight into that scary, unknown fog, even when every fibre of your being is screaming at you to turn back. Courage is about action, not intention. That's why so many people never find it – they're too afraid of what they can't see. We all want guarantees before we step onto that path. We want to know exactly what's going to happen: if we'll stumble, if we'll fall flat on our faces. But that's just not possible and here's a thought: why are you worrying about a fall that might never happen?

Why are you so focused on the possibility of tripping up, instead of planning for success? What if, instead of bracing for the worst, you prepared for the wins you're going to have on that foggy path? Notice how often we do this – how often we prepare for disaster instead of victory. Why waste time planning for a fall that may never come, when you could be preparing for the success that's waiting for you?

And please don't repeat my mistake and tell yourself that you have to wait until you feel 'ready'. I am going to tell you now, my friend, that day might never come. You don't have to wait for the fear to vanish – it probably never will. Instead, you move forward, scared, uncertain, unsure – and that's exactly where growth happens. That's where you start to become who you want to be.

It's not going to be easy, but nothing worth having ever is.

THE POWER OF IDENTITY SHIFTING

I've mentioned 'becoming' quite a bit so far. It's because I firmly believe that you can *become* your higher self, the next-level, 2.0 you. You know who she is. You've felt her tugging at your heart, whispering in your ear, urging you to finally break free from the constraints that have held you back. She's the real you – the woman you've always known you could be, the one who lives unafraid, unapologetic and full of life. She's not some distant fantasy; she's you, stripped of all the limiting beliefs, the doubts and the unhelpful stories that have been piled on you since the day you were born.

You've been wanting to be her your whole life, haven't you? That version of you who doesn't shrink when it's time to speak up, who doesn't hide when it's time to stand tall. The one who's free and completely untamed. The one who's not afraid to take up space, to shine, to be seen.

But to become her, you've got to face the part of you that doesn't believe it's possible. The part of you that's comfortable playing small, hiding in the shadows, muting your voice when it matters the most. The part of you that says 'yes' when she really wants to say 'no', the part of you that betrays you. That's the part you need to overcome, because it's the only thing standing between you and your next level.

Now, let's talk about identity. Your identity is essentially how you see yourself – the beliefs, qualities and characteristics that define who you are in your own eyes. It's made up of the roles you play, the labels you accept and the stories you tell yourself about who you are and what you're capable of. The identities we cling to can either elevate us or trap us. Think about it: if your entire identity is wrapped up in being a mother, what happens when your kids leave the nest? Or if your self-worth is tied to a certain level of financial success, what does it mean when that changes? Sometimes, we box ourselves into identities that no longer serve us, and if we're not careful, these identities can hold us back from becoming who we're meant to be. Maybe you picked up this book because a part of you feels that an identity shift is on the horizon. This is when you start to consciously change the way you see yourself. This shift is about redefining or upgrading your identity to align with the person you *want* to become, rather than being stuck in the version of yourself that you've always been.

WHY ARE YOU SO FOCUSED ON THE POSSIBILITY OF TRIPPING UP, INSTEAD OF PLANNING FOR SUCCESS?

Maybe your current identity is tied to being someone who always plays it safe, who doesn't speak up or who avoids taking risks. But if you want to become someone who is bold, confident and magnetic, you need to shift your identity to match that vision. It's a matter of adopting the mindset, behaviours and attitudes of that future version of you. If you're stuck in an identity that no longer serves you – like seeing yourself as someone who's 'just a mom' or 'not good with money' or 'not savvy enough to run a business' – you're going to limit what you allow yourself to achieve. An identity shift is crucial for stepping into your full potential. It's the bridge between where you are now and where you want to be. To step into your magnetism and reach your paradise island – your dream life – you've got to be willing to become someone else. You'll need to shed old identities that no longer serve you, parts of yourself that have been weighing you down. This isn't about losing who you are; it's about evolving into who you're meant to be.

To shift your identity, you start by getting clear on who you want to become, so it's not a daydream – it's really seeing that next-level version of yourself, the one who isn't held back by fear or doubt. Once you have that clarity, it's time to align your thoughts, beliefs and actions with this new version of you. It's like creating an 'alter ego' – or, as I like to call it, your 'alter she-go' – that embodies the best, most powerful version of yourself. Over time, as you consistently act in alignment with this new identity, it becomes your reality.

Don't think of this as pretending to be someone else. No, in fact you are uncovering and stepping into the truest, most powerful version of who you are meant to be. So, start envisioning who this magnetic version of you is. The more you can see her, the closer you will get to her. In the chapters to come, I'll share tangible steps you can take to step into her, but first, you need to think about who she is.

Think of it like summoning your own extra persona, just like Beyoncé has Sasha Fierce. Who is this alternative version of you? What does she believe in? What makes her feel powerful and confident? How does she carry herself through the world? Who is she surrounded by?

This requires more than just imagining; you have to embody this version of you. It's about seeing her clearly and then stepping into her shoes, even if they feel a little too big at first. You need to start making decisions from her mindset, acting with her confidence and living with her sense of purpose.

Take a moment. Close your eyes and picture her. See her in all her glory, living the life you've always dreamt of. Picture how she moves through the world – how she stands tall, how she speaks with conviction, how she navigates challenges with grace and power. Imagine the people she surrounds herself with, those who uplift and empower her, and the kinds of relationships she nurtures.

Think about what inspires her and keeps her aligned.

- What kind of mindset does she have?
- What are the thoughts that run through her mind daily?
- How does she approach her goals, her passions, her life?

This is your invitation to think about the version of you that you're stepping into. The version that doesn't shrink or play small but instead embraces her power fully and unapologetically. The truth is that you can become her, and it starts with the decision to let go of who you've been and step boldly into who you're becoming.

This journey is about more than just uncovering how you look or how others perceive you. It's about uncovering the very essence of who you are, aligning with your deepest values and inhabiting the power that's always been within you. It's about shedding the identities that no longer serve you and stepping into the light of your true, magnetic self.

What steps can you take today to start becoming HER?

THE POWER OF OUR ENERGY

A while back, I decided to take five days off at a wellness retreat, my first time really going away by myself. With the business booming and burnout creeping in, I knew I needed a break. A friend suggested I go as 'no one' – not as Erika the coach, the speaker, the 'Queen of Confidence' – but just as a woman who needed a break. She even recommended trying to stay silent, to focus solely on myself without the usual interactions.

When I got there, I embraced the idea. I sat by myself at meals, avoided eye contact and resisted the urge to chat. It felt so strange, almost like I was trying to be mean or dismissive. I did connect with a few staff members – because, let's be real, it was tough to completely switch off – but I kept it minimal.

On the last day, I made the choice to re-engage with the attendees. The moment I flipped that internal switch, it felt like I immediately snapped back into my usual self – chatting, smiling and effortlessly connecting with everyone around me. Looking back, I find it fascinating to see how I stepped into a different version of myself. Had I not consciously made that decision to 'shut off', I would have easily fallen into the familiar pattern of coaching and supporting others, which would have completely derailed my intention to have a break (the whole reason I was there!). This experience taught me that none of us is bound by labels like 'introvert', 'extrovert', 'the loud one' or 'shy.' These aren't fixed identities – they're just mindsets. You have the power to shift them with your awareness and energy. It's incredible how much we can influence our environment and the outcomes we create when we're conscious of the energy we're putting out into the world.

TIME TO MAKE A CHOICE

Stepping into your next level

This journey from pain island to paradise island is no joke. It's tough, uncomfortable and seriously challenging. But staying stuck in the same place – on that familiar, uncomfortable-comfort island – isn't doing you any favours either. You've picked up *Becoming Magnetic* because something inside you knows it's time for a change. Now it's time to take action. It's time to put this book down and make a choice.

I want to invite you to engage in some serious self-reflection (yes, right now, please!). We've covered a bit of ground and before we go any further, it's important you take time to draw a line in the sand. This is your chance to deeply reflect on your 'pain island', and to think on what is required for you to start sailing to your paradise island.

Grab a journal, open a new document or just find a quiet space to think. The intention of this exercise is about finding your clarity, courage and commitment to take the next step.

Exercise: Mapping pain island

You're standing at a crossroads – the messy middle where the old you and the new you are in a tug-of-war. Before you can move forward, you need to get clear on where you are right now. This is about facing the reality of your current situation – the things that are no longer serving you, the areas that are holding you back and the beliefs that are keeping you stuck. This is the part of the journey where you have to make decisions. And I'm not talking about small, everyday choices. I'm talking about the big ones many of us avoid, the ones that shift your entire life direction.

Here's what I want you to do.

‘It’s time to align your thoughts, beliefs and actions with this new version of you. It’s like creating an ‘alter ego’ – or, as I like to call it, your ‘alter she-go’.’

Step 1: Identify your pain island

- What's not working?

  Think about the area of your life that feels the most out of alignment. What's draining your energy? What are you tired of tolerating? Where do you feel stuck, frustrated or dissatisfied?

Step 2: Choose your focus

- Which area needs attention?

  From the list below, pick the one area that stands out to you the most – the area where you feel the most resistance or where you know something needs to shift:

  – family
  – relationships and friendships
  – health and wellbeing
  – mindset
  – purpose and fulfilment
  – career, work or business
  – money
  – faith, spirituality or religion

Step 3: Reflect on your current reality

- What needs to change?

  In this area you've chosen, what specifically is no longer serving you? What beliefs, habits or patterns are keeping you on your island of pain? Write down everything that comes to mind, no matter how uncomfortable it may be.

Step 4: Acknowledge the impact

- How is this holding you back?

  How is staying on pain island affecting your life? What opportunities are you missing out on because of it? Get real with yourself here – what is this costing you in terms of happiness, growth and potential?

The power to create the magnetic life you want is in your hands, and it starts with you making a courageous decision to step into the unknown with everything you've got. You are not just a participant in your life; you are literally the architect of your reality. And this decision to leave the old behind is the first step in building something extraordinary.

The choice is yours. Will you stay in the familiar, clinging to what's safe but unfulfilling? Or are you ready to step up, step out and claim the life that's waiting for you?

The choice is yours.

3

RADICAL SHIFTS REQUIRE RADICAL RESPONSIBILITY

RESPONSIBILITY

RESPONSIBILITY

Before we dive into all things magnetism, there's a crucial concept we need to address – a cornerstone in my journey that has shaped me into the person I am today. It's a topic that keeps coming up, whether I'm coaching women one-on-one, speaking on stage during a Q&A or sifting through emails from my online community. 'Erika, what was THE moment that changed everything for you?' I find this question so hard. It's tough to pinpoint just one moment that changed everything because, honestly, it wasn't just a single event that transformed my entire life. But there was one pivotal moment when I made the **decision** that I was ready to change. That decision became the catalyst for everything else – it's when everything, and I mean everything, began to shift. And that moment started when I learnt what the concept of 'taking radical responsibility' truly meant. I'd heard of the word 'responsibility' before, but I had no idea what it had to do with me.

Before we move forward, let's clarify what responsibility truly means. At its core, responsibility is about having the ability to respond – it's your response-ability. How you choose to respond to any given situation is entirely within your control. This means you have the freedom to decide how you will act, react and engage with the world around you.

But what does it mean to take radical responsibility? Unlike responsibility, radical responsibility is about taking extreme ownership of your life, regardless of the circumstances you find yourself in. It goes beyond simply responding to life as it happens. Instead, it's about actively seeking out and claiming ownership of every situation, every challenge, every experience. Radical responsibility means you're not just reacting to what life throws at you; you're looking for ways to take charge, to influence and to shape your reality – even when things feel beyond your control.

In other words, radical responsibility is about finding where you can exercise your power in every moment, even in the smallest details. Taking radical responsibility can be one of the most powerful shifts we can ever make, especially if we've been stuck in a perpetual cycle of feeling like life is happening *to* us rather than *for* us. Radical responsibility is the opposite of playing the blame game. Instead of pointing the finger at everyone else, you take an honest look at yourself and your contribution. You interrogate your actions, beliefs and results. You assess and inquire about the possibility of *you* attracting certain experiences into your life. It's one of the most important concepts I've learned in my journey to becoming magnetic.

Let me take you back to the moment when radical responsibility (*painfully*) changed the course of my life.

I was dumped on my twenty-eighth birthday. Nice present, huh? A couple of years before then, I had chosen to uproot my life in Florida, moving to Sydney, Australia, for a man I'd met in America – really, I was running away from my life. I didn't realise then just how wrong he was for me. And when that relationship inevitably fell apart, I gave myself no time to breathe – I jumped straight into another one. This time, I moved to Melbourne for a guy who, on the surface, seemed like a fresh start. As it turned out, he was just a different version of the same mess.

From the very beginning with him, I was told that who I was couldn't be talked about – not fully, not honestly. He had lied to his family about my upbringing, about my dad leaving when I was a kid. He said he didn't want them to know I came from a 'broken home', a term I hadn't even heard before. My past – being in foster homes, suffering abuse, breaking my back, losing my husband – none of that could be known. He made sure to bury it all deep down, as if my experiences were something to be ashamed of, something to hide. And the sad part? I started to believe him. I began to think that maybe he was right. Maybe I was damaged, that I needed to hide who I really was, that I wasn't worthy of being loved if people knew the truth about me.

Looking back, I find it almost unbearable to think about how much I allowed that terrible treatment and how long I lasted in that painful relationship. But I was so desperate to be loved, to be accepted, that I ignored the super-hot red, neon glowing flags telling me to run in the opposite direction. I knew deep down that it didn't feel right, but I was terrified to be alone. I had no one in Australia: no friends, no family. I only had surface-level friendships with my nail technician and personal trainer. As I mentioned, my service providers were my only friends, I mean – really, Erika?!

In this relationship, we fought constantly, and I had a daily knot in my stomach, which I now know was anxiety. I was always on edge around him, worried about saying the wrong thing, looking the wrong way. Being with him made me feel like I had to justify every part of my past, every choice I'd ever made. He constantly checked my phone, hacked into my email and wanted to know every detail of my previous relationships, grilling me about who I had been with and why. It was nuts.

One night, we had one of our usual arguments. He picked it over something so trivial – a person I had briefly dated before him. That argument spiralled into a week of tears. I cried myself to sleep night after night, desperate to fit into the mould he wanted, to be the 'cleaned-up' version of myself he'd dangled as the key to our

Blame keeps the focus on the past and what's been done to us, while on the flip side, responsibility focuses on the future and what we can do about it.

future together. He said he wanted to marry me one day but only if I could clean up my past, if I could somehow delete my history in order to be good enough to fit into his perfect world. And I was terrified I would mess it up. I wasn't happy, but I convinced myself this was my only shot at love. That no one else would ever love me if I let this relationship fail. And then, out of the blue, on my birthday, he called me and told me it was over. Just like that.

I, of course, was devastated. I had to go to work that day, but I was barely holding it together. During my lunch break, I stumbled into the food court at the mall across from work, feeling completely numb. As I wandered aimlessly, my glasses all foggy from the tears, I heard someone call my name. To my embarrassment, it was Hamish, my personal trainer. He was standing right in front of me, concern written all over his face.

'Are you okay?' he asked, his voice caring and gentle.

'I just got dumped, but I'll be okay,' I lied through a forced smile, trying to keep myself composed. 'I should come in for more PT sessions,' I added, desperate to change the subject. 'I'll message you about it later.'

He gave me a nod and a sympathetic smile, as if to say 'poor thing', and walked away.

That night, I tried to distract myself the best way I knew how. I grabbed a tub of ice-cream – because isn't that the best cliché heartbreak remedy? – and settled onto the couch to watch the girliest chick flicks I could find. I laughed, I cried and then I cried some more. The movies were a temporary (much-needed) escape, but the truth of my situation was always there, gnawing at me in the background. The next morning, I dragged myself to the bathroom and caught sight of myself in the mirror. But this time, something was different.

I had looked in mirrors millions of times before – checking my hair, my outfit, my make-up – but this time, I didn't just see my reflection,

I saw myself. I mean, I *really* saw myself, maybe for the first time in years. I stood there, staring into my own eyes, and what I saw wasn't just a broken woman; I saw someone who was lost, someone who had been running from herself for far too long. Damn, it really hurt.

As painful as that moment was, it became a turning point. I realised that in every failed relationship, in every mess of my life, the one constant was **me**. I was the common denominator. I was the one who had been stopping myself, hurting myself, neglecting myself. Sure, he had broken up with me, and sure, he wasn't very kind, but I had allowed him to treat me like that. I had ignored the signs, convinced myself that this was the best I could do. I had chosen to stay, out of fear of being alone, out of fear of not finding anyone better. That day, as the mascara dried and my reflection stared back at me with a mix of sorrow and newfound clarity, I knew something had to change. I mean, I had moved my whole life to the other side of the world! No longer could I blame my circumstances or the people around me. It was time to take ownership of my own happiness, of my own life. I didn't have a clear plan, and I certainly didn't know how the hell I was going to change everything, but I knew at that moment that I couldn't keep living the way I had been.

That moment in front of the mirror, broken and vulnerable, marked the beginning of a new chapter in my life. I realised that if I wanted to find happiness, to build a life that was truly mine, I had to start with myself. It was the first step toward taking radical responsibility, toward becoming the person I was always meant to be. It was the day I stopped waiting for someone else to save me and decided to finally save myself.

WHAT YOU NEED TO OVERCOME

You may find that you've struggled with the same issues for a very long time. I know I did. I would do the inner work on myself and think, *That's it! I am healed,* only to find myself struggling with the same issues again. I would feel insufficient and not good enough. I would be so puzzled: *Didn't I already work on this? When will this go away already!?*

Have you ever felt like that? Well, what if I told you that healing isn't linear, and even though you may have worked on something already, sometimes (most times) you have much deeper still to go.

Traumatic experiences in childhood and adolescence don't go away after three months of therapy; they imprint core beliefs and coping strategies deep into your being, and you might not know where to start. So how do you figure out what you need to work on? Look at your life, scan your work or your relationships, romantic relationship, friendships, family, health, wealth, your sense of purpose and joy. How are these areas of your life? Where do you want to get better results right now? What needs your attention?

If you tune into your life, you will be able to notice the area(s) that most need work. Choose the biggest one, then get to work. The 'work' can be done in all sorts of ways:

- committing to getting a therapist or coach
- going to a healing retreat
- joining a supportive community for accountability
- having regular sessions with a spiritual guide, healer or mentor
- cultivating a self-reflection or self-regulation practice, such as journalling or meditation
- enrolling in a self-development program.

I usually find that some sort of accountability with someone qualified to help you who won't let you hide works best. This isn't easy work, but I promise that you can let go of the heavy burdens you've carried throughout life. It's one of the greatest gifts you can give yourself.

AT ITS CORE, RESPONSIBILITY IS ABOUT HAVING THE ABILITY TO RESPOND – IT'S YOUR RESPONSE-ABILITY.

FOUR STEPS TO RADICAL RESPONSIBILITY

So, how do we start this?

There are four main steps to practising radical responsibility, and these practical yet powerful steps are essential for shifting you from self-sabotage and blame into self-belief and empowerment. By adopting radical responsibility, you're not just taking control; you're actively cultivating the qualities that make you magnetic. It's through this process of ownership and intentionality that you start to attract the life, relationships and opportunities you desire. These steps are your gateway to becoming the most empowered, confident and magnetic version of yourself.

Let's walk through them together. (And if you want to watch my TedX talk on these four steps, scan the QR code to watch it on YouTube.)

Step 1: Self-reflection

The journey toward radical responsibility starts with self-reflection. This is the moment when you truly look in the mirror and see yourself – not just the reflection staring back, but the person behind the eyes. This is one of the most powerful tools you have for stepping into your magnetism. Without this step, change simply can't occur. Without self-reflection, you won't figure out the mistakes you're making, the problems you're having or what doesn't feel good for you anymore. You've got to be willing to look in the mirror, literally and metaphorically. Self-reflection is where awareness meets authenticity. It's about acknowledging who you are, how you've shown up in your life and the beliefs that have shaped your world. This step is foundational because without seeing and understanding ourselves, we can't even begin to change our circumstances.

In the context of becoming magnetic, self-reflection is crucial. You can't attract what you truly desire if you don't first understand who you are and what you're projecting out to the world. The energy you emit, whether consciously or unconsciously, is what you attract back. By taking a hard look at yourself, you begin to see the patterns, the stories you've told yourself and the ways in which you've held yourself back. This isn't about self-loathing; it's about self-awareness. It's about seeing yourself clearly, so you can start to shift the energy you're putting out into the world.

Questions to reflect on

- What do you see when you truly look at yourself in the mirror? What thoughts and emotions come up for you?
- What are the recurring patterns or beliefs in your life that have held you back?
- How have these patterns or beliefs influenced your relationships, career, love life and overall happiness?
- What truths about yourself have you been avoiding, and what would it mean to face them head-on?

Step 2: A shift in perspective

After that moment of self-reflection, the next step of radical responsibility is a shift in perspective. This is where you move from seeing yourself as a victim of circumstance to becoming the creator of your reality. It's easy to get stuck in the narrative that life happens to us, but this perspective is disempowering. It keeps us in a loop of self-sabotage, waiting for things to change rather than actively changing them ourselves.

For me, the shift happened when I realised that blaming others – or even blaming myself – was keeping me stuck. Something needed to change. Blame keeps the focus on the past and what's been done to us, while on the flip side, responsibility focuses on the future and what we can do about it. It's the difference between waiting on the sidelines and stepping up to take control, knowing you're the one who can change the game. When you shift your perspective, the reality you see begins to shift too. This shift in perspective is about seeing beyond your circumstances, recognising your power to shape your life and understanding that you have the ability to respond in a way that serves your greatest good.

In terms of magnetism, this shift in perspective is vital. When you start to see yourself as the creator of your reality, you naturally begin to attract more of what you want. You're no longer waiting for opportunities to come to you – you're magnetising them. You believe that you have the ability to co-create with the powers that be and attract what you want as if it's already a done deal. This is the essence of becoming magnetic: actively shaping your life rather than being shaped by it.

Questions to reflect on

- How do you typically view challenges in your life? Do you see them as obstacles or opportunities for growth?
- In what areas of your life do you feel limited or unable to make change, and what truth are you avoiding that could shift your perspective and restore your power?
- What core story or belief are you holding on to that's defining your life right now, and if you were to rewrite it with full honesty and courage, how would it empower you instead?
- How might your life change if you started to see yourself as the creator of your reality, rather than a passive observer?

Step 3: Healing and reconciliation (the dark night of the soul)

The third step is what poet and priest St John of the Cross referred to as the 'dark night of the soul'. This concept comes from his writings in the sixteenth century, describing a spiritual crisis in the journey toward union with the divine. It's a period of deep, very painful introspection and soul-searching, where you feel completely disconnected, lost and sometimes drowning in darkness. But the good news is that this darkness is not here to break you – it's here to transform you. It's an initiation – one you must go through to reach a profound awakening and unveil the real you. Moving through this might feel like a death, but it's the spark that ignites the rebirth essential for your expansion.

The dark night of the soul represents the deep, often painful work of healing and reconciliation with yourself. It's about facing your deepest wounds, acknowledging the pain that's been buried and embracing forgiveness – both for yourself and for others. For me, this meant forgiving myself for the choices I had made, for the ways I had allowed myself to be treated, and for the times I had ignored my own self-worth. I had to find compassion for myself instead of judging myself. I've had a few dark nights of the soul, and each one allowed me to really understand myself and why I showed up with such a lack of confidence and low self-esteem in the first place. I spent eight years on my healing journey and a massive part of that time also involved forgiving those who had hurt me – not because they deserved it, but because *I* deserved the peace that came with it.

This step is where the real work of self-discovery happens. It's messy, it's uncomfortable and it requires a true commitment to your personal growth. But it's also where the most profound change occurs. When you heal those deep wounds, you free yourself from the chains of the past. You stop carrying the baggage that's been weighing you down, and you start to rise from the ashes, better than before. The dark night is where you confront your shadows, and in doing so, find your light.

In the context of magnetism, this step is crucial because you can't attract what you truly desire if you're still holding on to past hurts and resentments. Healing is what clears the way for new energy to flow

Radical responsibility means you're not just reacting to what life throws at you; you're looking for ways to take charge, to influence and to shape your reality – even when things feel beyond your control.

into your life. It's what allows you to move forward unburdened, open to receiving all the good that's coming your way.

Questions to reflect on

- What deep wounds or unresolved emotions are you carrying that need healing?
- How has holding on to past pain or resentment impacted your ability to move forward in your life?
- What does forgiveness – of both yourself and others – look like for you? How can it help you release the baggage you've been carrying?
- In what ways can you begin the process of healing, even if it feels uncomfortable or difficult? Who can you enrol to support you?

Step 4: A change in behaviour

The final step is a change in behaviour. This is where everything you've learnt through self-reflection, shifting your perspective and healing comes into play. It's the moment you start to embody the lessons you've learnt, making different, more aligned choices that reflect the person you *want* to become. This is where intention becomes action. It's not enough to just understand what needs to change – you have to actually change it.

For me, this meant stepping into the version of myself I had always wanted to be. It meant no longer tolerating relationships that didn't serve me, no longer staying silent when I needed to speak up and no longer making excuses for not living the life I truly wanted. It started with admitting I had a toxic relationship with alcohol, then with hiring a coach and committing to regular sessions, to journalling daily and making time in my day to process my emotions and learning the steps to regulate my nervous system. I left an unhealthy workplace and I committed to taking tangible steps toward self-care. Within twelve months of my moment in the mirror, I was a completely new person, and because I worked so hard at these four steps, I know their power.

In the realm of becoming magnetic, this change in behaviour is what solidifies your new reality. It's what takes your desires from being just ideas or dreams and turns them into your lived experience. When you start to act in alignment with your true self, you naturally begin to attract what you want into your life. You're no longer chasing after things – you're drawing them to yourself effortlessly. This is how you become truly magnetic.

Questions to reflect on

- What are the behaviours or patterns that you know you need to change in order to become the person you want to be?
- How can you start to embody the lessons you've learnt from self-reflection, shifting your perspective and healing?
- What small, actionable steps can you take today that align with your highest self?
- How will you hold yourself accountable to making these changes, and what support do you need to stay committed?

By integrating these four steps – self-reflection, a shift in perspective, healing and a change in behaviour – you begin to transform not only your life but also the energy you radiate out to the world. This journey to radical responsibility is the solid foundation on which your magnetism is built. It's what empowers you to attract the relationships, opportunities and experiences that truly align with your highest self. As you move forward in *Becoming Magnetic*, we'll dive deeper into the art of magnetism and the five phases that will guide you. It is with those five principles that things get real, your transformation takes root and you step into the life you've always known was waiting for you.

Once you assess the main themes in your life, your magnetism will go from hidden in your unconscious to becoming visibly there.

Taking radical responsibility is the reason I was able to transform my life and create the magnetism, the confidence, the authenticity, the joy, the fulfilment, the relationship, the successful business . . . the EVERYTHING I have today. And hell yes, it was ridiculously challenging, triggering and at times relentless, but once I understood and implemented it, I became unstoppable – and so will you.

In essence, you must overcome to become. Remove to improve. You must let go of the person you once were to become who you're meant to be.

When we choose to own our responses and actions, we can unlock our highest potential and start attracting not only what we want, but what we deserve. And when you do that, you're no longer at the mercy of your circumstances – you're in control, you're empowered and you're unshakable. This is the foundation of becoming magnetic. It's not about what happens to you; it's about how you choose to rise from it.

“In essence, you must overcome to become. Remove to improve. You must let go of the person you once were to become who you’re meant to be.”

4

UNVEILING YOUR MAGNETIC

POTENTIAL
POTENTIAL

POTENTIAL

Magnetism was in my blood from day one: even though my childhood was chaotic – bouncing between foster homes and constantly changing schools – I thrived on meeting people and connecting. But as I grew older, life started to hit harder, and it was really after Jeo's death that everything went downhill for me. I was drowning in grief, sadness and alcohol, completely severed from the vibrant, magnetic child I once was. My energy was pitch black, and it was no surprise that I kept attracting all the wrong people and situations into my life, so by the time I decided to take radical responsibility, you already know, I was a mess. Slowly, I started to see the light again. I dug deep into my trauma, my past, my pain, and finally began to reclaim my life. I learned about radical responsibility and finally realised that the power to change was in my hands all along. As I fell back in love with life and, most importantly, with myself, EVERYTHING started to open up again.

Something crazy happened.

I started caring about other people in a way I hadn't in years. My heart opened up, and with it, my magnetism began to show itself. The more I worked on myself, the more I peeled away the layers of hurt, anger and fear, the more I found the magnetic me underneath all that pain. I let go of the baggage, the stories that no longer served me and the old versions of myself that were outdated and holding me back. It felt like shedding a heavy coat I didn't need anymore.

I wasn't trying to be anyone else. I wasn't trying to fit into anyone's expectations. I was myself, and that was more than enough. This version of *me* was humble, friendly, open and unapologetically herself.

And today, this is who I know myself to be.

I learnt some very important things about magnetism during these experiences that I need to share with you:

- You won't (and can't) really care about others if you don't care about yourself.
- You can't connect with others if you aren't connected to yourself.
- If you don't accept yourself, how can you do this with others?

Once I started doing the internal work, that work started paying off. I began to love and accept myself *and* others. I wanted to connect. I wanted to meet people. I wanted to co-create with the world around me. **This** is magnetism, by the way. It's how you move in the world with others and the vibe you create around you. I started to build genuine connections, and that's when everything kicked off for me with magnetism.

I started to own my energy, building unshakable self-belief and standing firm in who I truly was. I realised that magnetism wasn't something I needed to find or chase – it was in me this whole time, I just wasn't aware of it. Every single day, we're attracting and magnetising, whether we're aware of it or not.

Think back on your life – those moments when you felt like everything just clicked, when things felt seamless, when people gravitated toward you, not because of what you were doing, but because of who you were being. When you weren't trying to force anything but were simply standing tall in your own authenticity, owning your space without apology . . .

These are the moments when your magnetism was in full effect. And guess what? You didn't have to do anything to make it happen. It was all about how you showed up in the world.

Take a moment to reflect. When have you noticed your own magnetism at play, even if you didn't recognise it at the time? What energy were you putting out? What were you attracting into your life? And most importantly, are you consciously tuning into that energy today, or are you running on autopilot?

(If it's tough to recall a moment like this, don't stress – you're now creating a life where moments like these become the norm.)

WE'RE ALL MAGNETIC

Whether we think about it or not, we are all magnetic. Every single one of us is constantly attracting or repelling things, people and experiences in and out of our lives. Think of it this way: every interaction you have, every room you walk into, every thought you entertain is either pulling things closer to you or pushing them further away – the good and the bad. This happens because of energy – your energy. So many of us think we're just unlucky, that things happen to us, but that's not how it works. The truth is, you're attracting your reality. Whether you're pulling in unhealthy relationships, negative experiences or constantly feeling stuck, there's something inside you creating that magnetic pull. And here's the bad news: most of us are doing this unconsciously.

Your energy is always moving, always interacting with the world around you. It's like a silent conversation happening between you and the universe. Whether it's tension or excitement, you can pick up on the energy. People feel yours, too.

“THE MINUTE YOU WAKE UP TO THE FACT THAT YOU’RE CO-CREATING WHAT YOU ATTRACT, EVERYTHING SHIFTS.”

ENERGY DOESN'T LIE

Think of your energy like a magnet. A magnet doesn't stop attracting or repelling just because you're not paying attention. Your energy works the same way. It's like you're tuning your internal frequency to fear, scarcity or doubt, and that's what's showing up in your life. On the flip side, when you're clear on what you want and confident in who you are, you start to attract the people, opportunities and experiences that match that energy.

Let's dig into the word *energy*.

When I say 'energy', I'm not talking about some woo-woo term reserved for spiritual circles, and it doesn't require a science degree to break it down. In the context of magnetism, energy is the vibe you put out into the world, the feeling people get when they're around you. It's the unspoken frequency of your being. People can sense it instantly. It's always flowing.

Imagine this: you've walked into a room where the tension was thick, even though no one was speaking. Or maybe you've been drawn to someone who wasn't necessarily the loudest, the flashiest or the best-dressed – but they had something about them, a certain pull. That's energy at play. You can't fake it, and you can't hide it. This is why we are always magnetising something.

Let me explain . . .

I don't know about you, but when I first heard terms like 'the universe', 'energy' or 'frequency', I remember being so confused. So before we go any further, let's get on the same page and translate some of these words into plain English: I know words like 'vibration', 'frequency', 'magnetic field' and 'aura' can sound a little vague at times, but they are powerful and important. Here's a real-talk breakdown of what I mean in the context of what I'm trying to teach you:

Buzzword	**What it really means**
Vibration	It's the overall feeling or mood you're radiating on a daily basis. Low vibe = blah, pessimistic, meh. High vibe = energised, positive, optimistic.
Frequency	The level of energy you're operating on. High-frequency people lift others up; whereas low-frequency people tend to drain the room.
Magnetic	When people and opportunities are naturally drawn to you; it's that inexplicable 'it factor' – a pull that's impossible to ignore.
Aura	The presence you give off, whether you're aware of it or not. Your personal energy bubble. Some say it's colourful, others just feel it. People pick up on it and feel it instantly. This is what announces you before you say anything.
Field	The invisible space around you that holds your energy. Imagine your energy stretching beyond your body to create a space that's full of everything you're thinking, feeling and sensing.
Intuition	Your inner GPS system. That gut feeling that says, 'Go this way' or 'Watch out for that'. It's not always logical, but it's usually right – if you're willing to listen to it. It's calm and internal (not loud and irrational like fear).

Now that we understand energy, this leads us to the **two types of magnetism** we all possess.

UNCONSCIOUS VERSUS CONSCIOUS MAGNETISM

Here's where it gets potent: there's a huge difference between being consciously magnetic and unconsciously magnetic, between actively working with your magnetism or being completely unaware of it.

Unconscious magnetism is when you're operating on autopilot. You're still attracting, but you're not aware of what energy you're putting out there or even *how* you're attracting what you are. This is when you find yourself getting things you don't want – negative relationships, environments or situations that seem to keep you stuck. This is when your unresolved fears, doubts or limiting beliefs are running the show, and you're not even cognisant of it.

You remember my not-so-nice boyfriend who wanted me to hide my past? I wasn't aware that I was putting out this energy of 'I am not good enough; I am damaged goods and broken; no one will want me' and, because of my lack of self awareness, I didn't notice the red flags until I was really faced with the reality eleven months into the relationship. And although it's **never, ever** too late to leave an unhealthy relationship, I definitely suffered more than I would have had I been more aware early on.

Conscious magnetism is when you know exactly what you're putting out there. You're intentional about the energy you carry, the thoughts you think and the way you show up. You know what you want, and you're actively working toward it. If you imagine a radio, you're in control of the volume and frequency you're tuning into, the song is rocking and you are jamming to the best tunes ever. As a result, you're calling in the things that align with your desires.

I remember preparing for a huge speaking event I'd dreamed about for years. This was more than just delivering a speech; it was a moment for fully owning my message and showing up as my most magnetic self. To do that, I focused on grounding myself, visualising the impact I wanted, and setting a clear intention to connect authentically with the audience.

Walking onto that stage, I could feel the energy shift in the room. I wasn't trying to impress – I was simply being present and open. People later told me they felt like I was speaking directly to them, like the message resonated on a deeper level. That's conscious magnetism in action. By intentionally aligning my energy and purpose, I attracted exactly the connections and impact I'd envisioned.

THE POWER OF AWARENESS

By now, you're seeing just how critical awareness is in the journey to becoming magnetic. This is the foundational step. Your energy, your vibe – it's all about what you're consciously putting out there. The minute you wake up to the fact that you're co-creating what you attract, everything shifts. You stop feeling as if life is just happening to you, and instead, you start steering the ship. You become intentional with the energy you carry into every situation, and that's when the real magic begins.

So, how do you become more aware of your magnetism?

Start by looking at your life.

What patterns are you noticing?

What thoughts are you entertaining?

What emotions are you holding onto?

What kind of people are you attracting into your circle? Are they supportive, encouraging and aligned with your values, or are they draining and always complaining? How do they make you feel?

What kind of experiences are showing up for you? Are you constantly hitting roadblocks or do you feel like things are flowing?

Your life is a direct reflection of the energy you're putting out. If you don't like what you're seeing, it's time to shift that energy. But first, you need to become aware of it. These are all clues to the energy you're broadcasting.

START OWNING YOUR ENERGY

Now that you know you're always magnetising, it's time to tune into what you actually want. Here are some real ways you can start becoming more aware of the energy you bring into the world:

- **Check in with your thoughts:** What's the first thing you think about when you wake up? Are you grateful, excited and ready to take on the day, or are you dreading what's ahead? Your thoughts set the tone for your energy. Make a habit of checking in with them, and if they're not aligned with what you want to attract, invite yourself to work on shifting them through deep inquiry.
- **Reflect on your inner circle:** Who are you allowing into your life? Who has access to you and your energy, and do they deserve it? Do they appreciate it? How comfortable are you with boundaries? Do you need to reteach people how to treat you? Does your inner circle or family give you energy, or do they drain your energy?
- **Tune into your vibe:** Forget about a 'fit' check, it's time to check your vibe. Pay attention to your emotions: how do you feel most of the time? Are you anxious, stressed or fearful? Or are you calm, confident and in control? Your emotions are a powerful indicator of the energy you're putting out. If you're constantly in a negative emotional state, you're attracting more negativity into your life.

Start noticing how you feel, and if it's not serving you, take steps to shift it.

- **Do an energy audit:** I get asked almost daily how I have SO much energy, and let me tell you: it's because I love my life and nothing (and I mean nothing) gets access to my world unless it's a match to my frequency, my vibe. And I vibe high – so you can imagine. Throughout the day, ask yourself: what energy am I bringing into the room, the conversation, the situation? Is this the kind of vibe I want to bring?
- **Manage the internal voices:** Imagine your mind like the *Inside Out* control panel, where emotions are individual characters battling to control the body they live in. Who's at the wheel most days? Is it sadness, anger, anxiety, joy? What's your inner dialogue? What are you saying about yourself? Your thoughts, the statements in **your** mind – they hold weight and they are a huge part of the energy you're sending out. Be mindful of the conversations that happen about *you* in your head, as they will impact the direction of your life.
- **Get real with yourself:** Results don't lie. Are you getting what you want? What would you like to draw into your life that you don't currently have? What's required for you to draw that in? Are you happy with the results you've been producing lately? If not, what needs to change in order for you to get the results you desire?

When you become aware of the energy you put out there, you start consciously tuning it to attract what you **actually** want. You stop repelling the things you desire and start drawing them into your life with clear intent. This is where the real power lies. Magnetism isn't just about 'being positive' or 'thinking good thoughts'; it's about taking radical responsibility for your energy, your actions and your life. Once you do that, you can create the reality you've always wanted. The more aware you become of the energy you're putting out there, the more control you have over what you consciously magnetise into your life.

Now it's time to reflect on what you've been drawing into your life. If you can start to see where you are actively and intentionally attracting versus allowing things to just be, you will be able to discover how to tune yourself to the frequency of what you want.

Take a moment to think or journal about what you actually want to attract moving forward.

- What kind of relationships do you want to be in?
- What kind of career or business do you want to build?
- What kind of environments do you want to surround yourself with, and are you aligning with them now?
- What kinds of opportunities do you want to attract, and are you positioning yourself for them?
- What kind of life do you want to wake up to every day?
- What type of energy do you want to attract, and are you reflecting that energy now?
- How can you align your actions today with the life you're trying to magnetise tomorrow?
- Who do you want to be in the next twelve months, and what energy do you need to embody to get there?

Magnetism isn't just about wishful thinking – it's about setting clear intentions and aligning your energy to match that vision. Who is the version of you that has everything you desire? How does she show up in the world? Can you start BEING her now? When you consciously show up as the woman who's already living her best life, you stop repelling the things you desire and you start drawing them in with ease.

THE FOUR BLOCKERS OF MAGNETISM

Now, wouldn't it be amazing if we could just sit back, relax and manifest our dream life from the couch? If we could chant a mantra, throw in a few positive affirmations and – boom! – everything falls into place. Sounds like a dream, right? But let me go ahead and tell you that unfortunately there are a few things getting in the way of that fantasy.

What if I told you that to truly become magnetic, you need to stop *trying* to be magnetic? Instead of forcing it, what if you simply allowed your natural magnetism to rise to the surface? The truth is, you already have what it takes, but the key is removing what's blocking it. For centuries, women have been conditioned to believe untruths about who they are and what they're capable of. These beliefs have been passed down from generation to generation, keeping us stuck and small. These are the real blockers to your magnetism – the barriers that stop you from stepping into your power, radiating from within and taking up your full space. If you're going to break free and let your magnetism shine, it's time to face these blockers head-on and dismantle them for good.

Blocker 1: No connection with yourself

Here's the hard truth – if you're not connected to yourself, your magnetism can't shine. It's like trying to run a car with no fuel. You can't expect to show up powerfully in the world when you don't even know who you are.

The biggest blocker to your magnetism is not knowing who YOU truly are. When you lack that deep self-connection, you start basing your worth on external validation – on other people's opinions, on societal expectations, on what the world says you should be. But let me tell you, looking outside yourself for your identity is a dangerous game. It leaves you vulnerable, constantly chasing approval that never

Magnetism isn't just about 'being positive' or 'thinking good thoughts'; it's about taking radical responsibility for your energy, your actions and your life.

fills the void. And as long as you're disconnected from yourself, you're not going to be the magnetic force you're capable of being. Disconnection happens when you numb out or avoid the hard truths. You know what I'm talking about – whether it's numbing yourself with food, alcohol, scrolling social media for hours, or getting lost in reality TV to avoid what's really going on. You end up running from yourself instead of sitting with your sh*t. Being busy all the time, needing to be productive or distracted – these are ways you avoid facing yourself. That's disconnection in action.

The deeper you disconnect, the deeper your magnetism lies buried because you're not showing up as YOU. You're showing up as some version of yourself you've created to please others, avoid pain or keep yourself safe. But here's the reality: magnetism is an inside job. It's about you knowing who you are, why you do what you do and what you actually want. When you have that connection with yourself, you show up differently. You move with purpose, you speak with conviction and people can feel that energy from a mile away.

That's why I believe so deeply in doing the work – journalling, personal development, therapy, hell, even just taking a walk by yourself in nature to reflect quietly. These aren't surface-level activities, they're tools to help you get to know yourself on a deeper level. Because when you get connected to your inner self, everything changes. Your intuition sharpens, your confidence rises – and your energy? Next level. Self-connection is your power source for magnetism.

Magnetic action:

Spend 15 minutes today journalling with this question:

Who am I, really, when no one is watching?

Let your thoughts flow without holding back. Write whatever comes to mind, no filters, no judgements. Allow yourself to explore your truest self, beyond the roles you play, the expectations you meet or the masks you wear. However, make sure you don't get trapped by internal negativity, as this is about getting curious.

What you uncover could be the key to unlocking your magnetism – the real you beneath all the noise.

Blocker 2: Impostor syndrome

I know so many incredible, high-achieving women who have a big, fat dose of 'impostor syndrome.' You'd be surprised – it's not just the newbies or the underachievers. We're talking about women killing it in their fields, smashing goals and yet still they're doubting themselves. A recent study even revealed that 75 per cent of female business executives experienced self-doubt about their ability to do their job. Here's the wild thing – it affects women more than men.

Impostor syndrome is like this mind distortion where no matter what you've achieved or how qualified you are, you feel like you're one mistake away from being 'found out' as a fraud. Even when the results are staring you in the face, you somehow convince yourself that it was just luck or you were in the right place at the right time.

Why do we feel like frauds? Well, there's a lot to unpack here. Some of it stems from the way we've been conditioned – no matter how incredible we are, there's this little voice inside whispering that we're not enough. We start believing that we just got lucky, that sooner or later, someone's going to catch on that we're winging it. But let me tell you, the only thing you're faking is this idea that you're an impostor.

Even some of the most famously accomplished people have admitted to feeling this. We're talking Charlize Theron, Michelle Obama, Dua Lipa, Billie Eilish and even the incredible Maya freaking Angelou. So if you think you're alone in this, you're not. But here's the deal – you're not an impostor. You're not pretending to be someone you're not. You're out here, doing the damn thing and learning along the way, just like everyone else.

I like to break it down like this – if you're feeling like an impostor, ask yourself: *Where am I actually pretending to be someone else? Am I really deceiving others?* Because the true definition of an impostor is someone who's intentionally pretending to be someone they're not to trick others. So, are you really doing that? Or are you just learning, growing and finding your way in a world that often makes us feel like we don't belong? Think of a child learning to walk – they fall down over and over again, but no one points and says, 'That baby is an impostor!' We all know that babies are learning. And guess what? **So are you.**

Impostor syndrome isn't a disease, it's an experience. We need to stop pathologising it like it's something we need to fix. Yes, it's real, and yes, it sucks. But it doesn't mean you're broken. It means you're pushing yourself into new, challenging spaces. That's growth, not fraud. So, what if instead of questioning our worth, we flipped the script? What if when that feeling popped up, we told ourselves, *I'm not an impostor, I'm learning. I belong here just as much as anyone else?* Let's start rewriting the narrative and stop letting this phenomenon hold us back. **You're not an impostor. You're a work in progress.**

Magnetic action

Step 1: Identify when and where you feel like an impostor

Take a moment to write down an area where you've been feeling like a fraud. Be specific. For example, maybe your self-talk has been, *I can't possibly go for that pay rise. I'm not good enough for that role.* But deep down, you know you've been working hard and truly want to go after it.

Example: Imagine you've been eyeing a promotion at work, but every time the thought crosses your mind, you hear that voice saying, *Who do you think you are? You're not qualified.* Write that down.

Step 2: Reality Check

Now, instead of running with that narrative, take a moment to look at the facts. Grab the job description of the role you're interested in. Review each requirement one by one.

Example: Let's say the job requires leadership experience, project management and a deep understanding of client relations. Reflect on your own experience:

- Have you led a team or managed a project?
- Have you built strong relationships with clients?
- Can you think of specific examples where you've nailed these tasks in the past?

Step 3: Reframe the narrative

As you look at the job description, start to challenge your self-doubt. Write down the reality: 'I have led a team of five people for over two years,' or 'I've successfully managed client projects that increased sales by 20%.' Notice how those statements feel different than your initial self-talk.

Example: Instead of telling yourself, *I'm not ready for that promotion,* you might reframe it as, *I've already got the skills, and this role is the natural next step for my growth.*

Step 4: Visualise the outcome

Take a minute to visualise what it would look like if you went for that promotion and got it. How would it feel to step into that role confidently? How would you show up differently? Allow yourself to fully step into the possibility.

Example: Picture yourself leading meetings, making decisions with clarity and getting recognised for your hard work. **How does that shift your energy?**

If you still feel unsure, ask for feedback from someone you trust – a colleague, mentor or friend who knows your work. Often, an outside perspective can help you see your value in a clearer light.

If you're still hesitating, ask yourself, *What's the worst that could happen if I went for it? And what's the best that could happen?* This perspective helps you assess the real risk versus the reward of stepping up.

Blocker 3: Believing you're not good enough (the victim mindset)

The beliefs we carry run the show when it comes to magnetism. Whether conscious or unconscious, they dictate what we attract into our lives. Unexamined beliefs act like faulty wiring, short-circuiting your magnetism and keeping you stuck. If you keep getting crap results in certain areas of your life, you can bet you've got some limiting beliefs playing out in those areas.

For example, I used to believe I was just a 'stupid Spanish girl'. I had a whole collection of mental 'evidence' to prove myself right: I didn't go to college, I grew up in the 'hood, raised on food stamps and food donations, and women like me weren't 'good enough' to teach or inspire others. I knowingly used those beliefs as a shield to hide behind. And we all do this. Every woman I've worked with has a set of limiting beliefs that hold her back:

- I'm not smart enough.
- I'm not attractive enough.
- I'm not capable enough.
- I'm not [fill in the blank] enough.

MAGNETISM IS COEXISTING IN HARMONY WITH THE PEOPLE AND ENERGY AROUND YOU.

This 'I'm not good enough' crap messes with so many of us. It's been passed down from society, media, childhood and the expectations we think we have to meet. I've coached women from all backgrounds and ages, and it doesn't matter how successful or polished they appear on the outside, they're often secretly fighting that same voice telling them they're not enough.

Oprah Winfrey has talked about this in depth. She said that after interviewing some of the most famous, talented people in the world, many of them – no matter how beautiful or successful – would ask her, 'Was that okay? Did I do a good job?' Even Oprah herself has experienced those moments of self-doubt. If people like that are struggling with feelings of not being enough, you'd better believe this mindset is real and widespread.

Let's get one thing straight – women have done extraordinary things. We've built empires, fought wars, raised entire generations, led revolutions and created world-changing technology. Women have stood on the front lines, curing diseases, breaking records and sending people into space. We are geniuses by nature, yet somewhere along the way, we got convinced that we weren't good enough. That's a damn tragedy. How is it that the same women who built civilisations, broke down walls and challenged the system are still questioning their worth? It's time to drop that old belief.

And we have the power and all the education and awareness available in this day and age to change that belief. It starts by doing the work, by really looking at where those beliefs came from. For me, it started in childhood when my dad left, and no one in my family stepped in to take me so I had to go into foster care and live with people I didn't know. I made it mean that, *No one wants me and my dad left us, so I must not be worth sticking around for.* That belief shaped so much of my early life. Maybe you have a story like that too – where the belief started early, and you carried it like a weight for years.

One of the biggest jobs we have in life is unpacking these beliefs and getting rid of the ones that don't serve us. I personally did this in therapy, at retreats and in one-to-one sessions with some of the most incredible coaches and mentors. I spent eight years healing and invested every dollar I had in the early days, as I knew this work would help me impact my future the most. Because here's the thing: You *are* good enough. You *are* more than enough. But you've got to recognise where you've been playing small and hiding behind those old stories.

My mother has been in the hospital most of my life. I've seen her depressed and struggling with bipolar disorder, and I've seen her neglect herself: not showering, not brushing her hair or teeth, not wanting to eat or drink water, not able to or having the desire to take care of herself. In those moments of neglect, I believe she really didn't feel enough. Yes, she was mentally unstable, but she didn't have the drive to even eat. Like her, many people struggle to feel good enough to simply get up to get dressed.

I meet so many women who come to my events around the world and they are goddesses. I mean – they are simply beautiful women. And it's not just their gorgeous hair, make-up, nails, clothes – it's their hearts! They look immaculate and their hearts are golden. These divine women often sit next to me on stage in my 'hot seat' for coaching and tell me, 'I just don't think I'm good enough. I'm not pretty enough. I'm not capable enough.'

And I ask, 'Who put mascara on your eyelashes today? Who washed your ass? Who brushed your teeth? Who dressed you in that nice outfit, or painted your nails?' And they look at me stunned. Like, 'huh?' But I'm dead serious. I mean, think about it. What part of you loves you so much that it put underwear on today? I'll tell you! It's the part of you that loves you so much it decided to curl the hair on your eyelashes and put on that stunning shade of lipstick. There is a part of you that loves you that much, that is so sure you're enough, that it actually did that. The problem is, we're so caught up in the 'I'm not good enough' line that we don't stop to notice the truth.

Often, we don't get quiet enough; we don't ask the deeper questions. We just go with the belief of *I'm not good enough* because it comes out, it rolls off our tongue and that's it. Case closed. But how long are we going to hand this crappy-ass UNTRUE belief around? Enough is enough.

When one of my clients struggles with this, I use it as an opportunity to enquire, to ask a better and deeper question. I ask them to get quiet. To close their eyes and put their hand on their heart and to truly check in with their inner self. I ask them: *Can you honestly say that you don't think you're good? You aren't good enough? You're not worthy or a good person deserving happiness? Are you not good enough to be given a chance to grow and develop?*

Many times, tears stream down their face while they hold their heart with their eyes closed. Often, most women discover that inside their golden hearts they know they are kind, capable and worthy of love and happiness.

Magnetic action

Give yourself a time-out: find a quiet space and put your hand on your heart. Close your eyes and take a few deep breaths. Ask yourself, *Do I truly, deeply believe I'm not good enough?* Stay with that question.

Now, write down everything that comes up – the thoughts, the doubts, the stories. Be brutally honest.

Next, for each thought or doubt, I want you to challenge it with something that's true or that you believe.

Example: Thought: 'I'm not good enough because I haven't achieved X yet.'

Challenge: 'But I've achieved Y, and that proves I'm capable of growth and success.'

Keep going until you have a list of thoughts you've flipped on their heads. Then, I want you to read through this list again and ask yourself: *Can I acknowledge that the part of me that dressed up this morning, that put on lipstick or shaved my legs, does believe I'm worthy? Why else would I even care about showing up?*

Now write this down and say it out loud to yourself: 'I'm more than enough as I am, and the part of me that already knows this is driving me forward every day.'

Blocker 4: Allowing others' opinions to control you – aka f*** what others think #FWOT

One of the most common reasons my clients struggle to speak up, to own who they are and to create the life they dream of is due to this final myth, so sit up: it's a big one. Giving a damn about what other people think may just be one of the biggest things holding you back from stepping into your true magnetism. Seriously, it's a killer. You might not realise how much of your life you're tailoring to fit into other people's expectations – suppressing parts of yourself, holding back your opinions or staying quiet when you need to speak up.

Let me break it down for you: we live in a world where everyone's got an opinion. The moment you start stepping into your power, wearing what makes YOU feel good, taking up space, speaking your truth and being unapologetically you, people are going to get ruffled. It's a given. You're going to trigger people, especially those who are uncomfortable with seeing others stand in their power. They will project their insecurities onto you because your growth may make them feel inadequate.

The question is: Why are you letting their opinions dictate your actions, or your life for that matter?

Let me tell you a little story. In one of my past relationships, my partner hated the way I sneezed. Now, I'm a loud sneezer – like a window-shaking, room-rattling sneezer. And I got it from my mom. And guess what? My son has the same sneeze too (it must run in the family). But in that relationship, my partner's family believed that it was inappropriate for a woman to sneeze like that. So what did I do? I started holding my sneezes in. And I mean really holding them in – so much so, I'm surprised I didn't burst a blood vessel trying to stop them. Guess what? Even with all that effort to please them, it still wasn't enough. I was bending over backward trying to be liked, trying to fit in, and it still wasn't good enough. Moral of the story? Don't let anyone else's opinions stop you from being who you are, even if it's about something as small as a sneeze. F★★★ what others think – aka FWOT. (If you have little people in your life, you can tell them to forget what others think. My son uses this a lot at school and it's been awesome to see how good it makes him feel.)

What if I told you that the opinions people have about you are not really about you? They're about *them*. People project their insecurities, their judgements and their unresolved issues onto others. So when someone has something to say about how you're living your life or who you're becoming, just know that it's not about you – it's about how you trigger something in them. Maybe you remind them of who they wish they were brave enough to be, or maybe your confidence makes them feel uncomfortable in their own skin. Either way, it's their problem, not yours. (I know, easier said than done, but I had to say it.)

When you stop worrying about other people's judgements, you give yourself the freedom to evolve, because you are always changing. The version of you that existed six months ago is not the version of you that exists today. The version of you that will exist in a year from now won't be the same as the one standing here today. That's growth. That's evolution. And no one can judge you because they can't even keep up with who you're becoming. They're judging their perception of you – who *they* think you are – not who *you* actually are. They're judging the old version of you that lives in their minds, not this version of who you really are. You are always evolving, growing and changing, so why let their opinion control your actions? Why let them keep you small?

It's time to get comfortable with the fact that not everyone is going to like you. In fact, if you're truly stepping into your power, some people are going to *dis*like you. But that's a sign you're doing something right. You're taking up space. You're standing for something. You're not being vanilla, one size fits all, trying to blend in with everyone else.

Magnetic action

Let's look at this fourth blocker in the context of navigating friendships. Just like at work, the fear of others' opinions can keep you from fully expressing yourself or setting necessary boundaries.

Identify the fear: Think of one situation in a friendship where you've held back from sharing your true feelings, opinions or boundaries because you were worried about being judged or causing conflict. Get specific about the type of conversation, gathering or dynamic where this tends to happen.

Calculate your cost: Reflect on the impact of staying silent. What important conversations have you avoided? What could this be costing you in terms of deeper connections, respect or your own peace of mind?

Example: By not expressing my feelings when a friend oversteps or dismisses me, I end up feeling unappreciated and disconnected. It's holding me back from building more authentic friendships and affects my self-confidence because I'm not fully honouring my boundaries.

YOU ALREADY HAVE WHAT IT TAKES, BUT THE KEY IS REMOVING WHAT'S BLOCKING IT.

Imagine the shift: Envision how your friendships could change if you started speaking up honestly. How might it deepen your connections, shift the respect others have for you and strengthen your own sense of self-worth?

Example: If I start sharing my thoughts and setting gentle boundaries, my friendships could become more genuine and supportive. I'd feel more confident, and my friends would appreciate and respect me for being honest.

Impact on others: Consider the ripple effect – how might your courage to speak up inspire your friends to be more open as well? Who else might benefit from seeing you honour your boundaries and express yourself?

Action step: Choose one honest conversation you'll have with a friend this week – whether it's addressing a small boundary, sharing something meaningful or gently voicing a concern. Make it a non-negotiable to honour your voice.

We've just walked through the biggest blocks holding you back from your magnetism, and now I hope you can see that it's not about *fixing* yourself; it's about *freeing* yourself from these beliefs and patterns that are weighing you down. Once you get these blockers out of the way, that natural magnetism that's been inside you all along can finally rise to the surface. No more dimming your light.

We're about to take a bold step forward into the next part of *Becoming Magnetic.* This is where we shift gears and dig into the good stuff – the Five Phases of Magnetism. These principles are the foundations for living in alignment with the energy that naturally draws what you desire toward you. It's time to learn how to tune into this power and use it with intention.

THE 10 MYTHS ABOUT MAGNETISM

Before we dive into the five phases of magnetism, let's clear up some of the most common misconceptions. When people hear 'magnetism', a lot of assumptions come up that can throw you off track. I want to make sure you know what magnetism isn't so you're fully equipped to step into the actionable steps in the chapters to come. These ten myths will help you get a clearer sense of true magnetism, leaving any illusions behind. Let's cut through the noise and understand what the heart of what being magnetic is really about.

1 Magnetism isn't about being beautiful or attractive

Magnetism runs way deeper than looks. Sure, you can be good-looking and magnetic, but one doesn't depend on the other. Societal beauty standards do not equal magnetism. Magnetism isn't about red lipstick or designer heels. It's about the energy you bring, that vibe that people can feel from you. You don't need the perfect body or bulging biceps to have it. Magnetism is an invisible power, and it doesn't come from your looks – it comes from your presence.

2 Magnetism isn't about people-pleasing

Please hear me: magnetism isn't about making everyone like you. This isn't a popularity contest, and it's definitely not about how many followers you have on social media. Magnetic energy doesn't scream for attention or validation – it just is. It's not fake; it's not performative. If you're people-pleasing, you're *trying* too hard and that energy feels forced and comes from lack, not magnetism.

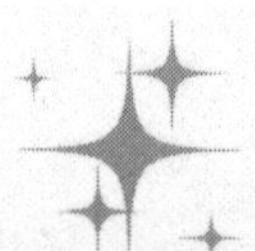

3 Magnetism doesn't mean weak boundaries

Being magnetic doesn't mean being a doormat. Just because people are drawn to your energy doesn't mean you're there to take on everyone else's baggage. Boundaries aren't preferences. Being magnetic means owning your energy, not absorbing everyone else's. You're not here to be a sponge for other people's drama.

4 Magnetism isn't loud and extroverted

You don't have to be loud to be magnetic. Magnetism isn't about volume – it's about energy. Introverts can be just as magnetic as extroverts (sometimes even more so). It's the energy that speaks, not how loud you are. A magnetic person draws people in with their vibe, not their words.

5 Magnetism isn't just for women

Even though *Becoming Magnetic* focuses on women, magnetism is for everyone. It doesn't care about gender, age or background. If you're paying attention, you'll notice magnetic people all around you, regardless of who they are. Magnetism doesn't discriminate. (Actually, a really fun exercise the next time you're out is to go 'magnetic people' watching.)

6 Magnetism is not selfish

Let's be real – some people use their charisma for all the wrong reasons. Manipulation, validation, deception, abuse . . . There are plenty of examples. The difference? Intent. Just because someone is trying to draw you in to take advantage of you doesn't mean they are magnetic. Watch out for people whose possibly hard-to-detect vibe is pure selfishness; they use a charismatic surface for shady purposes.

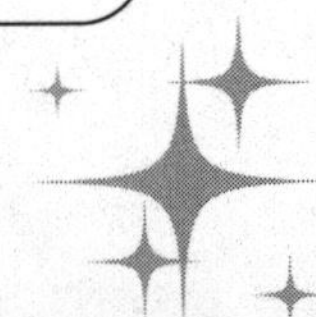

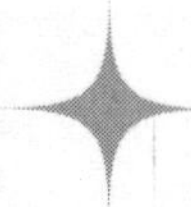

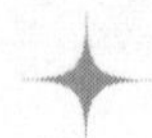

7 Magnetism isn't to blame for having negative people in your life

Being magnetic doesn't mean you have to let everyone into your space. This is especially important to those who identify as empaths or highly sensitive. You still need to filter who gets into your world. Just because you're attracting people doesn't mean they all deserve a spot in your life, so filter appropriately. Be smart, trust your gut and protect your space.

8 Magnetism isn't about performing

True magnetism isn't a spectacle – it's a natural force. You don't have to 'do' anything to be magnetic, because it's not about effort or seeking approval. It's about **being** – fully embodying who you are without effort or pretence. Your energy speaks for itself, and real magnetism draws people in without the need for performance or showmanship.

9 Magnetism isn't about other people

Magnetism starts within. It's not about what others think or say about you – it's about how you see yourself. Some people crank up their magnetism and attract everything they want, while others don't even realise they've got it. But at the end of the day, as long as you're good with you, trust you will attract the right things your way.

10 Magnetism isn't about changing to fit in

True magnetism comes from owning who you are, not bending to fit someone else's expectations. When you're magnetic, you don't need to change or mould yourself to be liked by others. It's about standing firm in your authenticity. Your energy naturally draws in the right people, opportunities and experiences – without needing to change to gain approval.

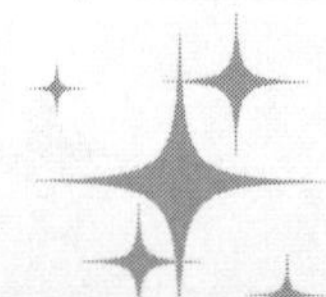

WHAT MAGNETISM IS: *CONNECTION*

The truest meaning of magnetism to me is connection. I use my magnetic energy to genuinely connect with others, to attract people, relationships, community and love. That's the real power of being magnetic. It's not about manipulation or forcing anything – it's about co-creating. When you're vibing with your energy dialled in, you're magnetic to the right people, opportunities and experiences. You move through life in sync, not just with yourself but with the world around you. It's a beautiful thing to witness.

When you're truly in your magnetic power, you connect on a much deeper level with those around you. You're not faking interest in order to get something from people – you *want* to connect. You *want* to build relationships, you *want* to engage, and you're not doing it for validation or approval. You're doing it because that's how we're wired as humans: to connect, to share, to lift each other up. Magnetism is coexisting in harmony with the people and energy around you. You're creating something beautiful together, whether it's just a smile shared with a stranger on the street or the energy you bring into a room. A single moment of kindness, of warmth, can shift the entire vibe of your day – and theirs. That's the kind of impact I'm talking about. It's real, it's powerful and it's yours to own.

THE FIVE PHASES OF MAGNETISM: DOING THE WORK

5

PHASE 1: SELF-MASTERY

SELF-MASTERY
SELF-MASTERY

'True mastery begins within. As long as you're alive, self-mastery will always feel just out of reach – because you're constantly growing, evolving, becoming. But it's in striving to master yourself that you gain the power to master everything else.'

You've probably heard it before – 'do the work' – but what does that **actually** mean?

'Doing the work' refers to the process of actively engaging in personal growth, healing and self-improvement. It means taking responsibility for your life by confronting your limiting beliefs, unresolved trauma and negative patterns. It involves deep self-reflection, emotional healing and the consistent effort to break old cycles and behaviours. The goal is to develop self-awareness, practise self-care and take tangible steps toward evolving into the best version of yourself.

In short, it's a commitment to ongoing self-development and inner transformation, not just through positive thinking, but also through real, intentional action. There's no one way or perfect formula to follow. It looks different for everyone. Some tangible examples of doing the work can be:

- therapy
- journalling
- art
- coaching
- crying
- sitting still
- healing through movement
- releasing emotions
- reflecting in nature

For some, it's those deep, messy moments where you confront your fears head-on. But whatever it looks like for you, one thing is clear: **if you avoid doing the work, the work will eventually do you**.

IF YOU AVOID DOING THE WORK, THE WORK WILL EVENTUALLY DO YOU.

The stagnation you feel when you avoid personal development is real. You stay stuck. You stay in the same patterns, taking two steps forward then four steps back. Growth stops. And that's not where we want to be. You're reading this because you want to grow. So, let me introduce you to the five phases of magnetism. These are the exact phases I and thousands of other women I've had the honour to work with have gone through. These steps are proven to shift your life. They are the steps that moved me from grief and doubt to a life filled with love, connection and opportunity. And these phases will move you too – if you commit to them.

In my first book, *Confidence Feels Like Sh*t*, I went deep into how confidence can be built from scratch, no matter how much you think you've lacked it. *Becoming Magnetic* instead follows the same logic. There are core phases that you must go through to truly own your magnetic power.

This chapter and the next four chapters will break down the phases to provide you with a clear step-by-step process on how to work through each stage in your day-to-day life. I've added powerful exercises to each phase so you can do the work in real time. Hear me when I say that if you actually do these exercises, your life *will* transform. These five phases are not just ideas – they're the building blocks that, when put into practice, allow you to embody a truly magnetic life.

MEET NINA

Nina grew up in a small suburb just outside of Christchurch, New Zealand, the middle child in a hardworking family. Her childhood was filled with love, outdoor adventures and a strong passion for sports. But as she got older, Nina started to struggle with body image – thanks to the harsh opinions of other kids at school and the relentless pressures of society. These insecurities didn't just disappear as she got older; instead, they followed her into adulthood, showing up as constant worry about how she looked and a need to drink at social events to feel like she fit in or was confident enough to hold her own.

Nina's twenties were spent looking for love and searching for something deeper, but she kept finding herself stuck in a loop of self-doubt and sabotage. She'd go out, hand out her number at pubs and parties, but never follow through – ghosting potential partners out of pure fear and insecurity. Then she met Tui, and he was different. He didn't back off when she put up her walls. He was patient, kind and came from a solid family that had showed him how to truly love. For the first time, Nina felt like she could actually build a life with someone.

But life had other plans. What should have been one of the happiest times in her life quickly turned into one of the most devastating. During a holiday in the North Island of New Zealand, her life took a devastating turn. Tui passed away from a sudden heart attack – right in her lap. The shock and trauma shattered Nina's world. The future she'd imagined with him vanished in an instant.

After Tui's death, Nina was completely lost – drowning in grief, depression and confusion. She moved to Australia to live with her sister in Melbourne, hoping for a fresh start, but finding her footing was hard. She couldn't shake the dark cloud that seemed to follow her everywhere. It was during this time that her sister, seeing the depth of her pain, suggested something different – a healing retreat. Her sister had been following me on social media and knew that I'd been through my own fair share of loss and grief. She thought maybe – just maybe – this could be the space where Nina could start to reclaim her joy and begin to piece her life back together.

When Nina showed up on the first day of the retreat, she seemed closed off and like she regretted coming. I could feel the weight of her grief and the sadness from losing her partner; it was almost like a shield she had up, blocking her from really connecting. Sure, she had said yes to attending, but her body language said 'I don't want to be here'. What's interesting is that Nina had no idea who I was or what kind of coaching I did. She hadn't listened to my podcast and didn't know that I, too, had lost my partner years ago. She wasn't aware that my journey had mirrored hers in many ways. But as the retreat unfolded, something clicked for her. She started to see that her healing wasn't just about losing Tui – it was about healing the relationship she had with herself. She went deep in that retreat and even though she was tough to crack initially, by the end of the retreat, Nina was almost unrecognisable – not just in how her face changed, but in the way she carried herself, the energy she exuded. She had begun to reclaim her story, and in doing so, her power. And with that came a new meaning for life. As we said our goodbyes on the last day of retreat, she was a brand-new woman.

After the retreat, Nina dove headfirst into one of our coaching programs, ready to go even deeper into her inner work and maintain the incredible momentum. During one of our calls, she casually mentioned that she'd been doing some social media management work. One of my team members picked up on that and suggested maybe Nina could support us in the business. The stars aligned perfectly, and we brought Nina into our team. From day one, she's been an absolute superstar and has become such an integral part of our team.

Given that my husband and I are all about self-development and growth, being part of our team isn't just a job – it's a commitment to doing the inner work daily, embracing radical responsibility, and constantly evolving. You've got to be all in, hungry for growth, and genuinely driven to make an impact. And Nina? She's shown up, not only for herself but for the business, in every way that counts. Since that first retreat, Nina has been on a relentless journey of healing. She faced her fears head-on and continuously pushed herself beyond what's comfortable. One of the key areas she wanted to focus on was attracting love into her life. As she worked on her self-worth, confidence and acceptance, it became clear just how important it was for her to call in a life partner. This sparked some powerful conversations about attraction and the art of drawing in what and who you desire.

Enter magnetism.

My husband Hamish, who is now a Shamanic practitioner and breathwork facilitator, works with individuals to help them gain clarity and realign with what they truly want. When Nina expressed her desire to find love again, Hamish guided her through a powerful session. Using visualisation practices, he helped her not just envision the type of partner she wanted, but also the life she dreamt of – happy, in love and fully fulfilled. In that moment, she could clearly see herself stepping into the future she desired, and from that point forward, her energy began to radically shift. What followed was nothing short of amazing. Nina dove headfirst into practising the phases of magnetism. She realised that it wasn't about big grand gestures, but small, intentional actions. She started greeting people with warmth, offering genuine compliments to strangers – little things that made a world of difference. And guess what? She began to notice how differently people responded to her. As she put more energy out there, more started flowing back to her. Her confidence grew, and she became more approachable, more engaging and more magnetic.

Fast forward six months, and Nina met the love of her life. This relationship was everything she'd dreamt of – and then some. Built on mutual respect, deep connection and a shared vision for the future, it was literally everything she had been calling in. Nina's life couldn't look more different today. She's a completely different woman now – more confident, more charismatic, and she's attracting incredible experiences and people everywhere she goes. Her boyfriend even tells her how magnetic she is, how when they're out it seems like everyone wants to talk to her – something she still finds hard to believe because, not long ago, she used to say the same thing about me whenever we were out together.

Nina didn't stop there. She kept applying the magnetic phases and saw how her life transformed even further. It wasn't just love she was attracting anymore – she started pulling in incredible opportunities, meaningful friendships and deeper connections across every aspect of her life. Today, Nina is unrecognisable in the best possible way. She radiates confidence, and her magnetic energy is undeniable – people are naturally drawn to her. She's no longer shrinking, playing small or holding back. Instead, she shows up without apology, takes up space and challenges herself to push past her fears.

Nina's built a life that's rich in love, connection and purpose – not just in her relationship, but in her career, her friendships and her vision for the future. And the best part? She recently received the incredible news that she's expecting her first child – a dream she held close for so long and something she vividly saw in her visualisation session. Now, it's all unfolding. Every desire, every dream she worked to magnetise, has become her reality. This is what happens when you become magnetic.

Nina's transformation wasn't luck – it was hard work. And this is the part where you have to get real with yourself. The truth is, you can't bypass doing the inner work if you want to live your most magnetic life. Believe me, the 'work' is real, and it's necessary. Nina created her beautiful life because she faced herself, she took the steps and she did (and continues to do) the damn work.

THE FIVE PHASES OF MAGNETISM

In the following chapters we'll be going deep into each of the five phases or magnetism. Here's a taster of what's to come.

Phase 1: Self-mastery

This is where everything begins. Self-mastery means truly knowing yourself – your thoughts, behaviours, triggers – through **self-awareness**, **self-reflection** and **self-acceptance**. It's about digging deeper, beyond the surface, to confront who you are at your core. This is the tough internal work – the uncomfortable reflection, the unfiltered honesty with yourself, then the healing. It's about asking the raw questions: *Who am I, really? Am I truly happy or fulfilled?* This phase requires you to face those truths head on and work through them so you can learn to accept yourself – flaws and all. If you're still seeking validation or approval from others, then this is where your work starts. You have to be grounded in who you are before you can start attracting the life you want.

Phase 2: Your true north

What do you stand for? What matters to you at your core? If you don't know, it's time to get clear – because your values are your internal compass, guiding every decision you make. This is where alignment begins. You can't live authentically if you don't know what drives you. When you define your values and stand firm in them, you build an unshakable foundation. The more you live by those values, the more magnetic you become. You'll start attracting people, opportunities and experiences that resonate with *your* energy because you're no longer swayed by external validation. It's not about fitting in – it's about showing up as the most authentic version of yourself. If you're still unclear about what truly drives you, then this is where your alignment begins.

Phase 3: Create your alter she-go

This is where you stop *thinking about* who you could be and start *being* her. No more waiting for the future version of yourself to show up – you step into her *now*. You make decisions, take action and show up in every area of your life as the woman who already has what she wants. We're not talking about 'faking it'; instead you'll be embodying the energy, confidence and mindset of the highest version of yourself, today. Your 'alter she-go' is the unapologetic, powerful woman you've been holding back. She's bold, she's decisive and she's already living the life you want. If you're still *dreaming* about who you want to be instead of *being* her, this is where you step in.

Phase 4: Your evolution

You've been embodying your new self, but now the universe is going to test you – are you truly ready to become this version of yourself? This phase is all about shedding your old skin, letting go of who you once were and stepping fully into your rebirth. It's not pretty, and it's definitely not easy – in fact, it's so damn hard. You'll face resistance, both from the world around you and from within. But this is where the deep transformation occurs. Shedding your old habits, limiting beliefs and stories that no longer serve you is necessary for growth. It might feel like you're being pulled apart, but that's part of the process. You're evolving into a stronger, more aligned version of yourself. If you're still clinging to old beliefs or scared to let go of past identities, this phase is where you'll have to dig deep, push yourself and stand your ground.

Phase 5: Magnetic aura

After all the inner work you commit to, you start to see the results – momentum, ease and flow show up in your life. You notice how effortlessly things start to align. People feel your energy the moment you walk into a room – there's a confidence, a presence that draws them in. You're no longer chasing opportunities; they come to you. It's not about magic or luck, it's about alignment. Your aura – the energy you project – becomes a magnet for what you want. The work you've done starts to pay off, and you step into your full magnetism.

Now that you've got a clear picture of the road ahead, it's time to dive in. These five phases aren't just for someone else's success – they're available to *you* too. I've witnessed this process work, not just in Nina's transformation, but in the lives of countless women I've coached. This is your opportunity to access that same power and create the life you've always wanted.

So, let's get started with Phase 1 – **Self-mastery**. If you don't truly know and accept yourself, you'll struggle to attract anything meaningful into your life. This is where you learn what it really takes to master yourself.

SELF-MASTERY

Self-mastery is where it all begins, because *you* are the foundation of everything you create, touch and bring into this world. Without knowing, understanding and owning yourself fully, nothing else you try to build can stand on solid ground. If you skip this work – if you avoid looking at your wounds or facing the hard truths – you won't have the strength or clarity to become magnetic. It'll all be forced, a facade, and that's the complete opposite of authentic magnetism. Authenticity is the cornerstone of magnetism. There's no 'fake it till you make it': that is a lie. You aren't fake and there's no place to 'get' to. It might be a common phrase people say, but it won't sustain the energy that truly draws what you want into your life. You want to live with a magnetic force? Then you need to be real. And being real means being honest and facing yourself – every dark and messy part of you.

Not many people talk about the gritty, raw work behind becoming magnetic. You hear a lot of 'love and light' and 'positive thinking', but where's the conversation about the pain, the healing, the dark nights of the soul? When I finally faced the pain of losing my husband – five years after his death because I'd been busy avoiding it – it hurt like hell. It wasn't pretty, and I sure didn't feel like sharing it on social media. It was private, excruciating, but absolutely necessary.

I had to feel it, reveal it and process it in order to heal. I had to make space in my heart and mind, to let go and create clarity for the future. I couldn't simply put on a smile or tell myself to 'stay positive'. I had to sit in that pain and choose to move through it, no matter how hard it was. That is the real work.

When I finally allowed myself to seek help and actually face the grief, it wasn't just the pain of losing Jeo that came up. It was like opening Pandora's box. Suddenly, there were all these other layers

I had to work through. Trust issues I didn't even know I had surfaced. I'd closed my heart off completely, scared to love again, terrified I'd lose someone else. I found out I had a pretty toxic relationship with alcohol too – something I wasn't even fully aware of. Every time I felt overwhelmed, I'd reach for a drink. It became my go-to and I didn't know when enough was enough. I didn't realise how destructive that was until I started unpacking all of this.

That's the thing with doing the work – it unravels *everything*. (That's one of the reasons so many of us try to avoid it.) Grief wasn't only about sadness for me; it was tied to so many other areas of my life. When I started healing one thing, I had to face all the other things I'd been avoiding, and in the end, it wasn't just about clearing Jeo's death. It cleared up so much more – my ability to trust, my relationship with myself, how I showed up in my friendships and my career. But what you're left with after you've moved through the process is clarity, peace and a lighter heart. It has been the one thing that allowed me to attract everything I have ever desired into my life. That's the power of doing this inner work.

Healing doesn't happen on its own. It requires support and dedication. I had to make my healing a priority, which meant saying no to social events, to binge drinking, to distractions. I chose to make time to sit in sessions for coaching, for quiet reflection, journalling and time to be with myself. It wasn't easy. I had to sit with my pain, and sacrifice things like my time and money to invest in my healing. Hamish and I didn't even have a big wedding because we decided to spend that money on a healing retreat instead.

But that choice changed my life. That retreat became a turning point in my growth, and I don't regret it for a second. If I hadn't made the decision to face myself and prioritise my healing, I wouldn't have the life, the love, the business or the relationships I have now. The truth is you can't skip this part. You can pretend, you can avoid, you can buy time, but in the end, you will know that you can't build something real if the foundation isn't solid. Your life will show you where it needs work, where it needs healing, where it needs acceptance. Self-mastery is where your magnetic power begins, because nothing real or magnetic can be built without first mastering *you*.

WHERE IT ALL STARTS: SELF-AWARENESS

Self-mastery is made up of three parts:

- **Self-awareness:** Knowing who you are at your core, recognising your strengths, patterns and blind spots without judgment.
- **Self-reflection:** Taking time to look inward, examining your thoughts, actions and motivations to gain deeper clarity and insight into your choices and behaviours.
- **Self-acceptance:** Embracing yourself fully, acknowledging all parts of you – flaws and all – with compassion, to create a foundation for genuine growth and change.

Before we can even begin that journey, we need to understand just how much of our lives we're living on autopilot. Studies show that we are only consciously aware and in control 5 per cent of the time; the other 95 per cent, we're sleepwalking through life. We don't even realise we're using the same strategies and the same patterns and getting the same results over and over again. This is why I couldn't find love; I was repeating the same cycles with similar men and wondering why nothing was changing.

When you step into self-awareness, you wake up from the dream. You realise you're not just along for the ride; you are the driver. You get to consciously decide where you want to go. Take a moment now – take a deep breath in through your nose, exhale slowly through your mouth. Blink a couple of times. You consciously made yourself do that. The beauty of self-awareness is that you realise you can actively choose how you show up in the world. Sure, autopilot serves us when we're doing mundane tasks, but we can't rely on it when it comes to building our magnetic selves. If we do, we'll keep attracting the same things we no longer want.

Action step: Journalling

A powerful tool for cultivating self-mastery (especially self-awareness) is journalling. If you don't have a journal yet, get one. Make time daily – whether it's first thing in the morning or before bed – to write. This practice will help you unlock a deeper awareness of your thoughts, feelings and patterns.

Think of this as a mind cleansing or a mind dumping, which allows you to get all your thoughts out onto paper* so that they are not cluttering up your mind anymore. You pull the thoughts out of your subconscious and allow them to be on the paper, which helps you to separate yourself from your thoughts, instead of believing that you are what you think. You get to see that you are not your thoughts; your thoughts are just sentences in your mind, things you are thinking.

Here are a few simple prompts to help you get started on your journalling journey. Ask yourself:

- How do I feel at this moment?
- What am I thinking about right now that might be causing this feeling?
- How long have I been feeling this way?
- What is this feeling trying to tell me or teach me?
- What would support me most right now?

* It's actually much more powerful to use pen and paper than a screen for this one.

AUTHENTICITY IS THE CORNERSTONE OF MAGNETISM.

When you've completed writing all of the thoughts that are in your mind on paper, be sure to view them with child-like curiosity. Judgement will not help you in this situation. The idea is to dump your mind on paper and understand with compassion; be prepared, you may feel anxious when looking at the thoughts you have been thinking. After doing this for a few weeks, you will get really good at understanding your mind, understanding why you think what you think, understanding who in your life is tied to certain feelings and thoughts. You will gain so much awareness of your own mind that when you are ready to begin shifting you will have a greater understanding of why you feel the way you do and what to do about it.

This process takes time. You must be consistent and do this for at least two to three weeks so that you can start seeing patterns. The idea for this is that you then understand the top three to five thoughts that mess with you the most. Many of my clients continue to do this process as it supports them to feel grounded, clear and aligned daily. It also motivates them to keep going.

Remember: this isn't about judging yourself. It's about getting curious.

SELF-REFLECTION

As we discussed in Chapter 4, self-reflection is a crucial step toward self-mastery. Once you become aware of your thoughts, actions and patterns, reflection allows you to dig deeper, to examine why patterns exist and how they've impacted your life. This process is about more than simply noticing your behaviours; it's an honest, compassionate exploration of your motivations, beliefs, and responses.

Self-reflection serves as a mirror for the inner workings of your mind and heart. It involves slowing down and taking the time to really notice how you're showing up in the world. It's here where you gain the tools to shift, grow and evolve. Self-reflection allows you to identify what aligns with your true self and what doesn't, helping you shed what's no longer in service to you. This gives you the necessary clarity to make intentional changes – changes that align with your highest potential and help you build a magnetic presence that's authentic, confident, and rooted in self-mastery.

Action Step: The 5-minute check-in

This 5-minute check-in is a quick, grounding practice you can fit into any part of your day. It's a moment to connect with yourself and get clear on your current state – no journal, pen or mirror needed.

Find a quiet spot to take a break in your day – whether that's in your car on your way to work, after a meeting or before bed – and pause. Close your eyes if it helps you to focus. Take a few deep breaths to centre yourself. Ask yourself these three questions:

- How am I right now? (Notice your current physical and emotional state without overthinking.)
- What would serve me most in this moment? (Reflect on what you need, be that rest, energy, connection or calm.)
- What am I truly grateful for right now? (Shift your perspective by acknowledging even one thing you appreciate in this moment.)

Observe without judgment: Simply let these answers come to you naturally. You don't need to change anything or take action; just let yourself witness what's there with compassion.

Close with a grounding breath: Finish by taking a deep, grounding breath. Feel free to take any small action that feels supportive, or simply continue with your day, carrying this awareness with you.

Practicing the 5-minute check-in regularly, even once a day, helps you build a steady habit of self-reflection. This simple practice keeps you aligned with what you need and can guide you to make decisions that feel authentic and supportive. Self-reflection can be woven into your routine effortlessly, empowering you to check in with yourself in real-time and adjust to whatever life brings.

SELF ACCEPTANCE

Self-acceptance is often spoken about, but truly living it is an act of courage. It's easy to chase growth and improvement, but without a foundation of acceptance, change can feel hollow. Real growth requires us to first accept where we are, just as we are. This isn't about fixing yourself to become 'enough' or 'worthy'. **You are already enough, right now, today.** Self-acceptance means embracing every part of yourself: the strengths and weaknesses, the light and the shadows, the parts you're proud of and the parts you'd rather hide. It's about welcoming the whole of who you are into the room, with kindness, compassion and understanding.

Self-acceptance is not a one-time achievement, it's a daily practice. It involves acknowledging the emotions you may have brushed aside, sitting with fears instead of running from them, and owning your past without letting it define you. It's a commitment to choose yourself, again and again, even when things feel challenging. True self-acceptance means you can look at yourself, flaws and all, and say, 'I am whole, and I am enough'. It's about being at peace with who you are in every stage of life, while still having the space and desire to grow. This phase of self-mastery calls you to stand fully in your truth, honouring both the work you've done and the journey still ahead.

Action Step: Promises to keep

Self-acceptance takes time and is a journey in itself. Remember, you are allowed to love yourself as you are and still desire to grow.

True change doesn't come from a place of self-judgement or harsh criticism; it comes from love, understanding, and compassion.

If you're committed to evolving into the magnetic woman you truly want to be, make these promises to yourself:

- I will treat myself with grace and kindness, especially when I stumble.
- I will honour my growth journey, embracing patience and compassion along the way.
- I will keep my word to myself, showing up even when it's challenging.

Embrace these promises and allow your journey to unfold with love, understanding and encouragement. You deserve your own kindness every step of the way.

NINA'S JOURNEY OF SELF-MASTERY

When Nina decided to take her sister's advice and say yes to attending the retreat, she was already inviting self-mastery into her life without realising it. That 'yes' was her first step toward investing in herself, in choosing herself, something she hadn't done in a long time. During those five immersive and intense days, Nina was forced to confront parts of herself she had been avoiding for years. She sat in her grief, journalled her thoughts and let herself feel every raw emotion she'd buried. There were tears, pain and moments when she felt like leaving, but she chose to stay, knowing this was her chance to change.

The retreat wasn't just about mental healing; it was about emotional and physical release too. Nina not only worked on her mind but also released the pent-up grief, fear and hurt from her body. That's what self-mastery looks like: staying present, facing the hard stuff and choosing to push through the discomfort. In Nina's case, breathwork and shamanic healing sessions facilitated the hard work of allowing herself to be vulnerable in a safe space, surrounded by other women who were also doing their work. (Different techniques work for different people.) She shared her truth, reflected deeply and held herself accountable long after the retreat was over by joining our coaching program and staying committed to the process.

Nina's self-acceptance came when she realised it wasn't just about healing from the loss of Tui. It was about healing the relationship she had with herself. For the first time, she saw her worth beyond external validation and what others thought of her. She stopped hiding behind a smile or pretending to be okay. She learnt to accept her flaws, her grief, her pain, and even her fears. Through self-acceptance, she freed herself from the pressure to be perfect, to meet societal standards and to constantly seek approval from others.

After the retreat, Nina made real changes in her life. She began practicing vulnerability, opening up to the people around her, sharing her feelings instead of burying them. She made a conscious decision to be honest about what she was going through, even when it was uncomfortable. And she continued to invest in her growth, both emotionally and spiritually. She didn't just stop after the retreat – she kept doing the work, day in and day out, and that's how self-mastery really happens. This isn't about achieving some final version of yourself. It's about learning to embrace the journey, the ups, the downs and the messy middle. It's about looking in the mirror, accepting what you see, and deciding to love yourself through it all. Like Nina, you don't have to have it all figured out; **you just need to be willing to start**.

IGNORANCE IS BLISS

Here's the bad news (or the good news, depending on how you look at it): once you've learnt this, you can't unlearn it. You can't go back to that 'ignorance is bliss' stage. Before, maybe you lived in the comfort of what you didn't know – because what you don't know can't hurt you, right? But now that you know all this, there's no going back. The veil's been lifted, and that ignorance you used to lean on no longer serves you. You've seen the truth, and it's both a blessing and a curse.

The truth is that 'knowledge' versus *truly* knowing are two different things. We've all read a bunch of self-development books, listened to podcasts, followed the gurus – and we think we 'know' because we've got all this information. But there's a huge gap between having knowledge and actually living it. Knowledge without knowing, without lived experience, is just data. It's just a bunch of information sitting in your head, and while that might make you feel smarter, if you're not embodying that knowledge, then you don't really 'know' it.

A lot of people in the personal development world get stuck here. They read the books, they attend the seminars and they consume so much content that they think, 'Yep, I get it, I know this.' But then, they look at their lives, and the results they want aren't there. And that's the hard truth – if you don't have the results you want in your life, consider that you don't truly know this yet. What you have is knowledge about the subject, but not lived experience. Knowing something intellectually doesn't mean you're living it. If you're not seeing the outcomes you desire, if you're not embodying these principles in your everyday life, then all you have is information – not transformation. And transformation comes from doing the work continuously, from integrating it, from actioning it until it becomes part of who you are.

If you're still stuck in the knowledge phase, it's time to move into knowing, because the more you embody this work, the more you will see it show up in your life.

MIXED SIGNALS

Many of us have big dreams, these clear desires for what we want to attract into our lives – a thriving business, deep friendships, more money or a fulfilling relationship. But here's the catch: while we might say we want these things, oftentimes our energy doesn't match up with them. There's this internal block, this part of us that isn't in true alignment with what we're trying to call in.

I see this time and time again with the female leaders I coach. They want to build powerful personal brands, make more money or create beautiful relationships, but something is stopping them. What they say they want, and what they believe they deserve, are two completely different things. That's where the mixed signals come in.

You see, we cannot attract what we are not aligned with. If you're constantly sending out doubt, fear or disbelief about what you want, it doesn't matter how much you say you want it – it's not coming your way. Let me break it down for you: let's say you want more money in your life, but you've been carrying around these old scarcity beliefs. Maybe you were taught that money is hard to come by, or that people who have a lot of money are greedy. You desire wealth, but at the same time, you're subconsciously repelling it because of the negative stories you've internalised. So, when you try to attract money, what happens? Nothing. Because deep down, your beliefs aren't aligned with your desire.

This is the misalignment we need to address. It's not that you can't attract what you want – it's that your underlying beliefs and energy are blocking it. You're sending mixed signals to the universe, and those mixed signals are holding you back.

You can't fake your way into magnetism. You just can't repeat mantras or affirmations you deep down don't truly believe. You have to get crystal clear on what's blocking you and aligning your energy to what you desire. If you don't fully believe you're worthy of the thing you want, it's never going to arrive. Period.

For example, I once coached a woman who desperately wanted to attract more girlfriends into her life. She felt lonely, disconnected and longed for deeper female friendships. But when I got to know her, I quickly realised she had this wall up – a huge, impenetrable fortress around her heart. She had been hurt by women in the past, and in response she decided she would never allow herself to be vulnerable with other women again. On the outside, she said she wanted connection, but on the inside, her energy was screaming, 'Stay away from me. I don't trust you.' That's mixed signals in action.

I see this happen all the time – people saying they want something, but energetically pushing it away because of past trauma, fear or limiting beliefs. They'll say they want love, but they're terrified of being hurt. They'll say they want success, but deep down, they don't believe they deserve it. The result? They send out confusing, conflicting energy, and what they want stays just out of reach.

So, how do you fix this? How do you align your energy with what you want? First, you need to get real with yourself. Be brutally honest about the stories and beliefs you're carrying around that are blocking you. What are you still holding onto that's not serving you? Maybe you've been hurt in the past, and you've built walls to protect yourself. Maybe you've internalised beliefs that you're not worthy of success, or that love always leads to pain.

Once you identify those blocks, it's time to start doing the work on yourself to break them down. (Coaching works a treat for this.) Allow yourself to heal, to feel the pain, to let it go. You can't just put a bandaid on these deep wounds and expect everything to be fine. You need to tear down the walls, brick by brick, and start sending out a clear, aligned signal for what you want.

Let me tell you, when your energy is fully aligned with your desires, you become unstoppable. The right opportunities, the right people and the right situations start flowing to you because you're no longer sending out mixed signals. You're clear. You're confident. You're magnetic.

This process is not easy. Sometimes it's painful as hell. But the alternative? Staying stuck, frustrated and wondering why nothing is changing. You have to be willing to stand for what you want, to believe you're worthy of what you want and to send out a signal that's clear and unwavering.

Time to do the work.

THE CIRCLE OF TRUTH EXERCISE

I've talked a lot about you doing the inner work. This exercise is an achievable start. It's extremely powerful to reveal the exact area(s) of your life that need your attention now. I've used this exercise countless times, both personally and with my clients, to cut through the noise and figure out exactly where you're feeling stuck in life. Beyond just identifying the areas where you're struggling, it helps with uncovering the thoughts and feelings behind those struggles so that you can start working on them head on. This is an awareness tool, designed to help you reflect deeply and pinpoint the stories you've been telling yourself that keep you from moving forward. Once you have clarity on where you're stuck, you can bring this awareness into therapy, coaching or your personal development work and start creating real change. You can do this exercise any time you want to gain clarity and understand why you're feeling stagnant.

If you want to stop feeling like you're spinning your wheels and finally break free from old patterns, this exercise is your next step in self-mastery.

Here's how it works: Draw three big circles in your journal: Stuck, Looping and Free.

1 Stuck This is where you feel completely frozen, like, no matter what you do, nothing changes. These could be areas like your relationships, money, career or health. Write down in the circle the parts of your life where you feel stuck.

Next, ask yourself: how does this feel? How does it feel to be stuck in your relationship, money or career? For example: you may feel angry, frustrated or sad. Write down the feelings that come up for you.

Finally, pay attention to the stories you tell yourself about being stuck. What's the narrative here? Are you telling yourself, 'I'll never get ahead' or 'I'm always going to be single'? Name the thoughts that keep you feeling trapped. In the circle, write out the thought or story you are telling yourself about this area.

2 Looping These are the areas of your life where you make progress, but you keep falling back into the same old patterns. It's that frustrating feeling of taking two steps forward and three steps back. Write down what's on repeat for you. Is it your finances, a relationship that you just can't get right or a personal goal that seems just out of reach? Then, ask yourself: What's the story behind this loop? Is it 'I'm so close, but I always mess it up' or 'It's just never the right time'? These stories keep you spinning in circles. Write down the parts of your life where you feel you're looping on repeat.

Next, ask yourself: how does this feel? How does it feel to be looping in your finances or friendships? For example: you may feel mad, overwhelmed or confused. Write down the feelings that come up for you.

Finally, pay attention to the stories you tell yourself about being stuck in a loop. What's the narrative here? Are you telling yourself, 'This

SELF-ACCEPTANCE ISN'T A FINAL DESTINATION; IT'S A CONTINUOUS PRACTICE.

never changes' or 'I'm always going backward'? Name the thoughts that keep you feeling trapped. In the circle, write out the thought or story you are telling yourself about this area.

3 Free These are the areas where you feel empowered, expansive and in flow. Life feels easy, and things are aligning. Even if this experience isn't happening for you right now, write down the area of your life where you feel free. It could be with your dog, when you sing, do art or are with your friends. Reflect on the thoughts and beliefs you have about these areas. Are you telling yourself, 'I'm capable and deserving' or 'Everything is falling into place'? Notice the difference in energy compared to the Stuck and Looping circles. Write down the parts of your life where you feel free.

Next, ask yourself: how does it feel? How does it feel to be free in this area of your life? For example: you may feel happy, fulfilled, proud or excited. Write down the feelings that come up for you.

Finally, pay attention to the thoughts you tell yourself about being free. What's the narrative here? Are you telling yourself, 'I am so grateful for the family I have' or 'I'm proud of the success I've built'? Name the thoughts that make you feel free! These should feel amazing and expansive. In the circle, write out the thoughts you are telling yourself about this area.

Note: many of us have much more in the looping circle and sometimes less in the free circle, so don't judge yourself. This exercise is about awareness, and these things change and shift; approach this exercise with curiosity and an open mind.

Once you've mapped out the circles, take a step back and look at the thoughts in each one. Where do you need to shift your narrative to move from Stuck or Looping into Free? Where are you letting limiting beliefs control your experience? What beliefs do you need to release in order to stop looping and step into freedom in every area of your life?

This exercise is about being honest with yourself and recognising that the stories you tell yourself can either hold you back or set you free. By identifying these patterns, you'll start to see exactly where you need to do the work. To help make change feel achievable, commit to work on one area so you aren't distracted by the fear of being overwhelmed.

One you work on the biggest area in which you feel stuck, it will positively impact all areas of your life. So focus on going all-in on the Big One, as this is such an effective awareness tool to take into therapy or coaching.

You've just taken a deep dive into self-mastery, the foundation of all magnetism. Don't expect to have everything figured out yet – this is a process, and you may have just started. But by becoming more aware of yourself, you're laying the groundwork for everything that follows. The big lesson here: you gotta be good with you before you do anything else.

In Phase 2, we'll take this to the next level by defining what you truly stand for. This is where your core values come into play.

6

PHASE 2:
YOUR TRUE NORTH

YOUR TRUE NORTH
YOUR TRUE NORTH

'People get lost chasing goals, forgetting that if you don't know who you are and what you stand for, those goals mean nothing. Get clear on your values first – own who you are – and watch how you attract everything you desire.'

One of the most attractive and powerful things a woman can do is have an unwavering sense of self. A woman who knows who she is and what she stands for is an undeniable force of nature. This isn't just surface confidence; it's a raw, grounded certainty, a conviction so deep it commands attention and magnetises people without her even trying.

You see, magnetism is more than energy or presence. It comes down to being rooted in who you are and what you believe. When you're deeply grounded in your core values and connected to your true north, you navigate life with a sense of clarity and purpose that others can't help but notice. Your values guide your actions, influence your decisions and dictate the kind of energy you bring into the world. When you know what drives you, you move through life with an authenticity that pulls people in.

Your clarity and conviction? Unshakable. And that's magnetic.

Here's the thing about values: they are more than words – they are what you live by. They shape how you show up in your relationships, at work and in the world. They help you set boundaries, align with what truly matters and allow you to stop being swayed by external opinions. Without clarity on your values, life feels messy, like you're always second-guessing yourself, chasing validation or living according to someone else's script. But once you define your true north, everything starts to align. You stop chasing; instead, you start attracting.

NINA'S JOURNEY: DEFINING HER VALUES

As Nina embraced her journey of self-mastery, everything began to shift. She was no longer willing to settle for the same things that once felt comfortable. The jobs that didn't fulfil her, the social drinking that numbed her, the relationships that drained her – all of it started to feel out of place in her new reality. Nina started prioritising her wellbeing, committing to fitness, healthy eating and aligning with natural remedies, things that had always called to her but had been buried under the noise of her old life. She started setting boundaries around her time, her energy and whom she allowed into her life. She valued connection, love and integrity more than anything, and it became clear that she needed to start living in alignment with those values.

For Nina, this shift was massive. She realised that her values had always been there, but the pain and grief she carried around had kept her from fully embracing them. She'd always valued family, and time spent with her nieces and nephews became even more precious. She knew deep down that one day she would start her own family, but first, she had to fully step into her truth. She realised she valued trust and loyalty in relationships, and for the first time, she was ready to demand that from her life partner.

In the past, Nina had chased external validation – she wanted to fit in and be liked. But with her newfound clarity, she no longer needed that validation. She no longer valued superficial things; she craved depth, authenticity and real connection. This clarity started showing up in her interactions, in her relationships and in the way she navigated her world.

Before this transformation, Nina had spent years hiding her true self, shrinking to fit what she thought others wanted from her. Afraid of being judged, she silenced her opinions, playing small in rooms where she belonged. Does this sound familiar? We've all been there, playing a version of ourselves that we think will be accepted, even though it leaves us feeling unfulfilled.

But as Nina deepened her self-mastery, she had a realisation – she had been living a life completely out of alignment with her values. Love, connection and integrity were some of her core values, yet they had been buried under layers of doubt and fear. Once she got clear on what really mattered to her, everything shifted. She no longer needed validation from anyone else, because she had given it to herself.

Nina began asking herself the tough questions: What's truly important to me now that I've faced my grief? What do I want for my future? What environments do I want to be in? Who am I when no one is around? Where have I been hiding and what personal values matter to me most?

With those answers came a sense of groundedness that she had never felt before. This was her true north. And when you get clear on that, the rest of your life aligns around it. That's exactly what happened with Nina.

In her personal life, she stopped seeking approval from others and started showing up as herself – unapologetically. And guess what? People could feel the shift. The right people began entering her life. People who respected and aligned with her values, new friends who connected with her on a deeper level and who celebrated her for being exactly who she was.

At work, she stopped holding back. She began stepping up and stepping into leadership, making confident decisions that were aligned with her values of authenticity and self-assurance. This newfound certainty made her magnetic – people wanted to be around her and work with her, not because she was trying to be something she wasn't, but because she was authentically herself.

Nina no longer shrank to fit into spaces or relationships that didn't align with her. Her clarity, her confidence and her unapologetic presence made her magnetic. She started drawing in amazing friendships, deeper connections with her loved ones and attracted the love of her life.

When you're living out of alignment with your values, you *know* it. You feel stuck, unsure and unfulfilled, like something's missing. But when you get clear on what really matters to you, everything else starts to fall into place.

WHAT ARE VALUES?

Values are the core beliefs that drive your actions, decisions and the way you live your life. They are your non-negotiables – the things you stand for, no matter what. These deeply ingrained principles act as your moral compass, guiding you through the world with clarity and purpose. Your values reflect what's most important to you, shaping not only how you see the world but also how you interact with it. They define your boundaries, dictate your behaviour and are the things you'll fight for and never compromise on.

Some common examples of values include:

- **integrity:** doing what's right, even when no one is watching
- **authenticity:** showing up as your true self, without masks or pretence
- **connection:** building deep, meaningful relationships with others

- **freedom:** having autonomy over your life, choices and actions
- **growth:** continuously evolving, learning and expanding as a person
- **respect:** treating others – and yourself – with dignity and care
- **contribution:** making a difference in the lives of others or the world around you.

These are just a few examples, but everyone's values will be slightly different. What matters to me might not be what matters to you, and that's the point. The key is discovering what resonates with you on a deep level.

Values are deeply personal and unique to each person. They are what grounds you when the world feels chaotic. When there's a misalignment, you'll feel it. For example, I've worked with clients who value integrity, yet find themselves in work environments where their supervisors value the bottom line above all else. The tension that arises isn't because either person is 'wrong', but because their values are out of sync.

LEARNT VALUES

Growing up, we often take on the values that are modelled to us by our caregivers, without ever realising it. Some of these values serve us well, while others can hold us back. In my case, my mom was obsessed with appearances and what others thought of her. She wouldn't leave the house unless her nails were perfectly matching her outfit, and as a kid, it drove me *insane*. But over time, I noticed that I had unconsciously adopted that same fixation. I became overly critical of myself, constantly trying to fit into this ideal mould that wasn't even mine. It kept me frozen, always seeking approval, always trying to live up to an impossible standard.

Without clarity on what you truly value, you'll be swayed by the noise around you – whether it's society's expectations, the opinions of others or even your own outdated beliefs.

It wasn't until I started doing the inner work that I realised something huge – I had taken on *her* value. It wasn't actually mine. I didn't care about appearances in the same way she did. That obsession with how others perceived me was something I'd absorbed, not something I truly believed in. And once I recognised that, I could let it go. That awareness set me free. Suddenly, I didn't feel the pressure to fit into anyone's expectations anymore, and I started stepping into *who I truly am*.

But not all values we inherit are harmful. My mom also had this deep love for connection. She could talk to anyone – a stranger at the grocery store, the neighbour or the mailman – it didn't matter. She valued friendliness, kindness and genuine connection, just because that's who she was. And that's something she passed down to me that I'm so grateful for. She taught me the importance of being a good person, of caring about others not for recognition, but simply because it's the right thing to do. That's a value I *definitely* embraced, and it's shaped how I show up in the world.

You see, we absorb the values of the people who raise us – sometimes without even realising it. It's crucial to do the work to figure out which values are truly *yours*, and which ones you've been carrying around because they were passed down to you. The truth is that not every value we inherit serves us. Some of them keep us small, stuck or out of alignment with our authentic selves.

When you start identifying those values, you gain the power to keep the ones that align with who you really are and the power to let go of the ones that don't.

Values aren't just something you 'know' – they're the filter for how you live your life. They influence every decision you make, from who you let into your life to how you spend your time, money and energy. If you're not clear on what you value, you could be running on autopilot. You might be spending all your time in the wrong places with the wrong people, wondering why you feel off. Maybe you're hustling at work when what you actually care about is spending time with your family.

In this chapter, we're cutting through the noise to figure out what actually matters to **you**, and how to align your life with the future you want, owning your values.

PURSUING VALUES VERSUS PURSUING GOALS

We live in a world where so many people are focused on goals, thinking, 'When I *have* this, then I will *be* that.' It's the 'when I, then I' fallacy and it's so pervasive. People think, 'Once I **have** the success, the money, the status, then I'll **be** free, at peace and generous,' but the truth is that when you pursue goals that don't align with your values, you're chasing things that will never fill you up.

Let me be real – there is nothing wrong with setting goals. In fact, goals give us direction. But goals without values at their core can feel hollow. You could be striving for success, but success for the sake of success is meaningless if you're sacrificing the things you truly value in the process.

Imagine you have a goal to become rich. Now, that sounds great on paper, right? But what happens if in the pursuit of that goal, you lose sight of your values? What happens if the money comes at the cost of your family, your health or your integrity? Too many people end up achieving the goal only to find themselves feeling empty. They've got the money but none of the fulfilment because the pursuit wasn't aligned with who they truly are.

I remember this one time Hamish and I joined a business program together. We didn't really know much about values at that point. The mentor was super-focused on helping people make money: he had a big thing for private jets, fancy restaurants and a high-flying lifestyle. Because Hamish and I weren't clear on our own values yet, we found ourselves getting swept up in his.

Every time there was an event or session, we'd leave feeling a bit off – disappointed and defeated. We still weren't multimillionaires, and it was like we were constantly chasing this dream that wasn't even ours. One day, though, it hit us like a ton of bricks. We looked at each other and realised, wait a minute . . . we don't even care about private jets. That wasn't our idea of success.

We valued something completely different. For us, it was about spending time together, contributing to the world and making an impact. Once we got clear on that, everything shifted. The pressure was gone. We didn't need to compare ourselves to that lifestyle because it wasn't in alignment with who we were or what we valued.

It's the same reason I can show up today, whether online or in person at an event, with so much energy and enthusiasm – because I'm aligned with what I value: impact. Making a difference in people's lives lights me up. Any success that comes as a result? That's a bonus. The real win is living in alignment with my true north.

Instead of chasing goals that may or may not bring you happiness, why not pursue virtues – those values that define who you are? Values like generosity, courage, integrity and kindness are the highest forms of human expression. And the beautiful thing is, values aren't something you pursue for applause or recognition. They aren't goals you achieve in public to show off. Values shine the brightest when no one is watching.

Let me say that again: **Values shine when no one is watching**.

That's the power of living in alignment with your values. When you lead with integrity, when you act with kindness, when you embrace generosity – not because you have to, but because it's who you are – you start living a life of substance. You stop caring about external validation because you're no longer comparing yourself to others. You're competing with yourself to become better, every single day.

This is where true magnetism flourishes. A woman who knows her values and lives by them is the kind of woman who commands respect without saying a word. She doesn't need to broadcast her achievements or flaunt her worth. Her value is in how she shows up, day in and day out, and that radiates more powerfully than any goal ever could.

Here's the shift I want you to make: Pursue values, not just goals. Because when you lead with your values, when you define success by how well you embody those values, everything else falls into place.

Goals are great, but goals without values are empty. It's the values you cultivate that truly matter. Values will guide you, ground you and ensure that you're living a life of meaning, not just achievement.

Action step: Discover what matters

Here's your challenge: Take some time to reflect on what you value. Ask yourself the following questions:

- What's truly important to me?
- What am I willing to stand up for, even if it's unpopular?
- When have I felt the most fulfilled or alive?
- When have I felt the most out of alignment or disconnected? What was missing?

Once you've done this, write your answers down. There's a deeper values exercise at the end of this chapter that will support you to identify exactly what's most important to you now.

WHY VALUES MATTER

If self-mastery is the foundation, then defining your values is the blueprint. After all, what good is mastery if you don't know where you're going? Defining your values gives you that direction. It's the next critical step in your journey toward becoming magnetic, because your values dictate how you show up in the world. They influence the choices you make, the people you surround yourself with and how you respond to everything around you.

Without clarity on what you truly value, you'll be swayed by the noise around you – whether it's society's expectations, the opinions of others or even your own outdated beliefs. You'll find yourself bending, compromising and questioning your own decisions because you lack a strong internal guidance system.

But when you're aligned with your core values, you stop over-complicating things because you're making decisions based on your values, not someone else's. You become clear about what matters most to you, suddenly life becomes much simpler and you stop over-complicating things.

When you're clear on your values, you start to see them reflected in your everyday choices. Your values influence everything – especially how you feel about yourself.

Let's break it down with some real-life examples:

If you value health, you'll prioritise activities like working out, eating nourishing food and getting enough sleep. But if you say you value health yet continue to neglect your body – skipping workouts or eating foods that aren't good for you – you're going to feel completely out of alignment. If your value is your health and physical wellbeing, these other options will have you living out of alignment with that value. And guess what? You'll feel it. You'll feel off-balance, frustrated and out of sync with yourself.

If you value connection, you'll make an effort to spend quality time with the people you care about, have meaningful conversations and foster deep relationships. But if you find yourself constantly overworking, neglecting friends or isolating yourself, you'll start to feel lonely, disconnected and unfulfilled.

If you value growth, you'll seek opportunities to learn, challenge yourself and expand your horizons. This might look like investing in personal development, taking risks in your career or stepping out of your comfort zone. But if you stay stuck in the same routine, avoiding new challenges or growth, shrinking yourself or playing small, you'll feel stagnant and frustrated, like something's missing.

LIVING OUT OF ALIGNMENT

When you live out of alignment with your values, you know it. There's this sense of unease, a nagging feeling that something isn't quite right. You feel stuck, frustrated or even resentful, but you might not know exactly why. That's because your actions aren't matching up with what you truly value, with who you deep down know yourself to be.

The more out of alignment you are with your values, the harder it becomes to attract what you want into your life. You'll feel like you're constantly fighting an uphill battle, trying to force things to work when, deep down, you know they aren't right for you.

Magnetism isn't just about being charismatic or confident; it's about being grounded in who you are. It's about having a clear sense of what you stand for, and letting that guide your every move. When you live in alignment with your values, people can feel that. They see someone who knows who they are, who's unapologetically themselves and who won't bend or compromise on what's important.

That's magnetic.

WHAT DO YOU MEAN YOU DON'T WANT SIX KIDS?!

One of the most effective tools I've ever used to stay aligned with who I am and ensure I'm living with integrity is a values exercise. It's simple, but damn, it's powerful. Hamish and I started doing this exercise early in our relationship, as we recognised how important it was to align as a couple, especially with our first baby on the way. As you've probably gathered by now, we were total personal-development junkies. We didn't just dip our toes into it; we dove in headfirst. You name it – we'd done it. Seminars? Check. Masterminds? Of course. Private mentoring? Weekly. If there was a way to learn, grow and align our lives, we were there, soaking it all in.

One of our mentors, a guy we deeply respected, was huge on values and creating personal mission statements. He lived by it. So, when we told him we were expecting our first baby, his face lit up, and without missing a beat, he invited us to his office. 'If you're not clear on your values as a couple and as a family,' he said, 'you'll struggle to find alignment. Your values are your anchor.'

He was right. At that point, we thought we had it all figured out. We were aligned in where we wanted to go in life and the business we were building, but throwing a baby into the mix? That felt like a whole new level of chaos. I mean, like most first-time parents, we had absolutely no idea what we were in for. And thank goodness for that mentor because that conversation – and the values exercise he walked us through – transformed everything. Not just our relationship, but how we approached parenting, our business and our lives. It shifted everything for us.

Let me set the scene for you. I'm seven months pregnant, waddling into a cute little cafe across from our apartment, ready to take on this values exercise. The plan was simple (or so we thought). First, we'd each write down our individual values – things that mattered most to us personally. Then, we'd make a list of what we valued in our relationship. Finally, we'd come together to combine our lists and create a set of family and relationship values we both agreed on.

Sounds pretty straightforward, right? Well, it wasn't.

Before we even got halfway through the exercise, things took a sharp turn. I was standing up in the middle of this crowded cafe,

PURSUE
VALUES,
NOT JUST
GOALS.

enormous and emotional like some kind of hormonal warrior, raising my voice and crying my heart out, absolutely convinced that I wanted six kids.

SIX.

Hamish, on the other hand, nearly choked on his coffee.

'Six kids, babe? You can't be serious,' he said, half-laughing, half-panicked.

Oh, but I was. I was dead serious. You see, growing up as an only child, I'd always dreamt of having a big, noisy, chaotic family. I wanted the house full of kids and all the mess that came with it. The foster homes I grew up in always had at least six or seven children running around, cats, dogs and havoc, and I just *loved* it. There was always this sense of connection, warmth and togetherness, lots of people at the dinner table, people all over the house – for me, that felt like family.

Hamish, on the other hand, came from a much smaller family: one brother, parents who were still together and a tight-knit circle of relatives. His idea of 'family' was very different from mine. And when I threw out the number 'six', he just . . . couldn't. He thought I was joking the whole time.

Well, I wasn't.

That's the beauty of this values exercise – it forces you to confront what really matters to you, even the things you didn't know were so important. We were sitting in a public cafe having a full-blown debate about how many kids we were going to have – me, pregnant and sobbing, and Hamish just sitting there with his head in his hands, wondering how he got himself into this. After two hours of going back and forth about the number of kids we wanted, we finally came to a compromise: one at a time and we'd check in after each one. (Hamish, always the diplomat.)

It sounds funny now, but at that moment, it was intense.

We were having one of the biggest, most emotionally charged conversations of our lives – about what kind of family we wanted to create. It forced us to get real with each other. And that's what the values exercise does – it forces you to peel back the layers and ask the hard questions: What do you really value? What's non-negotiable for you? What kind of life do you want to create?

The best part of that conversation was that it laid the groundwork for how we'd navigate everything moving forward. It wasn't just about kids; we talked about family, love, business, health, money and how we wanted to show up in our relationship. It allowed us to get real with each other about what we valued in life. By the end of that day, we didn't just have a plan for our family – we had a clear set of values that we'd created for our lives together.

It wasn't easy.

We spent a lot of time unpacking our pasts and figuring out where our values came from. As I've explained, I realised I'd inherited a lot of my mom's values, and I didn't even realise they weren't mine until I started questioning them. Hamish had his own stuff too. We had to get clear on what we wanted to keep and what we were ready to let go of.

That values exercise? It's a game-changer I have now integrated into my coaching practice because it lays the foundation for true alignment. When my clients get clear on their core values, it transforms everything – from how they make decisions, to how they show up in their personal and professional lives. It's the kind of clarity that cuts through the noise.

We've seen time and time again couples and individuals we've coached who aren't clear on their values, who haven't taken the time to sit with the discomfort and ask the tough questions. And guess what? That leads to marriages that don't last, careers they despise, lavish weddings they can't even remember and living a life that feels out of alignment. It leads to deep unhappiness and layers of resentment. The research backs this up too. The National Marriage Project found that couples who align on core values – particularly around family, finances and religion – are more likely to have long-lasting, strong marriages. Shared values help couples navigate life's challenges with resilience.

It's not just romantic relationships. Stanford University's WELL for Life study revealed that individuals who live in alignment with their core values are significantly more likely to experience higher levels of wellbeing and life satisfaction. They feel less stress, less anxiety and more fulfilment because their actions are in sync with their personal beliefs. When your actions and values are in harmony, life flows.

In the workplace, the impact is just as powerful. Gallup found that employees who work for companies that align with their values are 43 per cent more engaged. This leads to higher productivity and lower turnover. You can see how values don't just affect your personal life; they're the key to professional alignment as well.

That's why values matter so much. They're the blueprint of everything. Without clear values, you're navigating life without a compass. But when you define them, when you align your life to those values, everything falls into place. You stop living for other people's expectations, and you start living for you.

Whether it's in relationships or your individual wellbeing, your values play a massive role. When your actions, decisions and lifestyle are aligned with your core values, you live your life with so much more clarity, confidence and fulfilment. On the flip side, misalignment with your values leads to frustration, dissatisfaction and disconnection in both your personal and romantic life, and your work or career.

What do you really value?
What's non-negotiable
for you?
What kind of life do you
want to create?

Oh, and in case you're wondering . . . Hamish was right (don't tell him I said that). We ended up with two beautiful boys – and it was a decision we made together, consciously and with love. I honestly could never imagine myself with six kids now! Something I thought I wanted ended up not being the case, and that is what growth and self-reflection is all about. Our family is small and mighty and we couldn't be happier.

Time to do the work.

VALUES EXERCISE: FINDING YOUR TRUE NORTH

Step 1: Choose your words

Write down a list of ten to twelve words that resonate with you as values. These are things you deeply believe in, things that make you feel fulfilled, aligned and strong. Here are some examples to get you started:

integrity
growth
creativity
adventure
regularity
striving
competition
tradition
justice
personal presentation
relaxation
luxury

authenticity
contribution
family
autonomy
spontaneity
challenge
winning
peacefulness
sharing
efficiency
ease
sustainability

love
freedom
connection
safety
respect
achievement
faith
morality
nurturing
activity
simplicity

Step 2: Narrow them down

Now, refine your list. Are any of the values similar or overlapping? For example, if you have integrity and honesty, can they be combined into one word? Or do they mean completely different things to you? Keep narrowing your list down until you have around five to eight core values. These should be the most important ones to you – your true north.

Step 3: Define your values

For each value, write a sentence or two defining what it means to you. This isn't the dictionary definition – it's your personal definition. What does contribution mean to you? What does family or adventure look like in your life?

Step 4: Rate your alignment

On a scale from 1 to 10, rate how aligned you feel with each value in your life right now. For example, if you value creativity but aren't currently expressing it, your rating might be a 4 or 5. If you're living fully with integrity, that might be an 8 or 9.

Step 5: Create an action plan

For each value that's rated less than an 8, identify one small action you can take this week to move closer to living in alignment with it. For example, if you rated 'authenticity' a 5, maybe your action is to have a vulnerable conversation with a friend or show up more authentically on your social media. What's one small thing you can do to raise your alignment by just one number? Go do that. And then repeat the following week – and the week after that.

Defining your values isn't just some feel-good exercise. It's real work that can literally change the course of your life. It forces you to confront what matters most and lets you create a life that's in full alignment with who you are and what you stand for. But first, you need to make the time to do it. You need to make this a priority if you truly want to step into your magnetic self. Trust me, once you get clear on your values, everything else starts to fall into place. You'll stop chasing and start attracting. You'll stop bending to fit into spaces that don't align with who you are, and instead, create spaces where you can fully be yourself.

7

PHASE 3: YOUR ALTER SHE-GO

YOUR ALTER SHE-GO
YOUR ALTER SHE-GO

'When you commit to stepping into your future self – thinking, acting, and showing up as her – the world responds. It's not pretending; it's aligning with the woman you're destined to be, right here, right now.'

I attended a lot of programs when I first began my self-development journey. At one business program, I kept getting asked if I was a fashion stylist. Women would come up to me at the events and ask me to style them. I was so confused. Me! A fashion stylist? At first, I brushed it off. I was a hairdresser, after all. I spent years in hairdressing school learning how to make women feel good about themselves from the neck up, but dressing women? I hadn't even considered it. But as the questions kept coming – at almost every event – I started to think, *Maybe there's something here.* Why not try it out, right?

So, I dove in. And guess what? It was like finding a new love. Fashion styling wasn't all that different from what I did with hair. Both were about transformation, about helping women feel confident in their skin. It was about creating a look that matched how they wanted to feel on the inside. Before I knew it, I had a full-fledged side hustle. I was running styling sessions on weekends and after work. I even started getting media attention – next thing I knew, I was being featured on the news for my work! It was surreal, and honestly, it felt amazing.

There's something powerful about helping a woman see herself differently. I ran styling events where I taught women how to dress in ways that made them feel good and powerful. When you dress in a way that makes you feel good, you show up differently. It's not just about clothes; it's about what those clothes do for your confidence.

You take better actions, and when you take better actions, you create better results in your life. It's a ripple effect.

I loved watching that moment of transformation – the way a woman's eyes would light up when she looked at herself in the mirror and saw a more powerful, confident version of herself staring back. It wasn't just about looking good. It was about feeling good. That's where the magic was.

At first, I named my business 'The Queen of Curves' because I am curvy and I felt like it had a good ring to it. But it didn't take long for me to realise that I was unintentionally leaving some women out – women who didn't see themselves as curvy. And the last thing I wanted was to alienate anyone who wanted to be in my community or attend our events. One day in the shower, where all the wisdom comes to me, I had an 'Aha!' moment. *What's something all women want? Confidence!* And that's when I made the decision to rebrand as 'The Queen of Confidence'. It was a bold move, and honestly, it scared the hell out of me. *Like, who do you think you are, Erika?* Naming the business after confidence made *me* the Queen of Confidence, and I wasn't sure I was ready for that crown. It felt too big, too bold, too much. I tried to sabotage it and say 'The Queens of Confidence' or 'You are the Queen'. Hamish just shook his head. 'No, babe. You gotta be her.' He was right, once again.

Owning that name – The Queen of Confidence – wasn't just about branding a business. It was the first step toward becoming the woman I was meant to be. The more I leaned into it, the more I realised that confidence wasn't just something I was teaching other women; it was something I was also learning to master myself. Confidence is an inside job, and I had a lot of internal work to do.

In the beginning, my focus was all about external appearances – how to dress for your body shape, what outfits would flatter you or which clothes to get rid of because they no longer fit. I was a stylist who would go into women's wardrobes, helping them cull the pieces that no longer worked for who they were. But over the years, as I went deeper into my own personal development journey, I started to realise that real transformation had nothing to do with how we dressed on the outside – it was about how we felt on the inside.

Think of it like culling your *internal* wardrobe. You know that old sweater your grandma gave you when you were seventeen? It doesn't fit anymore, but you're still hanging onto it. It's outdated, it's stretched out, but there's sentimental value, so you leave it in the back of your closet. We do the same thing with beliefs. We hold onto old, outdated thoughts about ourselves – beliefs that we're not good enough, not capable or not worthy – just because they've been with us for so long. They no longer fit who we are, but we keep them anyway.

My work started to evolve from helping women clean out their closets to helping them clean out their minds. Instead of getting rid of old jeans that no longer fit, we were getting rid of a woman's belief that she wasn't good enough. Instead of tossing out a sweater from an ex-boyfriend, we were culling the idea that a woman had to be perfect to be loved. It became about identifying the limiting beliefs, the negative self-talk and the doubts that no longer served each woman, and replacing those with empowering beliefs that actually fit the **woman they were becoming**.

The real magic wasn't in the clothes or the styling; it was in helping them see themselves differently. Once they let go of those outdated beliefs, they started to show up as the confident, powerful women they were always meant to be. It was like trying on a brand-new outfit – except this time, it wasn't about the clothes, it wasn't about external confidence. It was about feeling confident from the inside out.

This journey was deeply influenced by my husband Hamish's obsession with superheroes. Random, I know. But it's true – this man loves superheroes. We're talking full-on fanboy status.

CONFIDENCE
IS AN
INSIDE JOB.

Hamish's obsession with superheroes didn't just centre on the characters; it was about what they represented – alter egos, and stepping into your true power. When Hamish was little, he and his brother Matthew used to play dress-up all the time. Hamish was always Superman, and Matthew was Batman. But one day, something serious happened. Matthew had an anaphylactic reaction to bunny fur in class. They didn't know what to do back then, so they laid him on the grass outside and told Hamish to take him home. Hamish, just eight years old, was left trying to save his little brother's life. Thankfully, a family friend happened to drive by and rushed Matthew to the hospital.

That night, Hamish's dad sat him down and said, 'You're a man now, son. You've gotta look after your brother.' Talk about pressure. From that moment on, Hamish stepped into the role of the rescuer. It shaped him for years. In every relationship, he played the hero, trying to save the damsel in distress.

When Hamish opened his gym, he called it 'Alterego' because he believed in the power of tapping into an altered version of yourself. His clients didn't just show up to work out – they stepped into their superhero selves. He created a whole process around this, asking his clients to picture the most powerful version of themselves and become that person in the gym, at work, when they ordered coffee – everywhere. It was incredible to watch. People transformed, not just physically, but mentally and emotionally. They became who they wanted to be.

Seeing the success Hamish had with his clients, I knew I had to bring this into my own work. That's when I launched my first coaching program, which was designed to help women step into their confidence. One of the most powerful modules in the program was all about creating your alter she-go. It's about tapping into that version of yourself we learnt about in Chapter 2, the version of you that is magnetic, confident and unstoppable. It's about naming her, defining her and becoming her.

Just like we all know that Beyoncé has Sasha Fierce, you have your own alter she-go waiting to be unleashed. We all do. It's the part of you that steps into the spotlight, owns the stage and doesn't apologise for taking up space. Your alter she-go is your permission slip to be bold, brave and fully expressed.

I'm not asking you to pretend to be someone you're not – it's about becoming more of who you *really* are. The version of you that isn't held back by doubt or fear. The version of you that shows up, commands attention and moves through the world with ease and grace. And listen, I get it. Stepping into your alter she-go can feel super uncomfortable at first. I didn't exactly feel like the Queen of Confidence when I started, but the more I practised, the more I embodied her. Now? She's a part of me. I want to help you unlock your own version of her too.

Over nearly two decades of working with women in hair, fashion and coaching – alongside my own journey – I've learnt that how we embody our values and beliefs, whether through clothing or mindset shifts, can radically transform our energy. The way we choose to show up in the world, how we dress, how we carry ourselves – it's all an expression of who we believe ourselves to be. That's where the alter she-go process comes in.

And here's the important distinction: it's not fake. It's not pretending. It's not about creating some false persona to hide behind. What you're actually doing is tapping into a version of yourself that's always been there, just waiting for permission to be unleashed.

This process isn't about playing dress-up for the sake of it or faking confidence until it magically shows up. It's about connecting with that future version of yourself – the you who already has the confidence, who already is magnetic, who walks around unapologetically as her authentic self. She exists, and she's not a far-off fantasy; she's real, and you're simply aligning with her.

You're tapping into her energy, thinking how she thinks, dressing how she dresses, speaking and carrying yourself the way she would. You're stepping into that future self and saying, 'I'm ready to live as her, right now.' This is about you embodying the qualities, confidence and energy of the woman you know you're capable of becoming – the version of you who is already thriving, already magnetic, already standing in her full power. The alter she-go process is just the tool to help you *unlock* her.

And for me? It started with the clothes, but it evolved into so much more. When you *look* the part, you start to *feel* the part. And when you feel the part, you **become** the part.

NINA'S JOURNEY: CREATING HER ALTER SHE-GO

After years of feeling disconnected from herself – hiding behind self-doubt, body image issues and the fear of standing out – Nina made the conscious decision to step into the version of herself she always dreamt of becoming.

As she moved through this phase, Nina began visualising the woman she wanted to be. Who was this next-level version of her? She saw someone who was **warm, magnetic, confident and unapologetically herself**. She was friendly, outgoing and naturally drew people in with her energy. Nina knew that this woman didn't shy away from people or dim her light in social settings – she was someone who radiated positivity and owned her presence. This is the essence of her alter she-go: someone deeply aligned with the traits she aspired to, already **embodying the energy of her future self**.

This wasn't just an abstract idea – it translated into real, tangible changes in how Nina showed up every day. She started by dressing the part. She loved crazy prints and colourful coordinated sets. At work, she began wearing the clothes that made her feel powerful and beautiful. She no longer hid behind oversized jumpers or tried to blend into the background; instead, she opted for the bold outfits that inspired her new confidence. The simple act of putting on clothes that made her feel good created a shift in *her* energy – which then affected the way *others* responded to her.

But it wasn't just about the clothes. Nina also changed how she interacted with others. She began to show up at work with a smile, engaging in more meaningful conversations with colleagues. At social events, she would compliment strangers, share stories, take up space by speaking up and putting herself out there. These small, intentional actions were part of her transformation – she was practising being her **alter she-go**.

The more Nina embodied this version of herself, the more magnetic she became. Her energy was contagious. People naturally gravitated toward her, curious about the shift they sensed in her (whenever anyone who attended Nina's retreat with her sees her, they say she is unrecognisable!). Nina noticed it in the way she effortlessly walked away from friend groups that were no longer aligned, in the way new friendships deepened, in the way colleagues began seeking her out for advice, and most importantly, in her romantic life.

When Nina met her partner, it wasn't some random stroke of luck – it was a direct result of her stepping into this new, confident version of herself. It all kicked off when she finally opened up to her hairdresser about wanting to find love, something she would have *never* done in the past. Back then, Nina was shy, closed off and avoided social gatherings like the plague – especially ones where she'd be meeting new people.

Talking about love? Forget it. After losing Tui, she couldn't even admit to herself that she wanted it.

But on this particular day, something shifted. Nina was getting her hair done, and she casually mentioned that she might see her hairdresser later at a party they were both attending. He was going with a group of friends, and in the past, Nina would have stayed on the sidelines, maybe even skipped the party altogether. But not this time.

That night, as she walked into the party, she spotted her hairdresser across the room with his group of friends. Without hesitation – something old Nina wouldn't have *dared* to do – she confidently waved and called out his name. She strutted right over, owning her energy, despite being surrounded by a group of men. She didn't shy away or play small; she stepped right into the conversation like she belonged there. And that's when it happened – one of his friends caught her eye, and that friend is now her partner.

They hit it off immediately, and Nina's confidence was undeniable. She was shining, owning her space and completely comfortable in her skin. Oh, and let's not forget the hot-pink pleather mini skirt she wore that night – totally her alter she-go's idea! Bold, unapologetic and magnetic, exactly the kind of energy that attracted her partner in the first place.

Nina's journey into her **alter she-go** was a powerful example of what can happen when you decide to embody the traits of the person you want to become. She wasn't pretending or playing a role – she was tapping into a future version of herself who was already confident, already magnetic and already living the life she desired. Through her actions, her energy and the way she presented herself, Nina became that woman.

And the incredible part? Once she started living as her **alter she-go**, her outer world began to shift to match her inner transformation. Opportunities, relationships and experiences started aligning with this new version of her. Nina became magnetic – not just to others, but to the life she truly wanted to live.

Her journey is a testament to the power of consciously choosing to step into the version of yourself you want to be and allowing that transformation to unfold in real, tangible ways. Nina's alter she-go wasn't just an idea – it was a reality she created, and she continues to live as that woman every day.

Through this process, Nina didn't just attract a partner; she attracted a whole new way of living – one that reflects her deepest desires and values. **And that's what stepping into your alter she-go is all about: becoming the woman who already has what you want, and allowing everything else to align around that.**

WHAT IS AN ALTER SHE-GO?

This idea of an alter ego isn't just some make-believe concept – it's actually grounded in psychological science. Cognitive psychologists have found that when people adopt an alter ego, they can bypass their limiting beliefs and step into a state of greater confidence and performance. One powerful concept behind this is called **enclothed cognition**, which is the psychological effect that clothing has on how we think, feel and behave. There is a symbolic meaning that influences our cognitive abilities. What we wear doesn't just impact how others see us – it changes how we perceive ourselves and our abilities, affecting confidence and performance.

Here's how it works: when you wear something that aligns with a particular identity – whether it's a sharp blazer, a flowing dress or even something as small as a specific accessory, like a hat – your brain begins to associate you with that identity. It's like sending a signal to your subconscious that says, 'I'm this person now. This is who I am.' And when your brain believes that, your actions, thoughts and emotions start to fall in line with that identity.

This is why athletes, performers and even public speakers use specific clothing, rituals or accessories to enhance their performance. Take Dr Martin Luther King Jr., for example, who used to wear glasses – not because he needed them, but because they helped him feel more distinguished and confident when giving speeches. It wasn't an effort to change who he was; it was a tool to unlock something that was already inside him. Similarly, Lady Gaga wears high heels not just as a fashion statement but as a way to tap into her powerful, larger-than-life stage persona, using the exaggerated height to boost her performance energy. Tennis champion Serena Williams had her own ritual – wearing the same pair of socks throughout a tournament to feel grounded and confident, tapping into the mindset of a champion. These are all small, intentional acts that help them step into a heightened version of themselves and deliver their best.

Let's come back to Beyoncé, one of the most iconic performers of our time. She's known for her stage presence, her powerful performances and her undeniable magnetism. But here's the thing: Beyoncé herself has openly said that she's a pretty quiet, shy and reserved person off-stage. In fact, during an interview with BET, the American TV network, she revealed that she could never do the things 'Sasha Fierce' does on stage. Beyoncé shared that Sasha is the bold, fearless alter ego she taps into when performing – someone completely different from her everyday self. People often confuse Beyoncé with Sasha Fierce, thinking they're the same person. But the truth is, Sasha is her alter ego – the unleashed, bold and unapologetic version of herself.

When Beyoncé steps onto the stage, it's not just her walking out there – it's Sasha. Sasha Fierce allows her to let go of any inhibitions or fears and fully embody her most confident, fierce self. Beyoncé has said that Sasha can do things she, Beyoncé, wouldn't dream of doing off-stage. That's the power of an alter ego. It's like putting on a suit of armour, a version of yourself that's fearless, unstoppable and fully in command.

In the same way, when you create and step into your alter she-go, you're telling your brain, 'This is who I am.'

Action step: Embodying your alter she-go

Before we dive into the complete exercise at the end of this chapter to completely unleash your alter she-go and start stepping into her every day, let's first lay out the foundational steps. These are key areas you'll want to consider as you begin thinking about who she is, what she stands for and how she shows up in your life.

1 Define who she is Start by getting crystal clear on your alter she-go. Who is she? What does she stand for? Is she fearless, adventurous, fashionable or effortlessly magnetic? What are her core values? Imagine her day – how does she navigate challenges, build relationships or stand up for herself?

2 Dress the part Step into her wardrobe. Think about what she wears when she feels her most powerful. It could be a statement blazer, bold accessories or even a signature lipstick. Use clothing as a tool to activate that mindset. If your alter she-go prioritises physical wellbeing, then runners or some other activewear might bring her to life. If she is creative, then perhaps a piece of handmade jewellery is what she wears. Remember: when you dress the part, you feel the part.

3 Create a ritual Anchor yourself with a ritual that gets you into her energy. It could be a playlist that pumps you up, a power pose in the mirror or journalling your intentions for the day. Rituals help you channel her energy and stay connected to her.

Clothing doesn't just affect how others perceive us, but also how we perceive ourselves.

4 Take aligned action Once you're tapped into your alter she-go, start acting like her. What decisions does she make? How does she set boundaries? What bold steps would she take today? Approach every task from her mindset.

ENCLOTHED COGNITION: THE SCIENCE BEHIND IT

There's real research to back this up. 'Enclothed cognition' was coined by social psychologists Hajo Adam and Adam Galinsky in a 2012 study. Their research demonstrated that clothing doesn't just affect how others perceive us, but also how we perceive ourselves. They ran experiments where participants wore a white lab coat. Half were told it was a 'doctor's coat', while the other half were told it was a 'painter's smock'. The results were stunning – the participants who believed they were wearing a doctor's coat performed tasks with heightened attention and precision, as if they had adopted the identity of a careful, detail-oriented professional.

This research shows how wearing specific clothing can activate certain psychological traits and behaviours. When we dress in a way that aligns with the version of ourselves we want to be, we begin to behave as that person. It's about more than just clothing – it's about shifting into an identity that allows us to think, act and feel in a way that matches the future self we aspire to be.

Why does this matter?

When you start to see yourself as that future you – the higher, more aligned version of yourself – you begin to create outcomes as her, because you're actively being her! It's like drawing a line in the sand and declaring, 'This is the new me, and I'm giving myself full permission to step into this version of myself.'

When you dress as your alter she-go, move as she moves and speak as she speaks, your entire world starts to respond differently (we'll dive deeper into this in Chapter 8). This process pulls you out of your comfort zone and allows you to challenge yourself in a real and tangible way, without waiting for 'some day' to arrive. It's not about faking it until you make it – it's about aligning with that future you *now* and operating from a place of embodiment.

I've even sent clients out on 'missions' where they visit coffee shops, airports or social events as their alter she-go, fully stepping into her energy. The feedback has been incredible. They've reported back with stories of how people reacted differently to them – being drawn to their openness, their energy and their confidence. This exercise becomes a fun, tangible way to test-drive your future self, allowing you to catch up with her much sooner than you think.

Your alter she-go doesn't play small – she owns her energy. It's about having fun with this. **We need to stop waiting for a special occasion to dress up for – your life is a special occasion.**

CREATING YOUR ALTER SHE-GO EXERCISE

All right, queen – it's time. This is where the magic happens! You're about to create and step into your alter she-go, the 2.0 version of yourself who is *already* that confident, magnetic, unstoppable woman.

This exercise is **fun** and **powerful**, but it's going to require you to dig deep. So, make sure you carve out some uninterrupted time for this process – give yourself space to *become* her. Let's go.

1 Name her

First things first – she needs a name. This is the version of you that commands attention, steps into any room and OWNS it. Who is she? What's her name? It can be playful, bold or something totally different from your usual self. Think of names like Beyoncé's 'Sasha Fierce' or my 'Queen of Confidence'. Maybe yours is 'Fearless Fiona' or 'Badass Bella'. Whatever you choose, make sure it resonates with the version of you who doesn't play small.

KNOW WHAT YOU WANT AND DON'T APOLOGISE FOR IT.

2 Define what she stands for

Now let's get your values from Chapter 6 in here. What does she believe in? What does she stand for? This version of you doesn't waver – she's grounded in her beliefs and values. Is she all about spontaneity, respectfulness and being relaxed? Write down her core values. Remember, this isn't a mask – it's about embodying the most aligned, real and powerful version of yourself.

3 Her outfit

How does she dress? Clothes have power – when you wear something that makes you feel unstoppable, you carry that energy. What is her go-to look? Maybe it's a leather jacket, a bold red lipstick, or a certain hat. When you put on these clothes and accessories, you should feel like you can conquer the world. Defining her signature look makes you feel confident and ready to take on anything.

4 Her theme song

Every queen needs a soundtrack. What's her anthem? This is the song that makes you feel like you could take over the world every time you hear it. Play it on repeat, get into the vibe and become her. Whether it's Alicia Keys' 'Girl On Fire' or Lizzo's 'Good as Hell,' this song should pump you up and connect you to your alter she-go.

★ *Head to the resources at the back and check out my alter she-go playlist on Spotify. You can even add your empowering song to the list!*

5 Her power pose

How does your alter she-go she stand? Shoulders back, chest out, chin up. This version of you doesn't shrink – she expands. Practise standing like her in front of the mirror. Own your space. Walk around your house like you're on the runway. The way you carry your body changes how you feel. Keep doing this until it feels natural.

6 Her superpowers

What are her strengths? What makes her stand out? Is she amazing at speaking up for herself? Does she walk into any room and light it up with her energy? Maybe she's a nurturing leader, or she's fierce in the boardroom. Define her superpowers – the things that make her extraordinary. Think big here; do not limit her.

7 Her power statement

What's her mantra? What does she say to herself to stay grounded, confident and unstoppable? This should be something you *believe.* Maybe it's 'I am creating the life I am worthy of living,' or 'I've got this! I was built for this!' or 'I can do anything I put my mind to.' This is the sentence she repeats in her mind when things get tough. Write down your power statement and start saying it every day.

8 Does she have a sidekick?

Some of the most iconic figures have sidekicks. Does your alter she-go have someone (or something) who supports her along the way? Mine is definitely Hamish. Maybe yours is a trusted friend, a symbol or even an imaginary figure that reminds you to stay focused.

9 What does it feel like to be her?

Close your eyes and imagine what it feels like to be your alter she-go. How does she walk into a room? How does she handle challenges? What's her energy like? What thoughts does she think, who is she hanging out with? Take a few moments to really visualise yourself as her. Feel it in your body – how does being this woman make you feel? If you can elicit emotion in yourself, even better.

10 Her rituals

What gets her into her zone? Does she have a morning ritual, a pre-meeting routine or a way she likes to unwind? Rituals can be powerful for grounding yourself in this new identity. Whether it's meditating, journalling, putting on her signature outfit or pumping her jams first thing in the morning, identify the rituals that help bring your alter she-go to life.

Alter she-go trait	Your version
Name her	(What's her name?)
Define what she stands for	(Her core values and beliefs)
Her outfit	(Her signature look)
Her theme song	(The song that makes her feel unstoppable)
Her power pose	(Her confidence stance)
Her superpowers	(Her unique strengths and abilities)
Her power statement	(Her mantra for when she needs to get back on track)
Does she have a sidekick?	(Any support she has – real or imagined)
What does it feel like to be her?	(Describe the feeling of being her)
Her rituals	(The routines and habits that help her show up as her best self)

This process is fun, yes, but it's also *transformational*. You're not just creating an alter she-go for the sake of it. You're tapping into a powerful version of yourself that's been waiting to emerge. The more you step into her, the more you'll notice that life responds differently to you. People will feel your energy shift, and opportunities will start flowing in.

This is your chance to become the woman you've always wanted to be. So, don't rush through the process. Take your time, get creative and build her. Because trust me – she's *already* there, waiting for you to mould her and then set her free.

EMBODYING YOUR ALTER SHE-GO: BODY, BEHAVIOUR AND MINDSET

While what you wear is important for your alter she-go, she also has a particular attitude, physical presence, set of behaviours and way of connecting with others that her clothes work in sync with, reinforcing and amplifying your empowered identity.

Confident body language and power poses

How you carry yourself speaks volumes. When you dress as your alter she-go you may find that you naturally stand tall, with shoulders back and chin up. Walk with purpose. Your body language should convey confidence, openness and warmth. Let your alter she-go take up space – own the room you're in.

Power poses have been scientifically studied, most notably by social psychologist Amy Cuddy and her team in a 2010 study. They found that holding a high-power pose, like standing with hands on hips, for just a few minutes can lead to increased testosterone (confidence) and decreased cortisol (stress), making you feel more assertive and ready to take on challenges. Which one of these power poses fits your alter she-go best?

- **The Superwoman:** Stand tall with your feet shoulder-width apart, hands on your hips and chin slightly raised. Feel your power!

- **The V is for Victory Pose:** Raise your arms into a V-shape above your head, hold your feet slightly apart and chest open. Embrace that triumphant feeling.
- **The She-EO Pose:** Sit or stand with your legs crossed and your hands behind your head. Lean back and exude authority.

These poses aren't just empty invitations – they work. Use them to summon your alter she-go before important meetings or social events to amplify your presence and feel more confident. (Yes, science backs this up too – see Amy Cuddy's research on power poses.)

Here are a couple of powerful moves your alter she-go can add to her toolkit.

- **Look people in the eyes:** Eye contact is a powerful skill that confident, charismatic and magnetic individuals master. It shows that you're comfortable in your skin, engaged, interested and trustworthy.
- **Smile more:** Now, I'm not saying 'be a good girl' and smile when you're not feeling it. I'm saying that a genuine smile can be incredibly contagious. When someone smiles at you, it's hard not to smile back, and it makes you both feel good. People are drawn to those who smile – it signals friendliness and approachability. Try it, and you'll see the positive impact it has on your daily interactions.

When you combine confident body language, a power pose, eye contact and smiling, you create in your alter she-go a magnetic force that makes an irresistible connection with those around you. People feel that you're someone they want to engage with.

Communication and charisma

Your alter she-go speaks clearly, confidently and with intention. Her voice should be strong, not apologetic. She is worth listening to, so let her words reflect that. People respect confidence, but also kindness – she strikes the right balance. How? Well . . .

- **Be interested, not interesting:** Confidence isn't about being the loudest person in the room. When you step into your alter she-go, you listen more than you talk. Ask thoughtful questions. People love to talk about themselves, and they'll appreciate you for making them feel heard. Active listening is key, so nod your head and hold eye contact.
- **Say their name:** As discussed in Dale Carnegie's classic book *How to Win Friends and Influence People*, using someone's name in conversation can have a powerful effect. It makes people feel recognised and valued, creating a personal connection that leaves a lasting impression.
- **Ask open-ended questions:** When embodying your alter she-go, you do this to lead a conversation and show genuine interest. Instead of basic small talk, try asking, 'Working on anything exciting?' or 'Anything good happen today?' This steers the conversation toward positive feelings and makes you more memorable, making them feel good – and because *you* made them feel that way, they'll associate you with those positive emotions. Magnetic people listen, mirror and paraphrase, creating a connection that goes beyond surface-level chat.
- **Active listening:** Next time you're in conversation with some-one, make an effort to use your alter she-go to listen to them and practise active listening. Focus on the person speaking, avoid interrupting them and respond thoughtfully. If they get interrupted

by something, bring them back to their conversation – remind them of what they were saying. Remember things about them and bring up what you know from last time you spoke if you're meeting them again.

- **Non-verbal cues:** The next time you speak to someone you don't know very well, pay close attention to your non-verbal skills. How is your body language? Is it what your alter she-go would show? See if you can keep your arms and legs uncrossed, maintain eye contact and use facial expressions that match your words and the message you're trying to convey.
- **Use hand gestures:** A study by Goldin-Meadow found that hand gestures are important in communication because they aid in clarifying ideas and making conversations more engaging. Gestures make information easier to understand and make the speaker seem more connected and expressive. Hand gestures can also regulate a listener's emotional response, putting them more at ease and helping them to build rapport. Using hand gestures while speaking not only makes your alter she-go's communication clearer, but also puts others at ease and makes you appear more open and trustworthy.
- **Own your oddities:** We're all a bit weird, and that's great! As your alter she-go, you own your quirks and unique traits. These are what make you special. Embrace the parts of yourself you might have been ashamed of or kept hidden. These oddities are often what others find most endearing and memorable about you.
- **Humility matters:** This is about being humble, listening, admitting mistakes, valuing others' contributions, being open to feedback and avoiding arrogance – all of which creates a respectful and engaging dialogue that fosters trust and connection. When you have done your work in self-awareness and in creating your alter

she-go, this skill is showcased (and is one of the most amazing skills to have, in my opinion!).

- **Give thoughtful compliments:** When you are conversing or meeting people as your alter she-go, don't go for basic compliments. Be specific and sincere – people will remember your words when they feel genuine.
- **Stay in your energy:** Stay grounded in your energy. Don't let other people's vibes pull you down. Confidence is about maintaining your inner power, no matter who's around.

You can see why people are drawn to your alter she-go! The skills you have given her work to form a magnetic energy that projects charisma and confidence.

Energy = Charisma

Your charisma is a blend of warmth and competence. You want people to get on with you, but also respect you. This balance of friendliness and authority is what makes your alter she-go – or anyone – truly magnetic.

- **Presence:** Are you fully 'there' with the person you're conversing with? Are you present, and is your presence, energy and full attention on them? People can feel this, and it's a skill magnetic communicators develop over time.
- **Warmth:** Be likeable, approachable and trustworthy. People are drawn to those who radiate warmth.
- **Competence:** When you step into your alter she-go, be assertive and show that you know your stuff, which will project confidence. Your alter she-go won't be afraid to take pride in herself. This balance is the sweet spot for charisma.

Emotional and mindset skills

The way you think shapes everything. Focus on giving your alter she-go empowering thoughts and aligning her mindset with your values. Know that you're worthy of what you desire and believe in your own magnetism. No one else will believe it until **you** do.

Your emotional intelligence plays a huge role. Emotional intelligence is the ability to recognise, understand and manage your own emotions while also being aware of and influencing the emotions of others. Your alter she-go will have this in spades.

To build emotional intelligence:

- **Practise self-awareness:** Regularly check in with your emotions and how they influence your actions.
- **Enhance empathy:** Actively listen to others, seeking to understand their feelings and perspectives without judgement.

Be aware of how you're feeling and manage your energy wisely. When you're grounded and vibing positivly inside, people naturally gravitate toward you.

When your alter she-go shows up, owning her space and magnetising the room, there are a few powerful traits she naturally taps into. It's not about pretending, it's about making sure these qualities are part of her mindset to keep her grounded and in her power.

- **Kindness:** Being kind goes a long way in making you approachable. Charisma isn't about being the loudest or flashiest person in the room; it's about being the person people feel safe and good around.
- **Warmth and openness:** This is about empathy – people need to feel your genuine care and authenticity. When you show up with warmth, people are more likely to trust you and feel comfortable around you.

- **Self-assuredness:** You don't need external validation when you know who you are and what you stand for. Confidence comes from being sure of yourself and not needing others' approval.
- **Presence:** Be present in the moment. When you're truly present, your energy is magnetic. You're not distracted or trying to prove anything – you're simply here. This kind of presence is powerful, and people can feel it.
- **Assertiveness without apology:** Know what you want and don't apologise for it. This doesn't mean bulldozing others; it means stating your desires with confidence and respecting yourself enough to ask for what you need.
- **Being memorable:** Create unforgettable moments. It's not just about the way you dress or the words you say – it's about the way you make people feel. People might forget what you did or said, but they'll never forget how you made them feel.
- **Embrace humour:** Humour is one of the greatest tools for connection. Magnetic people do not take themselves too seriously. They're not afraid to laugh at themselves and they take the opinions of others lightly. Humour is a great way to connect with people and show that you are approachable and down-to-earth.
- **F*** what others think (#FWOT):** You'll never be fully magnetic until you stop caring about other people's opinions. The less you give a crap about what others think, the more magnetic you become. It's the ultimate key to owning your space.

Time to do the work.

FINAL WORD: DON'T TRY – JUST BE HER

Stop trying. Stop wishing. Stop waiting. Decide who you are and be her. Your alter she-go already exists. It's time to bring her forward and let her live. Soon, you won't be stepping into your alter she-go – **you'll *be* her**.

Walk into rooms with these skills, stand tall, and know that you've *already* got what it takes.

8

PHASE 4: YOUR EVOLUTION EVOLUTION EVOLUTION

'When the student is ready,
the teacher will appear.'

In every transformative journey, there comes a moment when you have to leave behind who you once were and fully step into who you are becoming. This is the essence of Phase 4: Evolution – it's the point where the theory, the dreaming, and the envisioning all fall away, and the work you've done to reach this point gets tested. It's not enough to just dream about the person you want to be – you have to live her, breathe her and embody her in every aspect of your life. The only way forward is to let the old version of you fade, to make room for the new, fully integrated you to emerge.

Now, if we're being real, this isn't some quick overnight switch. The process of shedding who you once were is a gradual evolution, and it takes courage. It can feel unsettling, even terrifying, to step into the unknown of your future self. This is where so many people trip up – they get comfortable with the dreaming, but freak out when it comes to the doing. And if I'm honest? This is the part of personal development that frustrates me the most. I see people bingeing podcasts, devouring YouTube videos, buying all the books and signing up for course after course, hoping that more content will somehow shift their lives. But that's not how it works. That's just more noise in your head. You already have exactly what you need to transform into your most magnetic, powerful self. Now, it's about the integration – the consistent practice of being her.

This is the phase where we make it real. You've done the deep work of self-mastery. You've aligned yourself with your core values, and you've created your alter she-go. Now, comes the most exciting yet also the most challenging part of the journey – fully integrating all of this into your everyday life.

This is where you're tested. When you step out into the world as the new version of yourself, you're going to face resistance. There's no way around it. From yourself and from the people around you – your friends, family, your job and maybe even your partner. It's the pushback that happens when people – and you – realise that you're no longer showing up as the person they knew. That old version of you, the one they were comfortable with, is gone. And this new version? This next-level, unapologetic, confident YOU? Well, she might be a bit much for some people. She might challenge their comfort zones, and that's okay. This pushback is good news. It's feedback, a sign that you are truly stepping into the world as your most authentic and magnetic self.

This is what we call the 'death of the old self', a concept deeply rooted in the Hero's Journey – a classic narrative of personal evolution. This part of the journey feels like sailing away from pain island, where you've let go of your old identity but haven't fully grown into your new one. You're suspended in a kind of no-woman's-land, in what feels like a void. It's uncomfortable, sometimes even disorienting, because if you're no longer the old you, then who are you?

In the retreat Nina came to, Hamish and I saw this phase take shape during one of our most pivotal days – a day designed for integration, which we refer to as the 'death of the old self'. It's a symbolic moment where you consciously CHOOSE to start doing as 'she' does, to start showing up as the woman you are becoming. And let me tell you, that can be scary as hell. Because this is the moment to make the change real, to evolve into the woman you want to become. To take the scary action, to set and uphold boundaries, to be her unapologetically.

RESISTANCE: FROM YOURSELF AND THE WORLD AROUND YOU

When you evolve, the world around you will push back. You're no longer fitting into the mould others had for you. That old version of you – the one that was more accommodating, more apologetic or less confident – worked for people. They knew her. She was easy, predictable and comfortable. But this new you? She's a force, unapologetically stepping into her power, and not everyone will love that for you.

Some people may have become comfortable with the way you you might have shrunk or played small. When you start stepping into your truth – owning your space, using your voice and asserting your boundaries – guess what? They won't like it. Not because you've done anything wrong, but because your evolution challenges them. Your growth confronts their own insecurities, their own stagnation and their own unwillingness to evolve. You might not be shrinking anymore, but they still want you to fit into that smaller version of yourself.

Maybe they liked the old version of you because she was easier to handle. She didn't challenge them or demand more. But this new you? She might make waves, she might have strong opinions, she might not hold back when she's being mistreated. While this might ruffle some feathers, it's a sign that you are stepping into your full power.

Maybe you're no longer biting your tongue when someone crosses your boundaries. Maybe you're not shrinking or apologising for taking up space. Perhaps you're asking for what you deserve – whether it's in your career, relationships or friendships. As you stand tall in your power, expect some pushback. It's not just you feeling the discomfort – others around you will feel it too.

The truth is, some people liked the old you. They liked the version of you who didn't challenge them. The version who played small, didn't make waves and fit into their idea of who you should be.

If nothing changes,
nothing changes.
And right now you have
a real chance to make
some changes.

Now that you're stepping into your power, it shakes things up for them. It challenges the dynamics. They might resist your evolution, not because they don't care, but because it makes them uncomfortable to see someone shine so brightly when they're still playing in the shadows.

Questions to reflect on:

- Where do you think you'll get the most pushback?
- Who will be happy for your next level?

OPPORTUNITIES IN RESISTANCE: THE SILVER LINING

This pushback isn't a bad thing. In fact, it's an opportunity. When people react to your growth, they're giving you feedback. Feedback is a powerful mirror – it shows you where your boundaries are needed, where you're strong and where you still have work to do. Think of every difficult conversation, every bit of resistance, as a chance to reinforce this new, empowered version of yourself.

Maybe it's a friend who starts acting weird because you're no longer the people-pleasing, accommodating person they used to know. Good. This is a chance for you to practise setting boundaries. Maybe it's a co-worker who suddenly starts undermining you at work because you're speaking up in meetings now. Great. You get to stand in your confidence and assert your value. These aren't setbacks – they're opportunities. The more you practise holding your own, the more solid this new version of you becomes.

One of the books that has supported me and my clients most in the journey to becoming was Dr Joe Dispenza's *Breaking the Habit of Being Yourself*. Dr Dispenza's research shows us that our brains are wired to repeat familiar patterns – even when those patterns are no longer serving us. We are creatures of habit, and our bodies become so used to the emotions of our past selves. This is why the process of evolution can feel so uncomfortable, because on a biological level, you're literally rewiring your brain to become someone new. The brain loves the familiar, even if it's holding you back, and it will resist change at first.

THE TEST: ARE YOU REALLY HER?

Not only are you fighting your brain and the familiar, but you're also going to be tested. The universe (or life, or whatever you want to call it) will test you. You'll be asked to prove whether you're truly ready to embody this new identity. This isn't just about the big moments – this is about how you handle the day-to-day pushback, discomfort and friction that comes with levelling up.

Let's say you've decided to assert yourself more at work. You're speaking up in meetings, contributing ideas and holding boundaries around your time. Then, out of nowhere, you get a snide comment from a co-worker or passive-aggressive feedback from your boss. These moments are tests. They're life asking, 'Are you really ready to be this confident, assertive version of yourself? Or are you going to back down when it gets uncomfortable?'

As Dr Dispenza shares, in order to evolve into who you want to be, you have to continually make choices that align with your future self, not your past. Every test you face is an opportunity to rewire your brain, replacing old habits with new ones. The more consistently you choose the thoughts, feelings and behaviours of your higher self, the more you will condition your body and rewire your brain to accept this new version of yourself as the norm.

This is where the make-it-real work happens. The waves of resistance will come, and they'll feel overwhelming at times. It's easy to think that you're going backward when things get hard, but this is exactly where the magic happens. Responding to pushback is where you solidify your growth. You can either let those waves knock you down or you can learn to surf. And once you master riding those waves, they become a welcome part of the journey. You'll start to look forward to the challenges, because you'll know they're just strengthening your muscles.

When our clients leave our retreat, Hamish and I always remind them that this is where the real work begins. It's one thing to feel empowered in a safe, supportive environment, surrounded by people who are on the same path. But the true test comes when you return to your everyday life. This is where you'll be confronted with old patterns, old environments and old expectations.

It's the same with *Becoming Magnetic*. You can read all the chapters, nodding your head along and feeling inspired as you imagine your magnetic future self, but the real change happens when you put everything into action. This is when you have to embody your alter she-go – not just in theory, but in practice.

Integration is about choosing her every single day. It's about waking up in the morning and deciding, this is who I am. It's practising embodying her at work, in your relationships and even in your everyday routine. Integration means taking everything you've cultivated – self-mastery, values alignment and your alter she-go – and applying it moment by moment. This is where the future version of you becomes your present reality.

NINA'S JOURNEY OF TRANSFORMATION

Nina's journey reached a critical point the moment she left our retreat. After all the breakthroughs, the deep inner work and the shedding of her old self, she was no longer in the safe cocoon of the retreat environment. The real test was waiting for her back in her daily life – in the day-to-day grind, in the workplace, with her roommates at home and out in the social scene. This phase was about stepping into her evolution, where everything she had learnt would either stay with her and integrate into her life, or fall away like so many past self-help attempts.

Leaving the retreat is when Nina faced her first real challenge: consistency. It's easy to feel empowered when you're surrounded by people on the same journey, but once you're back in the real world, that empowerment is tested. Nina had to decide if she was really serious about her growth – about becoming her magnetic, confident self. Was she ready to step into that version of her, or would she retreat back into her old habits? This is where she was supported and mentored by our program; she communicated with the other members, and began committing to the inner work every day. She showed up for calls, filled pages of her journal and held herself accountable to the vision of who she wanted to be.

And then there was the world waiting to test her. Socially, she had always been the shy one, the one who avoided eye contact, who would shrink when people spoke to her. It would have been so easy for her to fall back into that pattern, to break eye contact, to let her nerves get the better of her. But Nina wasn't the same woman anymore. The confident version of herself – the one she had been working to bring out – didn't back down. She stood tall. She met the eyes of strangers with confidence. She let her energy fill the space. She let herself be heard and seen, rather than shrinking back into the shadows.

Her new-found confidence was tested in every area of her life. In her work, she was faced with challenges that pushed her to advocate for herself. Where once she might have stayed silent or avoided confrontation, she spoke up. She demanded what she was worth and didn't settle for less. In her health, she committed to routines and practices that helped her feel strong and vibrant, even when life got busy. She set boundaries in her friendships, refusing to tolerate toxic energy, and she cut ties with people who were no longer aligned with the woman she was becoming. This was not an easy process – there were tears, frustrations and moments of doubt – but Nina held her ground.

One of her biggest challenges came in her newly developing relationship. Relationships can be one of the most difficult spaces to evolve because they mirror back everything you still need to work on. But Nina faced these challenges head on, using her values as her guide. She had tough conversations right at the beginning, set boundaries and didn't shy away from the uncomfortable moments. She was clear about what she wanted from her partner and what she wouldn't tolerate, even if it meant risking the relationship. She was done playing small and done allowing her fears to dictate her choices.

Nina was tested over and over again. She was asked, 'Are you really her? Are you really this new, confident, magnetic version of yourself?' Each time, she showed up as that woman. She didn't go back to her comfort zone. She didn't let her old self take over. Instead, she made tough decisions and chose herself every single time.

But Nina didn't do this alone. She leant on her support team – the people in her corner who kept her mindset strong, the coaches and healers who held her accountable, and who supported her when the challenges felt overwhelming. She surrounded herself with those who uplifted her. Her self-care and spiritual health became non-negotiable, and she prioritised her wellbeing above all else.

In the end, Nina's evolution wasn't just about saying the right things or adopting new habits – it was about actually becoming the woman she always wanted to be. She embodied her values and stood firm in her worth.

Her journey was far from easy, but the results were undeniable. Nina walked away from jobs that no longer served her. She confronted the people she loved, had hard discussions and came out the other side stronger. She didn't let fear hold her back; she embraced the discomfort, knowing that it was a sign of her growth.

And the best part? She practised this every day but some days were harder than others. Eventually, her magnetic self wasn't just something she was wishing to be – it became who she was. Nina became the woman who stands in her power, who owns her space and who doesn't apologise for it. She became magnetic, not just to the people around her but to the life she had always dreamt of living. Because of that, she got the results. She attracted love, fulfilment and opportunities beyond her wildest dreams – all because she made the decision to rise to her highest self.

Action step: Responsibility in decision-making

When it comes to personal evolution, you cannot bypass responsibility. At this stage, it's crucial to understand that decisions must be made. The discomfort of avoiding decisions is much worse than the growth that comes from confronting them head on. Change doesn't happen by talking about it, **it happens when you make a decision**.

This is where you get to step into radical responsibility (remember Chapter 3?) and decide where you need to create shifts in your life. The discomfort, the fear, the anxiety – all of that comes up because these decisions have weight. But avoiding them only prolongs your discomfort and keeps you stuck. You are here because you're ready to change, grow and evolve. So let's get real about where decisions need to be made by taking a moment to reflect now on some questions.

What difficult conversations have you been avoiding?

There are always conversations we shy away from because we know they're uncomfortable. The truth is that those conversations hold the key to your growth.

Where in your life do you need to use your voice and claim your truth?

Where can you get real and share what's been on your mind, even though it may be uncomfortable?

Is it at work, in friendships, romantic relationship or with family?

Examples:

- Do you need to ask for a raise but have been too scared to?
- Are there friends in your life who no longer support who you're becoming?
- Do you need to set boundaries with a family member who doesn't respect your time or energy?

Decision: Write down exactly who you need to speak to, what the conversation is and why it's important. This isn't about confrontation: it's about claiming your voice and stepping into your power. (At the end of this section I'll share tips on how to have a difficult conversation.)

Where do you need to set boundaries?

Boundaries aren't just suggestions; they are absolutely necessary for protecting your energy and values. The new version of yourself that you're stepping into must have solid boundaries in place.

Examples:

- Maybe at work, you've been doing too much, taking on projects outside your role or staying late. It's time to decide when enough is enough.
- In relationships, maybe someone keeps crossing your emotional boundaries, and you need to clearly articulate what you will and won't tolerate. It may be time to reteach people how to treat you.

Decision: Identify where in your life you need stronger boundaries. What's currently happening that you're no longer willing to accept? Who in your life do you need to set clearer boundaries with to support your growth and wellbeing? Once you've identified this, the next step is enforcing those boundaries. What are the consequences?

For example: 'When you do *this*, I will do *that*.' A boundary with no consequences is just a preference.

Write out your game plan for holding these boundaries firm, even when it's uncomfortable.

Who will give you the most pushback?

Not everyone will be thrilled about the new, empowered version of you. You might already know exactly who's going to resist this change the most. Maybe it's a co-worker who's used to you saying 'yes' to everything, a friend who takes up all your energy or someone in your family.

Decision: Write down who you think will give you the most pushback. Prepare yourself for their reaction, and plan how you will stand firm. What will you say? How will you protect your energy and make sure you stay in your truth?

PUSHBACK ISN'T A BAD THING. IN FACT, IT'S AN OPPORTUNITY.

Who is in your support team?
Growth is easier when you have a solid support system. Who's got your back as you step into this next-level version of yourself? Maybe it's a mentor, a coach, your partner or a close friend. Maybe you need to find new mentors or communities who can hold space for your growth.

Decision: Identify and call in your support system. Who are the people who will champion your growth? And if you don't have that support right now, who do you need to enrol to help you stay accountable and supported?

SPEAK UP

You may notice after completing the Action Step that you have a list of conversations that desperately need to be had. Maybe you've avoided the conflict or steered clear of hard discussions, but the reality is that you will need to face them sooner or later. What I've seen in my work with women and couples is that most people don't have these difficult conversations and instead walk around the issues, but they only buy time because they cannot escape the reality. This leads to being stuck in relationships we're not happy in and building resentment, doing things we really don't want to do, staying in workplaces for too long or trying to run away from these difficulties only to be faced with the same or similar lesson at the next workplace or in the next relationship. I'd love to share some insights with you on communication in hopes that this section encourages you to gain the confidence to speak up, to have the tough chat(s) and to finally own your voice and take charge of the life you want to lead. If nothing changes, nothing changes, and right now you have a real chance to make some changes. When you communicate effectively, you build trust and rapport with others, and when people feel valued, they are more likely to be drawn to you. When you communicate clearly, you have an ability to influence others' thoughts and actions. If you are moving into leadership or positions of influence, communication allows you to impact others and build trust. Good communicators can connect deeply with others, as they show empathy and understanding. When you know how to do this, you create strong relationships that are mutually beneficial and supportive.

COMMUNICATION: THE FOUNDATION OF CONNECTION

Throughout my years of coaching women, I can tell you that communication is where so many people struggle. It's wild to me that in a world where we're constantly talking, texting and DMing, we still don't know how to communicate effectively. This skill, which is the foundation of any thriving relationship, is one of the biggest areas of opportunity for most of us. The truth is that so many women struggle to clearly express what they feel, need or want. Instead of being open and direct, we hold back. We filter our thoughts, water down our feelings or avoid sharing our truth altogether. And that creates a ripple effect.

I once had a client who was deeply unhappy in her relationship, but here's the problem – her partner didn't even know. She avoided telling him how she felt, opting for the classic, 'Yup, everything's fine,' even though it was far from fine. Over time, she bottled up her emotions until they exploded as outbursts, leaving him blindsided and confused. This communication breakdown created tension and resentment between them, and they both felt misunderstood.

See, communication isn't just about what you say. It's about what's going on in your head before you even say it, what the other person hears, and how they interpret what they heard. I call this the **communication cycle**:

1 What you think.
2 What you say.

3 What they hear.
4 What they make it mean.

No wonder we struggle to communicate, right? We've got four channels going on at once!

Now, here's where it gets even more interesting: communication is also about how we listen. And many of us listen just to respond, not to understand. We listen to defend ourselves, explain our side or 'win' the conversation. That's where we trip up. The most magnetic people? They listen. They truly *listen* more than they talk. They let others feel heard. (Trust me, I learnt this the hard way as a former chatterbox who always wanted to be right.)

The power of taking responsibility in communication

When my client finally realised that the lack of communication was harming her relationship, she decided to take responsibility. Not *blame*, remember? *Responsibility*. She recognised her role in the breakdown and chose to start a conversation by owning up to the fact that she hadn't been honest about how she was feeling.

Here's the magic in this: when you start a conversation by taking responsibility for *your* part, you instantly lower the other person's guard. They're more likely to listen without becoming defensive, which is half the battle.

She said something like this: 'I want to start by taking responsibility for not being open with you. I haven't been honest about how I've been feeling, and I've been holding back instead of sharing what's really going on. I want to own that. I realise this has affected our relationship, and I want us to have an open conversation about it.'

Instantly, her partner's walls came down, and they were able to have a real, honest conversation about their relationship for the first time in months.

If you don't communicate clearly, authentically and often, resentment, misunderstandings and disconnection will build up.

The script for those tough conversations

When it comes to having difficult or confronting conversations, here's an easy outline you can follow. Remember: communication is a skill, and just like any skill, it takes practice. The other person may not be learning this, but YOU are. This tool isn't guaranteed to work because we can't control how other people respond, but we can take OUR responsibility back. So focus on how *you* want to show up in this conversation. Check out the episode of my podcast on this topic, 'Confidently dealing with conflict':

Step 1: Start by taking responsibility

- Example: 'I want to take responsibility for how I've been showing up lately. I haven't been as open or honest as I should have been, and that's affected our relationship. I realise that's on me.'
- This lowers the other person's defences and shows you're not here to blame or attack but to communicate effectively.

Step 2: Be honest and direct

- Example: 'I've been feeling [insert your feelings here] lately, and it's been hard for me to bring this up. I want to talk about it now because it's important to me that we're on the same page.'
- Get to the point. Don't dance around the issue. Honesty is magnetic.

Step 3: Stay calm and present

- Make sure you're in a calm state before having this conversation. No distractions, no defensiveness. Your energy will set the tone for the entire interaction. Get rid of phones, TVs or computers.

Step 4: Listen to understand, not respond

- This is key. When the other person speaks, don't just wait for your turn to talk – really listen. Use active listening techniques like mirroring them, summarising what they've said or asking open-ended follow-up questions to show you're truly engaged.

Step 5: Seek resolution together

- Example: 'How do you think we can work through this? What's something we can both do to improve this moving forward?'
- This shifts the conversation from a confrontation to a collaboration. You're both on the same team and the goal is to strengthen your relationship.

Why this matters

The reason these steps work is because they create space for openness, honesty and respect. When you take responsibility for your role in the conversation, you make it easier for the other person to do the same (knowing that they might not, by the way!). We do this because this is who we are; we want to be self-aware. We want to be open and honest. We want to communicate with confidence and connection. You may not get the response you want from them, but you're taking response-ability, and that gives you power no matter how they respond. You're leading by example, 'being Gandhi', showing them that you're willing to grow and communicate differently, which invites them to do the same.

Remember: the goal of communication is not just to be heard but to *connect*. If you don't communicate clearly, authentically and often, resentment, misunderstandings and disconnection will build up. Your ability to have these tough conversations will make or break your relationships, especially your intimate ones. This is where your evolution begins – because without clear communication, it's impossible to integrate the growth you've been working on.

So, I'm inviting you, daring you: have the hard conversation. Stop avoiding it. Take responsibility, be open, listen to understand and watch as your relationships transform.

Practice this

Use this script as a guide for the next hard conversation you need to have. It could be with your partner, a friend, a family member or even your boss. The key is to keep practising this type of empowered communication. The power of communication is transformative – especially when you're willing to own your part, listen fully and show up with honesty.

THE FEEDBACK LOOP: GROWTH AND OPPORTUNITY

As you begin stepping into your power, something remarkable unfolds: the world starts to respond. Remember, no one knows that you've picked up *Becoming Magnetic* or that you've committed to taking action. No one is aware of the internal shifts you're already experiencing by simply reading these words. The only version of you they know is the one you've always presented. So, as you continue to evolve and change, it might feel unsettling for others – and that's okay. It's a sign that growth is happening. Embrace the test and keep showing up as *her* – the woman you are becoming.

As you do this, your relationships will begin to shift and new opportunities will naturally open up. The more you embody this future version of yourself, the more the external world will start to align with who you are now. You might notice that people treat you with more respect or that new doors seem to open effortlessly. You'll attract deeper, more meaningful relationships that resonate with your new energy. On the other side of any initial resistance is abundance – in your career, your relationships and your own self-worth. Life starts to mirror back the inner work you've been doing. Nina's journey is the perfect example – her commitment to showing up as her most magnetic self every day led her to finding the love of her life and discovering a sense of purpose she never thought possible. This wasn't luck; it was the result of her making the choice to evolve.

Let's wrap up Phase 4 with some tangible and powerful actions that will help you integrate everything you've learnt so far. These exercises are designed to make sure you are *living* as your most magnetic self, not just thinking about her.

Time to do the work.

Exercise: Fully stepping into your evolution

1 Build your self-care kit

This is about knowing what you need to feel your best. Take some time to reflect on the practices, routines and activities that fill your cup and keep your energy high. Self-care is not a luxury; it's a *necessity*. The more you thrive, the more you can show up as your most magnetic self.

- Do you need daily meditation, weekly yoga classes or long walks in nature?
- Is it journalling, therapy or dance classes that make you feel alive?
- What activities or habits consistently bring you back to centre?

Your Task: Write down 'The things I need in order to thrive'. What are the non-negotiable things that make you feel your best? What's missing that you need to start implementing? Write it all down and make a plan to prioritise these activities in your schedule no matter what. P.S. These should tie in to your values. Check out the episode of my podcast on this topic, 'Are you doing the things that make YOU feel good?':

2 Build your support team

Let's be real: *none* of us can do this alone. You need an A-team of people in your corner – mentors, coaches, therapists, friends – people who get you and want to see you winning. These are the people who hold you accountable and remind you of your power when things get tough.

A BOUNDARY WITH NO CONSEQUENCES IS JUST A PREFERENCE.

- Who is on your team right now?
- Do you need to enrol someone else to support you – like a coach, therapist or mentor?
- Who can you rely on when things get hard?

Your Task: Write down your 'My Support Team' – and list who's already on the team and who you need to enrol to help you step into your next level. If there are gaps, make it a priority to find those people and build that support system.

3 Have the difficult conversations

Hear me when I say that avoiding difficult conversations only creates *more* tension and discomfort in the long run. You need to tackle these head on if you want to evolve. I mean it. Whether it's setting boundaries, standing up for yourself or simply owning your truth, these conversations are *non-negotiable* for your growth.

- Who do you need to have a conversation with?
- Is it your partner, a friend, a family member or someone at work?
- What conversation have you been avoiding that you need to address?
- **When will you schedule it?**

Your Task: Using the script and outline provided earlier, write down the name of the person you need to speak to. Choose a date and time to have the conversation, and *stick to it*. It's time to clear the air and make sure your communication reflects the new, evolved version of you.

4 Make the decisions; set the boundaries

No more wavering. If you're going to step into your highest self, you need to make some real decisions and set some solid boundaries.

This is where the work gets real, and it's up to you to hold yourself accountable for making the changes you need to thrive.

- What decisions have you been putting off?
- Where do you need to set stronger boundaries?
- What changes do you need to make to fully evolve?

Your Task: Write down the decisions you need to make, the boundaries you need to set and the steps you will take to put them into action. Write down the consequences so you're clear on what will happen if someone oversteps your boundary. If you don't have solid consequences you won't uphold your boundaries. Then, set a date for when these will happen so you have clear accountability.

As you move through these exercises, you are preparing yourself for the final phase – the magnetic aura that comes from fully stepping into your power. Remember: the growth you've experienced so far is just the beginning. What's most important is how you *live* as this new version of you and how you handle the challenges that arise along the way.

Your next-level self is waiting for you, and it's time to finally claim her.

9

PHASE 5: YOUR MAGNETIC AURA AURA AURA

'I don't chase. I desire. I believe.
I act. I allow. I attract. I receive.'

In our fast-paced world, where it feels like everyone is hustling for validation and acceptance, where so many are caught up in perfectionism, obsessed with likes on social media and deeply worried about the opinions of others – you've somehow found a different rhythm.

It's like you've tapped into a secret flow, a groove that the rest of the world missed while they were too busy chasing the wrong things.

You glide through life with a kind of effortless grace. You draw opportunities in without even trying, moving through the chaos with a confidence and ease that makes people stop and wonder, *Damn, what's she got going on?*

When you step into your power, owning this energy, you don't just walk into a room. You own it. It's like you're the conductor, and the whole place tunes itself to your frequency. You exude warmth, self-assurance and a grounded sense of safety. People want to listen when you speak; they're drawn to you, and just being around you makes them feel more settled in their own skin. They want you in their lives. It's not just charisma – it's deeper than that. There's a magnetism about you that draws good fortune and great people toward you, while those who don't have good intentions keep their distance, sensing they can't disrupt your energy.

And here's the thing – you're not even trying to be the centre of attention. Attention naturally gravitates toward you.

When you walk into a room, it's as if the universe itself rolls out the red carpet.

You operate in 'solutions only' mode. Challenges shrink in your presence – not because they don't exist, but because you carry this unshakable self-belief that not only will everything be okay, but it will 100 per cent work out in your favour.

The best part? It almost always does.

This is because **you are magnetic**.

WHAT'S *REALLY* GOING ON

This is the final phase – the one that feels like everything's just clicking into place. Momentum builds, and it's like the universe is responding to you with ease. But don't get it twisted – this isn't magic or simply good luck. You've worked **hard** to get here, and you know it. You've committed to mastering yourself, embodying your values and stepping into your alter she-go. Now, the magnetic aura you give off is a reflection of that work, and people are drawn to it.

It's not that life has suddenly become easier; it's that you've developed an unshakable belief in yourself. You know things will work out because they *are* working out, because you've done and continue to do the inner work. That certainty? That's the force field around you. You move through life with a grounded sense of self-trust, and that's exactly why you're so magnetic.

This final phase is about living in alignment. You're tapped into a constant flow of giving and receiving, and because you're so in tune, more abundance naturally comes your way. You're co-creating with life now and it feels powerful AF.

Your presence? It is **next level**.

“This is the ultimate form of magnetism: trust. Trust that everything you need is coming, and everything you don't need is leaving.”

The energy you give off speaks before you even open your mouth. People feel it.

Your magnetic aura isn't just a vibe – it's real, tangible and almost electric. Every adjustment you've made, every shift you've gone through, led you to this point where your energy does the talking.

This phase is what gives you the freedom you've always wanted.
The freedom to show up without apology.
The freedom to claim your space.
The freedom to be who you are, as is; there is no filter needed . . .
because you are magnetic.

THE POWER OF YOUR PRESENCE

Let's break down what's happening here. At this stage, you've aligned your internal world – your mindset, your beliefs, your emotions – and it reflects outward in the form of a powerful, magnetic aura. Psychologists refer to this as **presence**. It's not about how loud or outspoken you are, but how grounded, aligned and certain you are in *yourself.* People who have a presence make others feel seen, heard and connected. It's one of the most magnetic qualities you can have.

Think about someone with an undeniable presence – whether it's a celebrity or someone you've crossed paths with. You know the type: they walk into a room and *own* it without even trying. It's not about their clothes or appearance – it's something deeper. The way they move, the way they hold themselves, it all draws you in. They stand tall, move with intention and exude a kind of energy that draws you in. It's an essence, a vibe, that radiates confidence and power. You don't just *see* them: you *feel* them.

NINA'S JOURNEY TO A MAGNETIC AURA OF CONFIDENCE

Nina's aura today is undeniable. The transformation is not just skin-deep – it radiates from within. She used to be shy, barely able to hold eye contact, let alone start conversations with strangers. Even when faced with friendly faces, she would shy away, doubting herself and her ability to connect. Now? She confidently walks up to anyone, no matter if they're warm or have a stiff, uninviting demeanour. This doesn't shake her any more. She takes up space and owns her power in every conversation. The once-quiet, reserved Nina is now a force – confident, present and bold.

Her transformation didn't stop with her confidence in social situations. She dresses in whatever makes her feel powerful in the moment. Whether it's sweatpants and a hoodie or pleather shorts with heels, Nina's style is now a reflection of her – not what society says she should be. She's embraced her freedom in a way that shows up not just in her wardrobe but in her energy. She lives on her own terms, completely detached from the judgements or opinions of others. She's set her own standards, and she's living life her way.

In her relationship, the changes have been profound. Nina has created deep love with her partner, and they're now co-creating an abundant life together, expecting their first child – a lifelong dream for her. It wasn't that she had every detail figured out when she visualised love and family. But what she did have was belief. She believed in the possibility and acted like the woman who could attract that love into her life. And it happened. In under two years, Nina found her partner, thrived at work, upgraded her friendships and set powerful boundaries to protect her mental health and wellbeing.

Nina's life is a masterpiece that she's actively creating. Every moment of joy, every relationship, every opportunity is a result of the hard work she's putting in. She's soaking in the abundance and happiness she earned. The most amazing part is that no one handed her this life; she fought for it. Yes, she was supported along the way, but she was the one who asked for it, invested time, energy and money toward it AND allowed herself to be open to receiving it. And then? She did the work and continues to do the hard yards to get here.

Through the grief of losing Tui, the heartbreak, sadness, confusion, being in a new country, battling a lack of confidence, a lack of self-belief and a lack of self-worth, Nina rose. She didn't just survive; she thrived. And she did it on her own terms. It wasn't easy, but the results speak for themselves. Nina now lives a life she's proud of, one filled with love, abundance and a magnetic presence that turns heads and opens doors. She's done it. And she did it her way. (Cue Frank Sinatra.)

DO YOUR RESEARCH

Throughout *Becoming Magnetic* I promised to make this concept of magnetism practical.

This isn't a science book, and I'm not here to present myself as an academic researcher (obviously) – that's not the point of *this* book. My goal has always been to keep things practical and grounded, helping my clients and those I serve cut through the fluff, bypassing the over-spiritualised language that is often found in this space. And while this isn't a textbook, there is some solid research that supports what we've been learning together. I'd love to share some resources you can look to for further exploration should you wish. Refer to the Resources and Next Steps section at the very end of the book.

PEOPLE WILL NATURALLY NOTICE YOU, BUT IT'S WHAT YOU DO WITH THAT ATTENTION THAT COUNTS.

Take Joe Dispenza's work, for example. In his theory, when thoughts and emotions are combined they become the conduit through which we can choose and change our reality and lives. Aligning *internal* energy with your *external* reality creates a powerful harmony between your body and the environment around you that draws people and opportunities toward you.

By now you may have come to understand that energy isn't just some abstract concept – it's frequency, carrying information. You can literally tune in to different frequencies by working with your thoughts and feelings. Your thoughts (up in your brain) are electric, and your feelings (from your heart) are magnetic. Together, the way you think and feel creates this powerful electromagnetic field that impacts your life in real time.

Studies show that your heart's magnetic field extends around you at varying degrees, and that the heart functions as a generator of information that is central to the functioning of the body. The heart is a powerful source of electromagnetic energy in the human body, producing a much larger rhythmic electromagnetic field than the electrical activity generated by the brain. Think of it like beating a massive drum: the stronger the beat, the more the sound waves resonate. Your heart is capable of generating waves of magnetic energy, and that energy is what people feel when they're around you, and you feel from others as well. It's real, and it's powerful. Studies have shown that we communicate energetically before we even speak.

Your magnetic aura is felt by others because it comes from a place of internal alignment. Imagine your energy as a constant flow – a give and take between you and the universe. You show up with gratitude, confidence and abundance, and that energy doesn't just stay with you. It extends outward, interacting with the world around you.

And guess what? That energy comes back to you. It's a cycle of giving and receiving that feels at times effortless. You're not just living in the world; you're co-creating with it.

It's not about your external beauty, the clothes you wear or how much money you have in your bank account – it's about the energy you emit. This is what draws people in, because your vibe becomes contagious.

This is what makes a person truly magnetic.

Connection versus attention versus attraction

One of the most misunderstood concepts when it comes to magnetism are the distinctions between *attention, connection* and *attraction*. A truly magnetic person knows how to move through these layers, going beyond superficial attention to build deep, meaningful connections and, ultimately, attract aligned opportunities to them.

Attention: the surface-level spark

Attention is often mistaken for magnetism, but in reality, it's the most surface-level form of interaction. In today's world, where people are fighting for clicks, likes and followers, attention has become a commodity. As one of my favourite expanders, entrepreneur Gary Vaynerchuk, often says, we live in an 'attention economy' – attention is the currency everyone is chasing. But here's the thing: attention alone doesn't equate to value or meaningful interaction. It's like glitter – it might catch your eye for a moment, but it doesn't last.

If you're magnetic, people will naturally notice you, but it's what you *do* with that attention that counts. Are you trying to get validation or recognition, or are you using that initial spark to build something deeper? If attention is just the glitter, connection is where the gold is found.

Connection: the real outcome of magnetism

True magnetism lives in the realm of connection. This is where relationships go beyond the surface and into something real and impactful. It's when people aren't just seeing you – they're feeling you. You're creating an energy exchange, a bond, where both people leave feeling enriched – it's amazing and my favourite thing about magnetism.

Magnetic people have a way of making others feel seen, heard and valued. They listen deeply, ask questions and engage with genuine curiosity. They aren't trying to impress; they're trying to understand and **connect**. This type of connection builds trust, loyalty and meaningful long-term relationships. It's the reason someone will remember you even after meeting dozens of other people at the same event.

Think of the difference between getting a bunch of likes on a social media post and having someone reach out to you personally to thank you for something meaningful you shared. One is attention, the other is connection – and connection is where magnetism thrives.

Attraction: the gravitational pull

When you reach the stage of attraction, you've moved into the deepest level of magnetism. Attraction is about drawing in the right things your way – not through force or manipulation, but through the power of your aligned energy. When you're truly aligned with your values, desires and purpose, you begin to attract like a magnet.

This is also the place where you start repelling.

At first, this can seem counterintuitive. After all, don't we want everything to flow toward us? It depends. In order to stay aligned with your highest self and your desires, you must also learn to repel what isn't meant for you. The beauty of this phase? You don't even need to consciously do it. **Your energy will do it for you.**

Attraction isn't just about pulling things in; it's about rejecting what doesn't serve you. You'll start to notice that things that aren't aligned with your values or desires will feel forced or uncomfortable. *It feels hard, there's no flow; instead, there's resistance.*

You won't have to push these things away; they will naturally fall out of your energy field. This is your signal to trust. Trust that if something is leaving your life or not flowing smoothly, it's either not meant for you right now, or it's not meant for you **at all**. This is where surrender comes in.

In my own life, I know that my relationship prior to meeting Hamish was all resistance, there was absolutely zero flow! But I wasn't listening to the signs. I wasn't aware enough to notice how hard that relationship actually felt. The powers that be were actually trying (so hard) to get my attention, poking me hard, but I wasn't listening. Thankfully, my ex removed himself.

When something is being repelled – whether it's a person or an experience – you'll begin to recognise (through self-reflection) that it's not a loss. It's protection. It's a part of the magnetic process that ensures you are only pulling in what is aligned with *your* highest self. The things that aren't meant for you? You'll see them trying to stay, trying to latch on, but it will feel like you're constantly swimming against the current. That's when you'll know: it's time to let go.

This was one of the hardest things for me to comprehend. I hated when people would tell me to just 'trust the process'. It would make me so angry because I felt absolutely out of control. *What process? And who's in charge of this so-called process?*

But when I learnt to reframe this as trusting MY process, that helped. *My process* was easier to trust because it allowed me the freedom to trust *myself* and the way *my* life was unfolding. Especially because *I* was the person trying to better myself and working WITH myself to get the outcomes I wanted. It made me feel as though I was my own

You don’t have to force what’s meant for you – and you don’t have to cling to what’s not.

cheerleader, on the sidelines doing things that would help me win in life, instead of sabotaging my own success as I had so often done in the past.

Trusting YOUR process means you don't chase what doesn't chase you. You don't force anything that feels hard, heavy or out of alignment. You trust that what's meant to be will flow easily into your life, and what isn't will be repelled. Repelling isn't negative; it's a part of your magnetism. It's what keeps your energy pure, your intentions clear and your aura powerful.

ATTRACTION AND REPULSION: TWO SIDES OF THE SAME COIN

In this phase, attracting and repelling are like two sides of the same coin. When you're aligned with your values, you'll attract things that resonate with you on a deep level. Simultaneously, the things that aren't in alignment will fall away. There's no struggle in this: you won't have to cut ties or burn bridges in a dramatic way anymore. It will happen with much more ease and flow. You'll recognise when something or someone isn't aligned, and it will start to move out of your space naturally (pay attention to this). Now, I am not saying you won't have to work on this – let me be clear, you will. (See Chapters 5–8.)

I'm saying that repelling isn't rejection – **it's redirection**. You're being guided toward what serves your highest good. When something isn't working, instead of forcing it, you'll trust that what's meant for you will flow. And what isn't? It will be released, leaving room for something better to take its place.

This is the ultimate form of magnetism: trust.

- Trust that everything you need is coming, and everything you don't need is leaving.
- Trust that the process is guiding you exactly where you need to go.

- Trust that you are exactly where you need to be at this moment.
- Trust that things are always working out for you.

That's why, when you're truly magnetic, you don't fear losing things that aren't right for you – you welcome it. You let go more easily. You have faith – real, embodied faith – knowing that the universe, life and your own energy field are always working in your favour.

The gravitational pull you've created doesn't just attract the good; it actively pushes away anything that would lower your vibration or throw you off course. It's your invisible force field that keeps you in alignment with your highest path. You're not losing anything; you're gaining space for what truly matters.

In essence, repelling isn't failure. It's freedom. It's part of the magnetic aura that allows you to navigate life with grace, trust and confidence.

You don't have to force what's meant for you – and you don't have to cling to what's not.

Your magnetism does the work, drawing in what's aligned and pushing away what isn't, leaving you free to focus on what really matters: becoming and embodying your most powerful, authentic self.

THE DIFFERENCE BETWEEN ATTENTION, CONNECTION AND ATTRACTION

- **Attention** is fleeting; it's the glance, the curiosity, the surface-level interest.
- **Connection** is where the heart of magnetism lies. It's when people feel drawn to you on a deeper level, resonating with your energy and what you stand for.
- **Attraction** is the natural result of being in full alignment with your higher self, and it works both ways. When you're deeply aligned,

you'll not only attract the right opportunities and people, but also naturally repel those who don't match your energy, creating space for what truly serves you.

DID THE PENNY DROP?

The work doesn't stop here. This magnetic aura you've built? It's not a one-and-done thing – it needs constant nurturing. This is about ongoing alignment with the five phases of magnetism. And trust me, your inner work and your values will evolve as you do. Your alter she-go? She's not stagnant either. She grows, adapts and shifts as you continue to step into your higher self, face new challenges, upgrade your desires and embrace the opportunities life brings you.

By now, I hope the penny has dropped. You are not just reacting to the world around you – you're influencing it. You're shaping it. The way you think, feel and act? It's changing your environment, your relationships, your results and your outcomes. And that's massive. Rather than being at the mercy of what's happening to you, you're co-creating with the universe itself.

Let that sink in:

You have the power to consciously shape your reality, to influence how things unfold and to decide what you attract.

It's no small thing. **You are more powerful than you ever thought.**

Take a moment to own that.

MICRO-SKILLS TO EMBODY THE WORK

Most people believe that being charismatic or confident is an all-or-nothing thing – you either have it, or you don't. But the truth? Charisma, confidence and magnetism are skills you can learn. They're a series of small, often unnoticed micro-actions that, when combined, create a powerful presence. The good news? You can start practising these today.

Here's a breakdown of essential micro-skills you need to start embodying your most magnetic self. Each one is a tool you can use to enhance your energy and interactions with the world. Walk into rooms with these micro-skills, stand tall and know that you've *already* got what it takes.

How you carry yourself: Your posture and body language send a powerful signal to others. Stand tall and confidently.
Action: Practice standing tall with shoulders back and head held high; imagine a string gently pulling you upwards.

Eye contact: Make and maintain eye contact. It shows confidence, interest, and engagement.
Action: When speaking or listening, hold eye contact for a few seconds to convey engagement and confidence.

Confidence: Believe in your abilities and decisions. Confidence is felt before it's seen.
Action: Remind yourself of a recent success before entering any room to reinforce your self-belief.

Self-belief: Trust in who you are and what you bring to the table. It's your foundation.
Action: List three qualities you love about yourself each morning to ground your day in self-assurance.

Unapologetic-ness: Own who you are without apologising or needing validation.
Action: Catch yourself whenever you're about to apologise for your opinion or presence – pause and own it instead.

Ownership of self: Be responsible for your actions, decisions and presence in the world.
Action: Take a few moments daily to reflect on your actions and how they align with your values.

Smiling eyes (warmth): Smile genuinely, allowing your warmth to shine through your eyes, making others feel welcome.
Action: Practice smiling in front of a mirror, letting the warmth reach your eyes and soften your expression.

Welcoming: Have an open, inviting energy. Be approachable and receptive to new connections.
Action: Approach new people with open body language and an easy smile; imagine welcoming them into your space.

Connection: Create a real connection by listening, engaging and showing empathy.
Action: Put away your phone or distractions when conversing to focus fully on the other person.

Stand out: Embrace what makes you unique and different, letting it shine through.
Action: Identify one unique quality or talent and look for small ways to let it shine in your interactions.

Difference: Celebrate and amplify your individuality – don't try to blend in.
Action: Choose one thing you love about your individuality and celebrate it today. Let it guide how you show up.

Image (personal style): Dress in a way that makes you feel powerful and authentic. Your style should represent who you are.
Action: Wear an outfit that makes you feel powerful and authentic; let your wardrobe reflect your inner self.

X-Factor: That intangible quality that's uniquely yours – find it, own it and let it shine.
Action: Reflect on what makes you truly unique and bring it to life in how you speak, move and connect with others.

Energy: Cultivate positive, confident energy. People will be drawn to your vibrance and enthusiasm.
Action: Take a few deep breaths before entering a room, focusing on positive, confident energy you want to share.

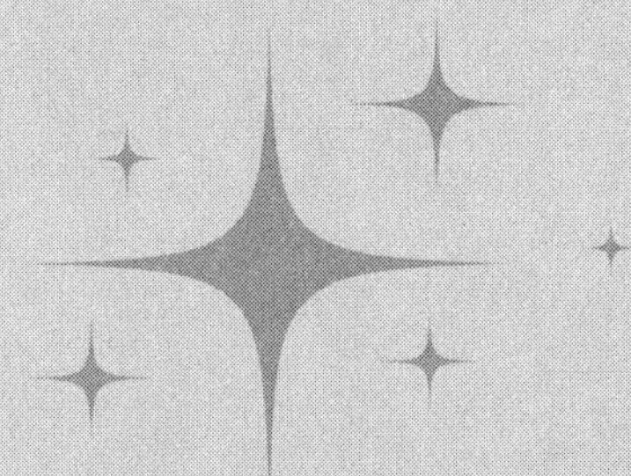

BEING MAGNETIC: LIVING THE WORK

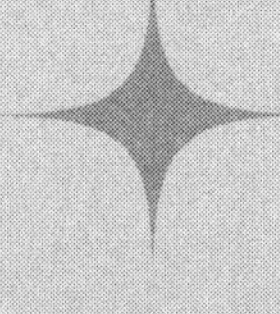

10

MAGNETISM IN YOUR PERSONAL LIFE

PERSONAL LIFE
PERSONAL LIFE

The five phases of magnetism are powerful, but how do they actually play out in your life? In the next two chapters I'll break it down and show you exactly how these phases – self mastery, defining your values, creating your alter she-go, the evolution and your magnetic aura – work in real-world scenarios.

First, we'll dive into magnetism in your personal life. This includes everything from cultivating magnetic energy to building magnetic friendships, finding magnetic love, flourishing as a magnetic couple and bringing that energy into your role as a magnetic parent. Each example will highlight how these phases can transform the way you connect, support and grow with those closest to you.

In Chapter 11 we'll move into magnetism in your career and business. Here, we'll explore how these same five phases empower you to become a magnetic leader, attract opportunities and elevate your presence in the professional world.

The following two chapters are where it all comes together – where you start putting the five phases of magnetism into action to create a life that's real, intentional and unapologetically yours in every area that counts.

One thing I've learnt from working with thousands of women in my coaching practice is this: how you show up in your personal life reflects how you'll show up in every other relationship you have. Whether it's with your partner, your children, your friends or colleagues – your energy in one space spills over into all the others. It all begins with the most private, intimate relationship you'll ever have – the one with yourself.

Many of my clients come to me because they are struggling in their relationships, wondering why things feel off or disconnected. What we always end up coming back to is this question: are you showing up fully in your relationship with *yourself*? When you're magnetic in your own life – when you're confident, in alignment and standing in your truth – that energy naturally expands into your relationships with others.

You might be focusing on your partnership or your friendships, but if you're not fully present or not embracing who you are at your core, this will affect how you relate to everyone else. Being in deep relationship with oneself is the bedrock of all other personal relationships and will enable you to carry the same magnetic energy into your romantic life, friendships, your family dynamics, and especially into how you parent.

In this chapter, we're going to dig deep into what it means to cultivate that magnetism in every relationship you hold dear. Magnetism is about truly owning who you are and letting that energy draw in the right connections, the real intimacy and the deep bonds you desire.

MAGNETIC ENERGY: YOUR VIBRANCY, COURAGE AND SPICE FOR LIFE

I had to include this here as I constantly get asked about how I have so much energy. THIS is how. Magnetic energy is about being the conductor of your own power, enthusiasm and resilience. It's the kind of energy that fills a room, draws people toward you and makes you feel invincible. When you embody magnetic energy, you wake up with passion and purpose, feeling alive and ready to tackle the day – no matter what challenges come up. You radiate positivity, optimism and resourcefulness, and others can't help but feel good in your presence.

This type of energy isn't about avoiding the hard stuff or pretending life is always perfect – it's about resilience. When challenges arise, you don't crumble; you rise with grace and strength, knowing that you'll find a way through as you have done before. With magnetic energy, you're operating at a high-frequency vibe, and this positive energy becomes a magnet for good vibes, opportunities and relationships. You feel empowered from within and nothing external can shake your core belief.

Magnetic energy – Phase 1: Self-mastery

For magnetic energy, self-mastery is all about owning your energy and knowing how to regulate it. To be magnetic, you must first be able to manage your emotions, thoughts and energy levels. Self-mastery means waking up each day with intention, knowing that you have the power to choose how you show up and how you respond to life's challenges.

- **Mastering your internal world:** Magnetic energy starts from within. Self-mastery involves knowing how to regulate your emotions, avoiding letting external circumstances dictate your mood and maintaining an optimistic, high-frequency state. You are responsible for your energy, and you decide how you want to show up.
- **Resilience and resourcefulness:** When challenges come, people with magnetic energy don't panic – they get resourceful. Self-mastery is about building resilience so that when things go wrong, you don't fall apart. Instead, you trust yourself to find a way through, you build confidence through self-trust, knowing that your internal belief and strength will carry you forward.
- **Daily energy practices:** Self-mastery also includes creating daily habits and rituals that support your energy. Whether it's morning routines, yoga, mindfulness, breathwork practices or exercise, these

practices help you keep your energy high and aligned with your goals.

Magnetic energy – Phase 2: Defining your values

To maintain magnetic energy, you need to be clear on your core values. Knowing what drives you and what you stand for creates a foundation for consistent, high-frequency energy. When your life aligns with your values, you wake up every day excited, passionate and full of purpose.

- **Living with purpose:** Magnetic energy comes from living in alignment with your purpose. When you're clear on your 'why', you have a natural enthusiasm for life. You wake up with a sense of purpose, knowing that you're doing meaningful work and living according to your values.
- **Clarity and focus:** Defining your values gives you clarity about what's important and what deserves your energy. You don't waste time or energy on things that don't align with your values, and this focus allows you to maintain high energy and enthusiasm for what truly matters.
- **Optimism and gratitude:** When you live by your values, it's easier to maintain an optimistic outlook. You're not just reacting to life – you're proactively creating it. This optimism, grounded in purpose, fuels your magnetic energy and helps you attract positive situations and people.

Magnetic energy – Phase 3: Stepping into your alter she-go

Stepping into your alter she-go in this phase is about fully embodying the version of yourself that is vibrant, alive and full of passion. This is where you stop holding back and start living life with full energy and enthusiasm, inspiring others with your high-frequency vibes.

How you show up in your personal life reflects how you'll show up in every other relationship you have.

- **Radiating high vibes:** In this phase, you become a source of high energy for others. Your enthusiasm for life is infectious, and people are drawn to you because of your positive energy. You step into your alter she-go by fully embracing your passion and letting it shine in everything you do.
- **Empowered and unshakable:** When you step into your highest self, no one can rock your energy. You're grounded, confident and strong from within. You're no longer swayed by negativity or external events because you're so internally empowered. Your magnetic energy becomes a shield that protects you from low-frequency vibes.
- **Inspiring others:** Your energy doesn't just impact you – it inspires everyone around you. When you're living in alignment with your true self, you naturally lift others up with your high vibes and positivity. This is where your magnetic energy begins to ripple out, influencing and inspiring others to rise to your level.

Magnetic energy – Phase 4: The evolution

In the evolution phase, your energy continues to grow and evolve. As you face new challenges and experiences, you learn to expand your capacity to hold more energy, more enthusiasm and more resilience. This phase is about growing your energetic capacity and learning to maintain high-frequency vibes even in the face of adversity.

- **Evolving through challenges:** Having magnetic energy doesn't mean everything is always easy. In this phase, you evolve by facing challenges head-on and learning how to keep your energy high, even when life throws you curveballs. You become more resilient and adaptable, which strengthens your energy even further.
- **Expanding your capacity:** As you evolve, so does your capacity to handle more – more success, more challenges and more opportunities.

You expand your ability to maintain high-frequency energy, no matter what's happening around you. This is where you grow into someone who can take on more, without losing your spark.

- **Continual growth:** In this phase, you're committed to continual growth. You know that your energy needs to evolve just like everything else in life. You keep pushing yourself to higher levels of positivity, resilience and enthusiasm, always seeking to grow your magnetic energy.

Magnetic energy – Phase 5: Magnetic aura

In Phase 5: Magnetic Aura, your energy is fully magnetic. You radiate positivity, purpose and high-frequency vibes, and people can't help but be drawn to you. You've reached a place where your energy is so strong, so grounded and so positive that you effortlessly attract good vibes, opportunities and relationships into your life.

- **Effortless magnetism:** At this stage, your energy is so magnetic that you don't have to force anything. People, opportunities and positive situations are naturally drawn to you because your energy is aligned with abundance, purpose and optimism.
- **Empowered and energised:** You wake up each day feeling energised and empowered, ready to take on whatever comes your way. Your internal energy is strong and unshakable, and no external circumstances can bring you down. You're operating at a consistently high frequency, and it shows in every aspect of your life.
- **Attracting high-frequency opportunities:** Because you're vibrating at such a high level, you naturally attract opportunities that align with your energy. Whether it's work, relationships or personal growth, everything you draw into your life matches the high frequency you're operating at. You're a magnet for success, positivity and growth.

Magnetic energy is about living life with passion, purpose and high-frequency vibes. Through the five phases of magnetism, you move from mastering your energy and aligning with your values to embodying your highest self, evolving with challenges and creating a magnetic aura that draws positivity, opportunities and success into your life. You become a beacon of high energy, resilience and optimism, inspiring others with your magnetic presence and creating a life filled with abundance and purpose.

MAGNETIC FRIENDSHIPS

Just like romantic relationships, friendships require effort, growth and alignment. Many of us carry wounds from childhood experiences – bullying, sister wounds* or trust issues – that play out in our adult friendships. If these wounds remain unresolved, they can affect how we show up in our friendships, leading to mistrust, lack of vulnerability and even one-sided or unhealthy connections.

Being a magnetic friend means being the kind of friend you wish to attract – someone who communicates openly, is vulnerable and builds trust through actions, not gossip or judgement. It's about understanding your values in friendships and knowing when to walk away from relationships that no longer align with who you are becoming. As you grow and evolve, your friendships must evolve too, reflecting your values and the kind of energy you want to cultivate in your life.

Magnetic friendships – Phase 1: Self-mastery

In magnetic friendships, self-mastery is crucial for understanding how your past affects your current relationships. Any unresolved issues

* The sister wound is the emotional pain from jealousy, competition or mistrust between women, often rooted in societal conditioning or personal experiences such as bullying or broken trust. It leads to comparison and rivalry instead of support.

from childhood can shape how we approach friendships in adulthood, often without us even realising it.

- **Healing past wounds:** If you've been hurt by past friendships, especially in your formative years, you might struggle to fully trust new friends. Self-mastery in friendships means taking the time to heal these wounds, so you're not bringing unresolved baggage into new connections. Otherwise, you may end up projecting old fears or insecurities onto current friendships.
- **Recognising patterns:** Do you find yourself stuck in the same kinds of friendships that feel one-sided, draining or unfulfilling? This phase is about recognising those patterns and taking responsibility for your part in them. It's not about blaming others, but understanding what you need to heal to show up fully in your friendships.
- **Trust and vulnerability:** To create magnetic friendships, you need to be emotionally available. That means mastering your own emotions, learning to trust yourself and allowing yourself to be vulnerable. Self-mastery in friendships involves being open and authentic, showing up as the kind of friend you want to attract.

Magnetic friendships – Phase 2: Defining your values

Just like romantic relationships, friendships need to be built on shared values. Defining your values in friendships means getting clear on what kind of friend you want to be and what you expect in return. Many people struggle with friendships because they've never defined what a healthy, thriving friendship looks like for them.

- **Clarifying friendship values:** What do you stand for in friendships? Is it loyalty, honesty, vulnerability or mutual support? Defining these values helps you understand what kind of energy you want to bring into your friendships and what kind of people you want to attract.

- **Vision for friendships:** Just like you might create a vision for your career or personal growth, it's important to have a vision for your friendships. What does your ideal circle of friends look like? Who are the people who inspire you to be better, to grow and to thrive? If your current circle isn't aligned with your vision, it may be time to re-evaluate.
- **Living your friendship values:** Attracting meaningful friendships starts with embodying the values you seek in others. Are you showing up as the friend you want to attract? Reflect on whether you're consistent, supportive and honest. Living by your values means being the friend who listens, communicates openly and values growth. The connections you draw in will often mirror the energy and commitment you put out.

Magnetic friendships – Phase 3: Stepping into your alter she-go

In this phase, you step into the version of yourself who embodies what it means to be a magnetic friend. Stepping into your alter she-go means no longer waiting for friendships to happen: you take action to be the kind of friend you want in your life.

- **Embodying your alter she-go in friendships:** Imagine the version of yourself who radiates confidence, warmth, and loyalty -- the ultimate magnetic friend. Stepping into your alter she-go means becoming that person, the friend who brings energy, authenticity and support into every interaction. This version of you isn't passive; she reaches out, initiates connection and shows up fully. As your alter she-go, you embody the values and qualities you want in others, setting the tone for genuine, trusting and growth-oriented friendships.

- **No gossip, all trust:** Magnetic friendships are built on trust, not gossip. If you want to be the kind of friend people can rely on, you need to eliminate gossip from your relationships. Stepping into this version of yourself means committing to honesty, transparency and kindness in your friendships.
- **Creating and maintaining connections:** Being a magnetic friend means you actively nurture your friendships. You don't wait for others to reach out – you make the effort. You stay connected, support your friends and create opportunities for deeper connection. This phase is about being intentional and proactive in your relationships.

Magnetic friendships – Phase 4: The evolution

Friendships, like any relationship, must evolve as you grow. In the evolution phase, you may find that some friendships no longer serve you, while others deepen. As you continue to evolve as a person, your circle of friends should evolve with you.

- **Outgrowing friendships:** It's natural to outgrow friendships as you evolve, especially if your values and priorities shift. In this phase, you may find that certain friendships no longer align with the person you're becoming. That doesn't mean those friendships were a failure – it means they served their purpose for a season.
- **Letting go of one-sided friendships:** If you find yourself in friendships that feel one-sided – where you're doing all the giving and none of the receiving – it might be time to let go. Magnetic friendships are reciprocal, where both parties energise the relationship. In this phase, you get clear on which friendships are lifting you up and which ones are draining you.
- **Evolving together:** The most magnetic friendships are those that grow and evolve together. When both people are committed

to their own growth and aligned in their values, the friendship becomes a space for mutual support, encouragement and evolution. In this phase, you nurture these aligned friendships and let go of those that no longer serve you.

Magnetic friendships – Phase 5: Magnetic aura

In Phase 5: Magnetic Aura, you have built a circle of friendships that radiate positivity, support and trust. The friends you have now are those who align with your values and help you thrive, just as you do for them. There's no more forcing connections or holding onto relationships that drain you. Instead, your friendships flow naturally and support your highest self.

- **Effortless friendships:** At this stage, your friendships feel easy, natural and reciprocal. You're surrounded by people who uplift you, inspire you and share your vision for growth. There's no drama, no gossip – just mutual respect and connection.
- **Thriving together:** The friends you attract now are those who are on the same path of growth and evolution. You push each other to be better, celebrate each other's wins and support each other through challenges. Your circle is full of people who are as committed to their personal growth as you are.
- **Boundaries and balance:** In this phase, you've set healthy boundaries in your friendships. You know when to give and when to step back. You respect each other's space, and your friendships are balanced, with both people contributing equally to the relationship.
- **Expanding your circle:** The energy you project in Phase 5 naturally attracts more like-minded people. You may find that new friendships come easily, as others are drawn to your magnetic energy. Your aura is one of openness, trust and authenticity, and it attracts friends who resonate with that same energy.

Magnetic friendships are built on trust, vulnerability and aligned values. Through the five phases of magnetism, you move from healing past friendship wounds to becoming the kind of friend you wish to attract. You learn to let go of friendships that no longer serve you and embrace those that evolve alongside you. By stepping into your power as a magnetic friend, you create deep, meaningful connections that support your growth and reflect the energy you've worked so hard to cultivate.

MAGNETIC LOVE

Single ladies, this one's for you.

When it comes to attracting love, magnetism starts from within. Often, when we're single, we may find ourselves repeating patterns, making choices from a place of lack, desperation or fear. It's easy to feel like we're swimming against the current – constantly chasing, waiting and hoping for the right person to finally show up.

But here's the truth: love isn't just about luck or timing. It's about alignment. We attract what we are, not necessarily what we want. If we're out there dating from a place of insecurity, scarcity or desperation, those are the energies we'll continue to encounter. The key to magnetic love isn't about finding someone – it's about becoming the version of *ourselves* who naturally attracts love, effortlessly and on our own terms.

You may find that before calling in the right partner, there's inner work that needs to happen. This work helps us shift from chasing to attracting – and trust me, the difference is profound.

Let's walk through the five phases of magnetism as they apply to being single and wanting to attract love. These phases will support you in stepping into your magnetic self and drawing in the love that's aligned with who you are becoming.

Magnetic love – Phase 1: Self-mastery

This begins with addressing your limiting beliefs and confronting past heartaches. This phase is crucial, because without doing the inner work and healing, you risk attracting the same unhealthy dynamics over and over again.

- **Attracting from fear of being alone:** If you're afraid of being by yourself, you may settle for less than you deserve, choosing relationships out of fear rather than from a place of desire. You become driven by a need to fill a void rather than a genuine connection.
- **Operating from scarcity:** If you believe that 'all the good ones are taken', you're already limiting yourself. This mindset leads to settling or holding onto relationships that aren't serving you because you don't believe something better is out there.
- **Unhealed past relationships:** Without healing from previous heartaches, you're likely to attract the same energy in new relationships, just in a different form. It may be a different person, but the emotional wounds will keep drawing in partners who mirror your unresolved issues.
- **Co-dependency and trauma bonds:** When self-worth isn't addressed, you might find yourself in co-dependent relationships or trauma bonds, clinging to partners who don't serve your growth. This could manifest in repeatedly attracting emotionally unavailable partners or people who manipulate and take advantage of your vulnerabilities.
- **Hooking up with manipulative people:** If you haven't worked on self-love and healing, you'll attract people who can sense that you aren't fully grounded in yourself. This can lead to relationships where you're manipulated or mistreated because you're looking for validation outside yourself.

- **Feeling incomplete or not whole:** When you don't feel whole on your own, you seek someone else to complete you. This is a dangerous place to be because it often leads to relationships built on shaky foundations, ones where both parties are looking for the other to fill in the gaps they haven't addressed within themselves.

In this phase, your focus is on self-love and healing. It's about recognising your worth, doing the uncomfortable work to heal your past, and breaking the cycle of attracting partners who reflect *your* insecurities.

When you master this phase, you start attracting people who match the love and respect you've cultivated within yourself.

Magnetic love – Phase 2: Defining your values

Once you've done the deep inner work of self-mastery, the next crucial step is getting crystal clear on your values. So many single women have a long list of qualities they want in a partner – someone kind, successful, loyal, driven – but they rarely stop to ask themselves if *they* embody those values. How can you attract someone who aligns with your desires if you're not living in alignment with them **yourself**?

Here's the reality: if you're unclear about what truly drives you, you're likely to bend, twist and change to fit what someone else wants. You'll play games, pretend and even ghost people because you're not rooted in your own truth. Defining your values gives you an unshakable foundation, and when you live by them, you naturally start attracting people who align with your energy.

- **Clarity on your own values:** It's easy to have a checklist of what you want in someone else, but, before you focus on that, turn the spotlight on yourself. Ask, *Do I embody the values I want in a partner?* If you want someone who's honest, loyal and hardworking, are you living those qualities? If not, this is where you need to start. You can't expect to attract someone living in alignment with these values if you aren't there yourself.

- **Attracting from authenticity:** When you define and live by your values, you become magnetic to the right people. There's no need to play games, pretend to be something you're not or mould yourself to fit what others want. You stand firm in who you are, and the people who are meant to be in your life will be drawn to that authenticity. No more bending or twisting to fit someone else's expectations.
- **Avoiding misalignment:** Without knowing your values, you may fall into relationships where you're out of alignment – trying to please someone or playing by their rules. This leads to superficial connections or relationships built on shaky foundations. Defining your values helps you avoid falling into situations where you're not being true to yourself, which ultimately leads to healthier, stronger relationships.
- **Emotional stability:** When you're grounded in your values, you make decisions from a place of clarity and stability, not out of fear or scarcity. You're less likely to chase or cling to people who don't align with your core beliefs because you know what matters to you and won't settle for anything less. This is where real confidence comes from – knowing who you are and standing firm in it.
- **Boundaries and self-respect:** Living by your values naturally leads to stronger boundaries. You know what you stand for, so you're not easily swayed by external pressures or people who don't respect your standards. This self-respect radiates outward, and others will treat you the way you treat yourself.

In this phase, the focus is on aligning your life with the values you want to attract in a partner. When you live in alignment with your values, you stop chasing and start attracting. You'll notice that the right people, the right opportunities and the right relationships flow into your life effortlessly because you're living as the most authentic version of yourself.

Magnetic love – Phase 3: Stepping into your alter she-go

Now that you've done the inner work of mastering yourself and defining your values, it's time to step into your alter she-go. In this phase, you stop holding back and start making decisions from a place of empowerment and clarity.

- **Becoming her now:** Too many women hold off on living their best lives, thinking they'll be confident once they find the right partner or when they lose weight, or after they achieve a certain milestone. But the truth is, the more you delay stepping into your true power, the longer you'll wait for those things to show up. The key to this phase is being the woman you want to be *now*. If you want to attract love, show up as the woman who already has it: confident, self-assured and complete in herself.
- **No more masks:** This phase is where the masks come off. If you're still pretending to be someone else – whether that's playing small, acting 'cool' or avoiding vulnerability – it's time to let that go. The woman who has stepped into her alter she-go is unapologetically herself. She's bold, she's real and she's not afraid to set boundaries or be vulnerable. She knows her worth and attracts people who recognise it too.
- **Stop waiting for permission:** Often, we wait for someone else to validate us or give us permission to step into the life we want. In this phase, you give yourself that permission. You make decisions from a place of worthiness, not from fear or self-doubt. You don't wait for the right moment – you create it.

If you've been holding back in love, afraid of being too much or not enough, this is where you drop that narrative and step fully into your power.

- **Boundaries and decisiveness:** When you embody your alter she-go, you're not afraid to set boundaries or make decisions that honour your highest self. You respect yourself deeply, and that respect sets the tone for how others treat you. This is the phase where your boundaries are clear, and you no longer waste time with people who don't align with your values or vision.
- **Being in flow, not force:** The energy of your alter she-go is rooted in flow, not force. You don't need to chase or force connections. You don't have to overextend yourself to keep someone's interest. You know that you are enough, exactly as you are. You attract effortlessly because you're aligned with who you truly are and what you deserve. This is where dating and relationships start to feel lighter, more fun and filled with ease.

When you step into this phase, you're no longer hoping or wishing for a relationship to fill a void. You've done the work to heal, you know your values and now you show up as the person who already has what she wants. You're magnetic because you're fully aligned with yourself – grounded in confidence, authenticity and decisiveness.

Magnetic love – Phase 4: The evolution

At this point, you've been doing the work – embracing self-mastery, defining your values and stepping into your alter she-go. But now comes the real test, the evolution phase is where the universe tests you. You've stepped into this new version of yourself, but old patterns or red flags might still show up.

You might think you're done with old patterns, but evolution isn't linear. Sometimes, you'll face familiar temptations – people or situations that test your boundaries. This is where you truly step into your power and show that you've outgrown the versions of yourself that no longer serve you.

- **Tests and triggers:** This phase often feels like the universe is sending you red flags disguised as green ones. Maybe someone shows up looking like everything you want on the surface, but deep down, you sense the same toxic patterns you've worked so hard to break free from. These moments test whether you're going to fall back into old habits or if you've truly evolved into the woman who knows her worth. The question is: will you listen to your intuition – or ignore it?
- **Letting go of old identities:** Evolution requires letting go of who you used to be – the woman who accepted less than she deserved, who doubted her worth, or who attracted emotionally unavailable partners. This isn't easy. It's like shedding old skin, and sometimes it feels raw and uncomfortable. But this is the only way to step fully into your new self. If you're still clinging to old beliefs about love or yourself, this is where your work lies.
- **New perspectives on dating:** As you evolve, you might notice that your 'type' starts to shift. The people you were once drawn to no longer feel like a match, and you begin to open up to new possibilities. This phase is about recognising that your growth may attract a different kind of person – someone more aligned with your values and your new self. Dating might start to feel easier, more abundant and less like a struggle.
- **Dealing with resistance:** It's normal to feel resistance in this phase – both from within and from the people around you. You might encounter moments of doubt, wondering if you're truly ready for the kind of love you say you want. Old fears or insecurities may bubble up, but this is where the true transformation happens.

“MAGNETIC FRIENDSHIPS ARE BUILT ON TRUST, NOT GOSSIP.”

It's about staying grounded in your growth and not slipping back into familiar, yet limiting, patterns.

- **Trusting the process:** Evolution is not a smooth, easy journey. It's full of tests, setbacks and uncomfortable moments. But through it all, you're evolving into the most powerful, aligned version of yourself. Trust that every challenge you face is shaping you, pushing you closer to the love you truly deserve. Stay persistent, hold onto your boundaries and trust that what's meant for you will arrive in its own time.

In this phase, the focus is on persistence and alignment. You may face people or situations that test your growth, but this is where you prove to yourself that you've evolved. You'll likely find that the kinds of people you attract are shifting, and the dating pool that once felt scarce now feels abundant. You no longer have to work so hard to find connections because you're stepping fully into your magnetism.

Magnetic love – Phase 5: Magnetic aura

This is the phase where everything starts to flow with ease – where your energy, confidence and presence become magnetic. You meet great people, form connections without pressure and allow relationships to grow organically. There's no scarcity mindset or rush. You trust yourself, and when the right person shows up, you'll feel it deeply. Your aura, aligned with your values and self-worth, draws in the right energy: people who are in tune with your essence.

- **Effortless attraction:** At this stage, you don't need to force anything. The relationships, connections and opportunities that align with your energy start to show up without you having to chase or manipulate anything. You're in a state of flow, and people can feel it the moment you walk into a room. You're magnetic because you're deeply grounded in your self-worth and authenticity.

- **Confidence and presence:** Your aura is undeniable. When you've done the inner work and stepped into this evolved version of yourself, your confidence is palpable. You don't need to do anything extra – the energy you project speaks for itself. It's the kind of confidence that comes from within, not from external validation. People are drawn to you because they sense your grounded, authentic presence.
- **No rush, no pressure:** In this phase, there's no urgency to rush into relationships or force connections. You've moved beyond scarcity and the fear of missing out. You're content in yourself, and this allows you to approach dating and relationships with patience, trust and ease. There's no pressure to label things, no need to fast-track anything – you're able to let things unfold organically because you trust that what's meant for you will come at the right time.
- **Surrender and trust:** One of the most powerful aspects of this phase is the ability to surrender. You no longer need to control everything or have all the answers. You trust yourself, and you trust the process. This isn't about passivity – it's about knowing when to lean back and allow things to come to you. When you've done the work, you don't need to micromanage every detail of your love life. You're in flow with the universe, and you trust that the right person will enter your life when the time is right.
- **Aligned connections:** The people you attract in this phase are aligned with who you truly are. They see you, respect you and honour the work you've done to get to this point. You're no longer attracting people who are misaligned or playing games. You know the difference between someone who truly resonates with your energy and someone who doesn't. It's green flags all the way – people who match your values, your authenticity and your level of self-awareness.

- **Enjoying the journey:** There's a sense of freedom and joy in this phase. You're no longer fixated on finding 'the one' or ticking off relationship milestones. You're enjoying the process, having fun and forming genuine connections along the way. Whether it leads to a committed relationship or not, you're at peace with the journey because you know that the right person will come into your life when it's time. Until then, you're thriving, attracting meaningful friendships and connections, and enjoying the flow of life.

In Phase 5: Magnetic Aura, you've reached a point where love and connections flow to you effortlessly. You're not chasing anyone or anything because you've done the work to align with who you truly are. The pressure is gone, and in its place are ease, joy and trust. Your magnetic aura pulls in people who are aligned with your values, and you're no longer in a rush to define or label relationships. Instead, you're content, confident and fully surrendered to the process of loving.

MAGNETIC COUPLES

In any strong, thriving relationship, both partners need to commit to their own personal growth and self-mastery. This is the must-have foundation of becoming a magnetic couple: two individuals who are whole, complete and doing the work on themselves, coming together to create something even greater. It's the opposite of a trauma bond or co-dependency. Instead, it's an inter-dependent relationship, where both people are independent, yet they support, depend on and uplift one another.

Hamish and I have had the pleasure of coaching couples on building these powerful, synergetic partnerships. We've seen firsthand the difference between couples in which both partners are committed to growth and those in which only one is interested in evolving. When both individuals are doing the work, they become unstoppable – thriving in their individual lives, in their relationship and family life as a unified, magnetic power couple. They communicate intentionally, respect each other and create a partnership where both people's dreams and growth are supported.

The five phases of magnetism for couples will take you through the journey of how to build a relationship that's deeply connected consistently, evolving and truly magnetic.

Magnetic couples – Phase 1: Self-mastery

Just as for individuals, self-mastery is the foundation of any magnetic couple. Both partners need to commit to doing the inner work, confronting their limiting beliefs and building a strong sense of self-worth. In a relationship, this means each person takes responsibility for their own growth and healing. You can't expect to have a thriving partnership if one or both of you are still carrying unresolved trauma, insecurities or emotional baggage.

- **Individual growth:** Both partners need to be on their own personal journey of self-awareness and self-acceptance. Without this, you risk bringing old wounds and unhealthy patterns into the relationship.
- **Avoiding trauma bonds:** Relationships built on unhealed trauma often lead to co-dependency, where both partners rely on each other for validation or emotional stability. In contrast, self-mastery allows each person to be whole and grounded in themselves, avoiding the trap of needing the other person to 'complete' them.
- **Taking responsibility:** In this phase, it's crucial that each person owns their own emotional triggers and reactions. You can't rely on

your partner to fix or heal you. This self-mastery is what allows both individuals to come together as equals, rather than rely on the other to fill their respective gaps.

Magnetic couples – Phase 2: Defining your values

In a magnetic relationship, both partners need to have clarity on their individual values and align those with the values of the relationship. Defining your values as a couple is essential for creating a unified vision and moving forward together. Without shared values, even the most passionate relationships can become strained as conflicts arise over fundamental differences.

- **Individual and shared values:** While each person should have their own individual values, it's important to define what you both stand for as a couple. What do you prioritise together? What matters most in your relationship?
- **Alignment in growth:** Couples who thrive share a commitment to growth. When one person values personal evolution and the other is content with staying comfortable, conflict often arises. When both people value self-improvement, they can grow together rather than grow apart.
- **Intentional communication:** Values also affect how you communicate. A couple who values honesty, respect and compassion will approach disagreements with a focus on resolution and growth, rather than defensiveness or blame.
- **Avoiding misalignment:** Couples who don't take the time to define their values often find themselves out of sync. This is where frustration builds, as one partner feels dragged by the other or doesn't feel supported. Alignment in values creates harmony and respect in the relationship.

Magnetic couples – Phase 3: Stepping into your alter she-go

In this phase, both partners are stepping into the highest versions of themselves – the alter ego. This isn't about pretending or acting like someone you're not. It's about embodying the energy of who you aspire to be, both individually and within the relationship. Each person shows up fully as their best self, and together, they create a powerful, magnetic partnership.

- **Empowerment in the relationship:** When both partners step into their alter ego, they bring confidence, strength and decisiveness into the relationship. They stop playing small or holding back, and instead, make decisions and take action from a place of alignment with their highest selves.
- **Supporting each other's growth:** In this phase, the relationship becomes a space where both individuals are supported in stepping into their fullest potential. Each partner encourages the other to grow, learn, change, evolve and pursue their goals and dreams. There's no jealousy, competition or holding each other back – only empowerment, support and mutual respect.
- **Mutual respect and boundaries:** Stepping into your alter egos means setting healthy boundaries and respecting each other's needs and individuality. The relationship is not about control or dependency but about lifting each other up as independent, powerful individuals.

Magnetic couples – Phase 4: The evolution

In the evolution phase, both partners have already stepped into their empowered selves, but now comes the true test. Relationships evolve just like individuals do, and this phase is about weathering those changes together. As you grow, the relationship will face challenges, and how you handle them will determine whether you continue to evolve together or grow apart.

- **Embracing change together:** A magnetic couple understands that relationships, like individuals, need to evolve. This means being open to change, adapting as needed and supporting each other through the process. As one or both partners grow, the dynamic of the relationship will shift, and it's important to be flexible and willing to evolve together.
- **Facing challenges as a team:** In this phase, the universe will test the strength of the relationship. External challenges, personal growth shifts or even new desires can arise, but magnetic couples face these challenges together, communicating openly and staying grounded in their shared values.
- **Resisting the old patterns:** Like individuals, couples may be tempted to fall back into old, familiar patterns, especially when things get tough. This phase is about resisting those temptations and staying true to the new, evolved versions of yourselves and the relationship.

Magnetic couples – Phase 5: Magnetic aura

This is the phase where the relationship flows with ease, joy and connection. As a couple, you become a magnetic force – both individually powerful and even more so together.

- **Effortless synergy:** At this stage, the relationship feels like it's in a state of flow. There's no need to push or force anything because both partners are deeply aligned with themselves and each other. Communication is effortless, decisions are made together and both people feel supported and appreciated.
- **Magnetic together:** As a couple, your energy radiates outward. You attract opportunities, success and positive relationships as a

unified front. You're no longer two individuals just coexisting; you're a power couple whose combined energy creates abundance and success, and when you're out in public people can FEEL it.

- **Keeping the spark alive:** Even in the most powerful relationships, it's essential to keep the connection and intimacy alive. Magnetic couples continually charge their relationship – through date nights, quality time, fun and adventure, and intentional communication. They nurture the relationship, knowing that, just as individuals need growth, so does the partnership.
- **Unshakable trust and connection:** In this phase, both partners trust each other deeply and are connected on all levels – emotionally, intellectually, physically and spiritually. There's no fear of losing the other or being left behind because both people are fully committed to the partnership and to each other's growth.

Magnetic couples are built on the foundation of two individuals doing the work on themselves. Through the five phases of magnetism, couples who commit to self-mastery, align their values, step into their highest selves, evolve together and cultivate a magnetic aura become unstoppable. These relationships are deeply connected, filled with trust and radiate synergy. Both partners are whole and complete on their own, but together they create something even more powerful – an unbreakable, magnetic union that thrives on mutual respect, growth and love.

MAGNETIC PARENTING

Parenting is one of the most powerful areas where magnetism can create lasting impact. Becoming a magnetic parent doesn't require you to be perfect – it's about being committed and willing to heal your past, breaking generational cycles and raising emotionally intelligent, confident children by leading through example. The goal is to create a safe, nurturing environment where your children feel loved, heard and supported. This requires a deep commitment to personal growth and conscious parenting (and sometimes re-parenting yourself).

This is *especially* important for those who are single parents or caregivers, or sharing care with an ex-partner. Co-parenting or raising children on your own brings its own set of dynamics, but it's crucial to remember that magnetism in parenting does not depend on family structure – it's about the energy, love and presence you bring to your relationship with your children.

When you do the inner work – healing your wounds, regulating your emotions and aligning with your values – you become the type of parent who teaches by example. You model confidence, compassion and connection, showing your children how to navigate the world with emotional intelligence and resilience. In magnetic parenting, it's not just about teaching your children, but also embodying the values you want to pass on to them.

Magnetic parenting – Phase 1: Self-mastery

In magnetic parenting, self-mastery is where everything begins. Before you can be the parent your children need, you must do the inner work on yourself. This means healing your own childhood wounds, addressing any unresolved trauma and breaking the cycles of generational patterns that no longer serve you or your family.

- **Healing past wounds:** If you haven't healed from your own upbringing, you risk unconsciously passing down the same trauma or dysfunction to your children. Self-mastery as a parent means recognising where those wounds exist and committing to breaking the cycle for your children.
- **Emotional regulation:** Magnetic parents don't just talk about emotional intelligence – they model it. By mastering your own

> Magnetic parenting is about breaking generational cycles, healing your own wounds and creating a safe, emotionally intelligent environment where your children can thrive.

emotions, you show your children how to handle frustration, anger, sadness and disappointment in healthy ways. Forget about being perfect; the aim is being self-aware and accountable for how you show up.

- **Leading by example:** Your children learn from what they see, not just what you tell them. In this phase, self-mastery means being the person you want your children to grow into. If you want them to be confident, compassionate and resilient, you must embody those traits yourself.
- **Emotional intelligence:** Whether you're a single parent or co-parenting with an ex, this phase calls for deep emotional mastery. You may find that taking care of yourself emotionally is even more important, as you're navigating additional challenges. This phase is about learning to manage your emotions and responses, ensuring that you show up as the best version of yourself for your children, regardless of the circumstances.

Magnetic parenting – Phase 2: Defining your values

As a magnetic parent, defining your values is essential to creating a cohesive, aligned family environment. What kind of parent do you want to be? What are the values that will guide your parenting? These are crucial questions because your values shape how you communicate, discipline and connect with your children.

- **Clarifying family values:** In this phase, take the time to define what matters most to you as a parent. Is it open communication? Emotional safety? Independence? By knowing your values, you can align your actions with the parent you aspire to be, ensuring consistency in how you show up for your kids.
- **Modelling values for your children:** It's one thing to talk about values, but living them is where the real work lies. When your children

see you living your values – whether it's through honesty, kindness or resilience – they internalise those traits. They learn through your actions, not just your words. Many children won't listen to what we say as parents, but they will model who we are being.

- **Creating a family vision:** Magnetic parents, coupled and single, often create a vision for their family, rooted in shared values. What does a healthy, thriving family dynamic look like to you? Defining this vision helps guide your decisions, making sure every interaction is aligned with the values that matter most.
- **Defining your parenting vision as a single parent or co-parent:** Your parenting values may look different if you're sharing care with an ex or navigating single parenthood. Here, you focus on aligning your actions and decisions with what you believe to be most important for your family – whether it's consistency, love or emotional safety. Co-parenting may require clear communication and flexibility, while single parenting may call for a strong sense of independence and resilience.

Magnetic parenting – Phase 3: Stepping into your alter she-go

In this phase, magnetic parents fully step into the version of themselves they want to be as parents. This is where you stop wishing to be a certain kind of parent and start embodying it every day. Your alter she-go is the parent who models confidence, love and emotional intelligence – not through perfection but through consistency and authenticity.

- **Becoming the parent you want to be:** Stepping into this phase means you're no longer waiting to become the ideal parent – you are actively being that parent right now. You embody the traits you want your children to learn, like resilience, patience and confidence. You show up as the best version of yourself, even on the tough days.

- **Modelling confidence and emotional intelligence:** Magnetic parenting is about teaching by example. You model how to handle conflict, how to navigate difficult emotions and how to communicate effectively. Your children learn these skills from watching you regulate your emotions and communicate with them openly and honestly.
- **Stepping into your power as a parent:** This phase is about realising that you have the power to shape your children's emotional and mental wellbeing. By stepping fully into your role as a conscious parent, you create a safe and nurturing environment where your children can thrive.
- **Stepping into your power as a single or co-parent:** In this phase, you embody the highest version of yourself as a parent, regardless of your family structure. You don't let external factors dictate your ability to be a magnetic parent. Whether co-parenting or raising children solo, you step into the version of yourself that is confident, empowered and fully present for your kids. You own your unique circumstances and use them as a way to strengthen your connection with your children.

Magnetic parenting – Phase 4: The evolution

Just as individuals grow and evolve, so do parents and family dynamics. The evolution phase in magnetic parenting is about adapting to the changes that come with raising children. As they grow and change, so must your parenting approach. This phase is about evolving together and being flexible in your methods while staying grounded in your values.

- **Adapting to your children's growth:** As your children grow, their needs change. What worked when they were toddlers may no longer apply when they're teenagers. Magnetic parents are flexible and willing to evolve their parenting style to meet their children where they are developmentally.

- **Adapting to challenges of co-parenting or single parenting:** Co-parenting or solo parenting often brings additional challenges, such as navigating different parenting styles or managing your energy without the constant support of a partner. This phase is about embracing these challenges as part of your growth. You remain flexible, resilient and committed to creating a loving, stable environment for your children, even when circumstances are complex.
- **Staying committed to growth:** Just as you evolve individually, you must also evolve as a parent. This means continuing to learn, adapt and grow in your parenting approach. It's about being open to feedback – whether from your partner, your children or your own self-reflection – and adjusting as needed.
- **Navigating challenges together:** Parenting comes with its share of challenges, and in this phase, the key is facing those challenges together as a family. Magnetic parents maintain open communication, model conflict resolution and stay united in their commitment to creating a loving, supportive environment, no matter what obstacles arise.

Magnetic parenting – Phase 5: Magnetic aura

In Phase 5: Magnetic Aura, you have created an environment where love, connection and trust flow naturally. Your children feel safe, supported and heard because they are growing up in a home where emotional intelligence, communication and compassion are prioritised. This phase is about reaping the rewards of the conscious parenting journey you've been on.

- **Deep connection and trust:** In this phase, you and your children have developed a deep sense of connection and trust. They feel safe coming to you with their challenges because they know they will be heard and supported. This creates a bond that allows your children to thrive emotionally and mentally.

- **Effortless communication:** At this stage, communication within the family becomes effortless. You've modelled openness and honesty, and now your children reflect that back to you. There's no fear of judgement or rejection because they know that they are loved unconditionally.
- **Creating a thriving environment:** Your home has become a space where everyone – parents and children – can grow, learn and evolve. There's a sense of ease and flow in the family dynamic because everyone is aligned with the values of love, respect and emotional intelligence.
- **Creating a magnetic environment despite family structure:** Whether you're a single parent or co-parent, you've built a magnetic environment for your children by focusing on emotional regulation, resilience and self-love. At this stage, the love and connection you've nurtured with your children radiate outwards. You're proof that magnetism in parenting does not depend on family structure, but on the energy and care you bring to your relationship with your kids.
- **Modelling for future generations:** The work you've done doesn't just benefit your children; it sets a foundation for future generations. By raising emotionally intelligent, confident children, you're breaking generational patterns and ensuring that one day they carry these lessons into their own relationships and families.

Magnetic parenting is about breaking generational cycles, healing your own wounds and creating a safe, emotionally intelligent environment where your children can thrive. Through the five phases of magnetism, parents who commit to self-mastery, align their values, embody their best selves, evolve with their children and cultivate a magnetic aura create deep, meaningful connections with their kids. This approach fosters trust, open communication and a thriving family dynamic where everyone can grow and evolve together.

11

MAGNETISM IN YOUR CAREER CAREER CAREER & BUSINESS BUSINESS BUSINESS

'How you do one thing is how you do everything': this phrase of Martha Beck's has stuck with me for years, and has become a cornerstone of how I now live my life. It's a reminder that the energy, mindset and behaviours we bring to one area of our life tend to show up in every other area as well. Whether you realise it or not, the patterns you follow at work, in your relationships and even in your everyday habits are interconnected.

Think about it: if you're someone who shows up fully at work – paying attention to detail, striving for excellence – it's likely that same energy carries over into your relationships, your home and your health. On the flip side, if you're avoiding taking risks, staying quiet in meetings or holding back in one area, chances are that pattern is playing out elsewhere in your life too. Trust me – I've seen it time and time again.

I've run countless live events over the last decade and one thing I notice is the same pattern over and over. The person sitting quietly at the back, not raising their hand, trying to be invisible, not stepping up – that's usually the same person who's 'sitting in the back' of their own life too. They're not showing up fully, they're not taking up space and they're missing out on the real opportunity to intentionally step into their magnetism. The way we do anything is how we do everything – *unless* we make the conscious decision to change it. That's when we become magnetic in all areas of our life.

BEING A LEADER ISN'T JUST ABOUT MANAGING OTHERS; IT'S ABOUT LEADING YOURSELF FIRST.

You're reading *Becoming Magnetic* because you're ready to step up. Maybe you've started to build magnetism in one part of your life, but I'm willing to bet there are other areas where you're not showing up as your most magnetic self yet – and that's completely okay. This is a journey of rediscovering how you've been showing up, and more importantly, how you *can* start showing up.

In this chapter, we're going to dive into what it means to be magnetic in ALL areas of your working life – business, money and more. And once you consciously bring energy to one area of your life, you will see everything start to shift; other areas of your life will also be transformed.

In your work and career, magnetism plays a crucial role in attracting the right opportunities, creating a fulfilling professional life and allowing you to thrive in your chosen field. Becoming magnetic in your career isn't about luck or chance – it's about aligning your values, stepping into your highest potential and cultivating an energy that naturally draws success toward you. Whether you're climbing the corporate ladder, building a business or navigating a career change, being magnetic in your work means you're showing up confidently, authentically and with intention.

By working through the five phases of magnetism, you'll learn how to master yourself, align with your core values, step into your power, evolve with challenges and create a magnetic aura that attracts opportunities, success and fulfilment in your career.

Magnetic career – Phase 1: Self-mastery

In your magnetic work and career, self-mastery is foundational. To thrive in your professional life, you first need to do the inner work of mastering your mindset, habits and emotional responses. Self-mastery means taking full responsibility for your career path: no longer blaming external factors for where you are, but instead looking inward to see where you can grow.

- **Owning your career journey:** Self-mastery is about recognising that you are in control of your career. Whether you want a promotion, more opportunities or a career shift, it starts with you. It's about being proactive in your personal growth and knowing that your professional success is a reflection of the work you do on yourself.
- **Mastering your emotions:** In your career, emotional regulation is key. Stress, frustration and setbacks are inevitable, but how you respond to them defines your magnetism. Mastering your emotions means you remain calm and grounded, even when things get tough. People who handle challenges with grace and resilience naturally attract more opportunities and trust in the workplace.
- **Breaking limiting beliefs:** Many people hold limiting beliefs about what they can achieve in their careers. Self-mastery requires you to confront and break those beliefs – whether it's thinking you're not good enough for a promotion or that you're stuck in a role you don't enjoy. By mastering your mindset, you open yourself up to new possibilities.

Magnetic career – Phase 2: Defining your values

To create a magnetic career, you must have clarity on your professional values. Defining your values for your work and career helps you identify roles, opportunities and workplaces that resonate with who you are and what you stand for. Without clear values, it's easy to fall into jobs that don't fulfil you or to compromise on what truly matters to you for the sake of external rewards.

- **Clarity on professional values:** What do you stand for in your career? Is it growth, creativity, impact, service, leadership or work–life balance? Defining these values is crucial for making decisions that align with your long-term vision and avoiding career paths that don't resonate with your core beliefs.

- **Aligning with your purpose:** When you're clear on your values, you attract work that feels purposeful and aligned. If you value leadership and personal development, you'll naturally seek out roles that allow you to grow and mentor others. If you value creativity, you'll be drawn to environments where innovation is encouraged. Your values guide your career choices and ensure that the work you do feels meaningful.
- **No more settling:** Defining your values helps you stop settling for jobs, roles or projects that don't fulfil you. When you know what's important to you, you no longer waste time in positions that drain your energy or don't align with your goals. Instead, you focus on creating a career that reflects your highest potential.

Magnetic career – Phase 3: Stepping into your alter she-go

In Phase 3, you step fully into your alter she-go in your career. This means showing up as the person who already embodies the success, confidence and professionalism you aspire to. It's about owning your power, making bold decisions and carrying yourself as the leader or expert you know you can be. In this phase, you stop accepting less than you deserve and start confidently communicating your needs and worth.

- **Embodying success and worth now:** Instead of waiting for the perfect opportunity or the right time to step into your power, you begin to embody that energy now. You make decisions as if you've already achieved your goals, and you carry yourself with the confidence of someone who knows they are worthy of success. This shift in energy attracts opportunities and people who are aligned with your vision.
- **Asking for what you deserve:** This is the phase where you stop accepting less – whether that's working overtime without

compensation, being underpaid or undervalued. You know your worth, and you confidently ask for more. Whether it's negotiating a higher salary, requesting a promotion or setting boundaries around unpaid overtime, you step up and advocate for yourself. You're no longer afraid to ask for what you need. And if your workplace is not prepared to give you what you need, then look for a workplace that will.

- **Communicating boundaries:** In this phase, you also learn to communicate your boundaries clearly and assertively. If you've been taking on more than your fair share of work or staying late without compensation, this is where you set limits. You're no longer available to be taken advantage of, and you make sure your time, energy and expertise are respected.
- **Taking bold action:** You stop playing small and start taking bold, decisive action in your career. Whether it's going for a promotion, launching a business or pivoting to a new field, you move with purpose and confidence. You're no longer waiting for permission – you give yourself the green light to pursue what you truly want and to ask for the compensation and recognition you deserve.

Magnetic career – Phase 4: The evolution

The evolution phase in your work life is about embracing the changes and challenges that come with professional growth. This is where you face the tests – whether it's navigating a difficult transition, handling increased responsibility or evolving into a new role or industry.

- **Embracing growth and change:** Just like individuals evolve, your career will too. The roles you take on, the skills you develop and the challenges you face all contribute to your professional evolution. In this phase, you embrace change rather than resist it, knowing that every challenge is an opportunity for growth.

- **Navigating setbacks and tests:** In your career, there will be moments when things don't go as planned – setbacks, failures or difficult projects. How you handle these challenges defines your magnetism. Do you crumble, or do you use these moments to evolve and become stronger? This phase is about showing resilience and adaptability in the face of obstacles.
- **Evolving into new roles:** As you grow professionally, you may find that your career path shifts in unexpected ways. You may outgrow your current role or industry, or you may be called to take on leadership positions that require you to evolve. Magnetic professionals are willing to step into these new challenges and trust the process of growth.

Magnetic career – Phase 5: Magnetic aura

In Phase 5, you've cultivated a magnetic aura in your work and career. This is where success, opportunities and recognition come to you effortlessly because you've done the inner work, aligned with your values and stepped into your power. You're no longer chasing success; it comes to you because you are in flow with your purpose and potential.

- **Opportunities flow toward you:** At this stage, you no longer have to push or hustle endlessly. The work you've put into mastering yourself, aligning with your values and stepping into your power attracts opportunities that reflect your goals and vision. Promotions, collaborations or new roles come to you naturally because you're in alignment.
- **Confidence and ease:** In this phase, you exude confidence and ease in your professional life. People notice your presence, your energy and your competence, and they want to work with you. You've put a halt to trying to prove yourself – your work speaks for itself, and your confidence creates an undeniable magnetic pull.

- **Aligned success:** The success you attract now is fully aligned with your values and purpose. It's not about chasing external markers of success like titles or money – although those may come – but about creating a career that is fulfilling and resonates with your true self. You're thriving in your work because it reflects who you are at your core.
- **Continued growth and expansion:** Even though you've reached a point of flow, the journey doesn't stop here. Magnetic professionals continue to grow and evolve, always seeking ways to expand their skills, impact and influence. In this phase, you remain open to new possibilities and opportunities for growth, knowing that your career will continue to evolve.

Being magnetic in your work and career is about aligning with your values, stepping into your highest potential and cultivating an energy that attracts success and opportunities naturally. Through the five phases of magnetism, you move from mastering yourself and defining your values to embodying your professional power, evolving with challenges and creating a magnetic aura in your career. This approach allows you to build a career that is not only successful, but also fulfilling, authentic and aligned with who you truly are.

MAGNETIC LEADERSHIP

At the core of magnetic leadership is self-leadership. Being a leader isn't just about managing others; it's about leading yourself first. A magnetic leader is someone who embodies personal growth, self-awareness and authenticity, and in doing so, naturally attracts people who want to follow their vision. Self-led individuals, whether in formal leadership roles or not, exude the kind of energy that makes others feel inspired and connected.

True magnetic leadership is rooted in authenticity, empathy and a commitment to personal evolution. Leaders who are constantly growing and pushing themselves inspire others to do the same. They don't lead by just telling others what to do – they lead by example, by being deeply connected to their values, their mission and their purpose. In this space, leadership and magnetism become intertwined, creating leaders who don't chase success, but attract it through their energy and impact.

Magnetic leadership – Phase 1: Self-mastery

In magnetic leadership, self-mastery is the foundation of everything. Before you can lead others, you must first learn to lead yourself. Self-mastery is about owning your personal growth, developing emotional intelligence and aligning with your values. The more you master yourself, the more magnetic your leadership becomes.

- **Leading yourself first:** Leadership starts with the self. A magnetic leader takes full responsibility for their actions, mindset and growth. They're constantly working on themselves, knowing that their personal evolution will have a direct impact on how they lead others.
- **Emotional intelligence:** Great leaders are emotionally intelligent: they're aware of their emotions and how those emotions affect others. Self-mastery in leadership means being able to regulate your emotions, remain calm under pressure and respond rather than react in difficult situations.
- **Building self-trust:** Leaders who trust themselves inspire trust in others. Self-mastery means developing a deep sense of confidence and self-trust. When you know your own capabilities and can trust your instincts, others will naturally follow your lead.

Magnetic leadership – Phase 2: Defining your values

Magnetic leaders are clear about their values. Defining your values as a leader ensures that your decisions, actions and leadership style are always aligned with your core principles. Without clearly defined values, it's easy to lead from a place of insecurity, indecision or people-pleasing.

- **Leading with integrity:** Values-driven leadership is rooted in integrity. When your leadership is aligned with your core values, people can feel it. They're drawn to leaders who are consistent, honest and true to their principles, even when it's difficult.
- **Clarity in decision-making:** Defining your values gives you clarity when making decisions. Instead of wavering or doubting, you can make confident choices that align with your vision and mission. This clarity creates a magnetic pull, as people naturally trust leaders who know what they stand for.
- **Attracting the right team:** As a leader, your values not only guide your decisions but also attract the right people to your team. People who share your values will gravitate toward your leadership, creating a unified and aligned team dynamic.

Magnetic leadership – Phase 3: Stepping into your alter she-go

In leadership, stepping into your alter she-go means becoming the leader you aspire to be today, instead of waiting for permission or the perfect moment. This is where you fully embody the traits of a magnetic leader: confidence, authenticity and the courage to lead boldly.

- **Embodying leadership now:** You don't wait to be given a leadership title to act like a leader. You start leading by showing up as your most empowered self, whether you're managing a team or working solo. You step into the energy of someone who leads with purpose, vision and integrity.

- **Authenticity and charisma:** People are naturally drawn to authentic leaders. When you show up as your true self, unafraid to be vulnerable or real, you attract people who are inspired by your authenticity. Charisma isn't about being perfect – it's about being real and confident in who you are.
- **Taking bold, decisive action:** Magnetic leaders don't hesitate when it comes to making decisions. They act with boldness and clarity, trusting their instincts. In this phase, you step into your power as a leader by taking decisive action and moving forward with confidence.

Magnetic leadership – Phase 4: The evolution

Leadership, like personal growth, is an ongoing process of evolution. In the evolution phase, magnetic leaders understand that they must constantly evolve to meet new challenges and lead effectively in changing environments. This phase is about adapting, growing and leading through change.

- **Evolving with the times:** Leaders who thrive are those who are willing to evolve with the world around them. Whether it's learning new skills, adapting to technological advancements or shifting your leadership style, you're constantly growing and evolving to stay relevant and effective.
- **Embracing challenges:** In leadership, challenges are inevitable. The evolution phase is about meeting those challenges head on and using them as opportunities for growth. Magnetic leaders don't shy away from difficulties; they face them, learn from them and come out stronger.
- **Inspiring growth in others:** As you evolve, so do the people you lead. Magnetic leaders inspire growth in their teams by encouraging continual learning and development. They create an environment

where personal and professional growth are not only valued but expected.

Magnetic leadership – Phase 5: Magnetic aura

In Phase 5: Magnetic Aura, your leadership reaches a point where your presence, energy and impact are undeniable. You no longer need to push or strive to lead – people are naturally drawn to your leadership because of the energy you exude and the trust you've built.

- **Effortless leadership:** At this stage, leadership feels natural and effortless. You've built a level of trust, authenticity and respect that draws people to you without you having to force it. People seek your guidance because they know you lead with integrity, empathy and purpose.
- **Creating a collaborative environment:** Magnetic leaders don't just lead; they create environments where others can thrive. You attract talented, driven individuals who are aligned with your vision and values, and together you create a culture of collaboration, trust and growth.
- **Leadership beyond titles:** In this phase, your leadership is no longer about your role or title – it's about the energy you bring. Whether you're officially in charge or not, people look to you for guidance because of the energy you radiate. Your leadership is magnetic because it's grounded in who you are, not just what you do.

Magnetic leadership is rooted in self-leadership, authenticity and personal growth. Through the five phases of magnetism, leaders move from mastering themselves to aligning with their values, stepping into their leadership power, evolving with challenges and cultivating a magnetic aura that naturally attracts followers and opportunities.

Your leadership
is magnetic because
it’s grounded in who
you are, not just
what you do.

Magnetic leaders lead with empathy, integrity and courage, inspiring others through their energy, vision and unwavering commitment to growth.

MAGNETIC BUSINESS

Magnetic business is where expansion, success and abundance become the natural by-products of living and working in alignment with your purpose. It's the space where your vision becomes reality, where you attract opportunities, collaborators and wealth through focused action and passion. In magnetic business, you operate with such energy, enthusiasm, passion and purpose that everything you touch turns to gold. You're not just working for success – you're on fire for life, waking up with excitement for what each day holds.

When you tap into this magnetism, you enter a state of flow in which abundance surrounds you. You're focused on both the micro and macro steps that move your business forward, collaborating with influential people and making a massive impact. It's a field where you serve others, and in turn, receive abundance.

Magnetic business – Phase 1: Self-mastery

In magnetic business, self-mastery is essential because your business is a direct reflection of you. The energy, passion and commitment you bring to your work come from the inner alignment you've crafted yourself. To create a thriving business, you must first master yourself – your mindset, habits and emotional wellbeing.

- **Mastering your energy:** Your energy is your greatest asset in business. Self-mastery means taking responsibility for how you show up each day. Are you passionate, focused and driven, or are you scattered and overwhelmed? Mastering your energy ensures that you bring your best self to your business every day.

- **Doing the inner work:** If you're unhappy, disconnected or not addressing the deeper issues within yourself, your business will reflect that. Self-mastery in business means healing your past, facing your fears and doing the internal work that keeps you aligned and energised. When you're clear and connected to your purpose, your business thrives.
- **Emotional intelligence:** In business, emotions like fear, doubt and overwhelm can sabotage your success. Self-mastery means being emotionally intelligent – knowing how to manage stress, setbacks and challenges with grace. When you master your emotions, you can navigate the highs and lows of business without losing momentum.

Magnetic business – Phase 2: Defining your values

Magnetic businesses are built on strong, clearly defined values. Defining your values in business means aligning every decision, partnership and action with your core principles. Without values, your business can become directionless, and you may find yourself chasing money or success at the expense of your true purpose.

- **Business with purpose:** What are the core values that drive your business? Do they include service, innovation, integrity or growth? Defining these values ensures that your business is built on a solid foundation of purpose, not just profit. When your business is aligned with your values, everything you do feels authentic.
- **Attracting opportunities and partners:** When you're clear on your business values, you naturally attract opportunities, clients and collaborators who resonate with those values. People want to work with and support businesses that are mission-driven, values-aligned and operate with integrity.
- **Making aligned decisions:** Defining your values helps you make decisions with clarity. Whether it's choosing partners,

making investments or deciding the direction of your business, your values guide you. This alignment creates a magnetic pull, attracting success and growth that feels aligned with your long-term vision.

Magnetic business – Phase 3: Stepping into your alter she-go

In business, stepping into your alter she-go means showing up as the entrepreneur or business leader you aspire to be, right now. This phase is about embodying the energy of success and purpose in your daily work, taking bold actions and leading your business from a place of confidence and vision.

- **Owning your success:** Instead of waiting for external validation, you step into the energy of someone who is already successful. You make decisions from a place of confidence and abundance, acting as the CEO of your life and business, fully embodying the role you aspire to.
- **Laser focus on micro and macro:** Magnetic business leaders have both a micro and a macro focus. They execute the small daily actions while keeping their eyes on the big vision. You know that every decision and action you take is contributing to the long-term success of your business, and you operate with precision and clarity.
- **Attracting big opportunities:** When you step into your alter she-go, you begin attracting big opportunities – whether they are lucrative deals, high-profile clients or major collaborations. This is the phase where your confidence, drive and focus create a magnetic pull, drawing opportunities to you effortlessly.
- **Passionate enthusiasm:** You wake up each day with fire and enthusiasm for what you're creating. This passion is contagious; it influences your team, collaborators and clients. People are drawn

to your energy because you're living your purpose, and they want to be part of that success.

- **Building a magnetic personal brand:** Your personal brand is the embodiment of your business and your values. In this phase, you don't just build a business – you create a powerful, authentic personal brand that reflects who you are and what you stand for. Your brand is an extension of your alter she-go. It's how you show up in the world, how people perceive you and what they feel when they interact with you or your business.
  - **Authentic brand identity:** You step into the version of yourself that you want to present to the world – authentic, confident and bold. Your personal brand becomes a magnet for the right clients, collaborators and opportunities because it's aligned with your true self.
  - **Visibility and influence:** In this phase, you focus on building visibility and influence through your personal brand. You show up consistently online, in person and in your industry as the leader you aspire to be. This is where you establish yourself as an authority, build trust and create lasting impact.

Magnetic business – Phase 4: The evolution

As your business grows, so must you. In the evolution phase, magnetic business leaders understand that they need to constantly evolve, adapt and grow alongside their business. This phase is about embracing change, scaling your business and navigating the challenges that come with growth.

- **Scaling with purpose:** As your business expands, you stay aligned with your purpose and values. Magnetic business leaders grow their businesses with intention, making sure that every step of expansion aligns with their long-term vision and mission.

- **Embracing challenges:** Growth doesn't come without challenges. In this phase, you'll face new obstacles – whether it's scaling your operations, managing a larger team or dealing with increased competition. The key is to embrace these challenges as opportunities for growth, learning and evolution.
- **Adapting and innovating:** The business world is always changing, and magnetic leaders know how to adapt and innovate. You stay ahead of trends, evolve with your industry and continually seek out new ways to serve your clients and customers better. This constant evolution keeps your business fresh, relevant and magnetic.

Magnetic business – Phase 5: Magnetic aura

At this point your business exudes success, abundance and influence. You've reached a level where everything you touch turns to gold because you're so aligned with your purpose and values. Opportunities flow to you, and your business is thriving on all levels – financially, creatively and interpersonally.

- **Effortless expansion and abundance:** At this stage, abundance flows naturally into your business. Clients, collaborators and opportunities come to you effortlessly because your energy is magnetic. You're no longer hustling or grinding for success; it comes to you because you've done the work to align with your purpose and vision.
- **Impact and influence:** Your business is not just financially successful, but it's also making a significant impact. You're influencing your industry, leading by example and making a difference in the lives of your clients, customers and community. This impact fuels even greater success and expansion.
- **Collaborating with power players:** Magnetic business leaders attract high-level collaborators – people who are equally driven,

successful and aligned with your vision. These collaborations create exponential growth, influence and financial success for both parties.

- **Thriving in flow:** In this phase, you're in a state of flow. You wake up excited to work on your business because it aligns with your passion and purpose. There's no struggle or resistance – everything feels aligned, abundant and full of potential. This is where your business becomes truly magnetic.
- **Magnetic personal brand:** By Phase 5, your personal brand is thriving. You're known for your expertise, authenticity and the value you bring to your industry. Your brand radiates magnetism, and you effortlessly attract opportunities, clients and collaborators because people are drawn to your energy and reputation.
- **Effortless attraction through your brand:** At this stage, your personal brand is fully aligned with who you are and what your business stands for. People trust your brand because it's a reflection of your authentic self and your unwavering commitment to your values and mission.
- **Influencing and inspiring others:** Your personal brand has become a source of influence, inspiring others in your field and beyond. People seek your guidance and want to collaborate with you because your brand is a beacon of success, confidence and purpose.

Magnetic business is where passion, purpose and financial abundance converge. Through the five phases of magnetism, you move from mastering yourself to aligning your business with your values, embodying the energy of success, evolving with growth and cultivating a magnetic aura that effortlessly attracts opportunities, wealth and influence. In this state, your business thrives because it's built on purpose, passion and intentionality, drawing in success, collaboration and expansion at every step.

MAGNETIC MONEY

Money is energy. It flows in and out of our lives, reflecting the stories, beliefs and emotions we hold about it. To become magnetic to money, you must first shift your mindset from scarcity and lack to abundance and gratitude. You can't attract wealth if you're holding on to beliefs that money is hard to come by, that you're unworthy of financial abundance or that you're not good with money. By stepping into the energy of abundance, expressing gratitude for what you have and what's on its way to you, and addressing deep-seated beliefs around money, you can attract wealth and financial success into your life.

Magnetic money isn't about hustling harder; it's about aligning yourself energetically with abundance. When you shift from negative states like fear, frustration or scarcity to gratitude, joy and expectation, you open yourself up to receive money with ease. Money flows where energy goes, and when you're in alignment with that flow, you start to experience financial freedom and wealth in ways you've never imagined.

Magnetic money – Phase 1: Self-mastery

For magnetic money, self-mastery is about understanding and transforming your relationship with money. Most of us carry deep-seated beliefs around money that we inherited from childhood or past experiences. These beliefs can create blocks that prevent us from attracting the financial abundance we desire.

- **Understanding your money story:** What was your first memory of money? For many, it was hearing phrases like 'We can't afford that' or 'Money is hard to come by'. Self-mastery in money requires that you examine your personal money story without judgement and identify the beliefs that have shaped your financial life. Are you carrying beliefs that money is evil, that rich people are greedy or that you have to work hard for every dollar?

- **Healing money wounds:** Just like emotional wounds, money wounds need healing. If you've grown up associating money with shame, guilt or lack, it's time to heal those feelings and create a new, empowered relationship with money. Self-mastery means doing the inner work to release those old beliefs and step into a mindset of abundance.
- **Shifting to abundance:** Once you've identified your money blocks, it's time to shift your mindset. Self-mastery in this phase involves training your brain to see money as an abundant resource, always available to you. Gratitude is a powerful tool here: being grateful for what you have now and what's on its way helps shift your energy into abundance.

Magnetic money – Phase 2: Defining your values

Just like in other areas of life, defining your values around money is crucial. What does wealth mean to you? Is it simply about accumulating money, or is it about freedom, security or being able to give back? When you define your values around money, you align your financial actions with a greater sense of purpose, making it easier to attract and manage wealth.

- **Aligning money with purpose:** Money is a tool, not the end goal. Defining your money values helps you connect your financial goals with your bigger purpose in life. Do you value financial freedom, philanthropy or creating generational wealth? Align your actions with these values, and money will flow to support your greater mission.
- **Value-based financial decisions:** When your financial decisions are rooted in your values, you stop spending money frivolously or feeling guilty about making money. Instead, you begin to view money as a resource to further your purpose and create impact.

You no longer chase money just for the sake of it; you attract it because it's aligned with your values and goals.

- **Abundance mindset:** Defining your money values also reinforces an abundance mindset. Instead of focusing on what you lack or what's missing, you focus on the opportunities and possibilities that money can bring when used in alignment with your values.

Magnetic money – Phase 3: Stepping into your alter she-go

In Phase 3, stepping into your alter she-go means embodying the version of yourself who is already financially abundant. This is where you stop worrying about money, stop stressing over bills and start behaving like someone who has already mastered their finances. You act, think and move as if you're already living in financial freedom.

- **Embodying financial success now:** Instead of waiting for your bank account to grow before you feel abundant, you begin to embody that energy now. You make decisions from a place of financial confidence and abundance, not fear or scarcity. Whether it's negotiating a higher salary, raising your rates or investing in yourself, you act as someone who knows their worth.
- **Attracting opportunities:** When you step into your alter she-go, you open yourself up to opportunities for wealth. Gone are the days when you're hesitant or doubtful when opportunities for financial growth present themselves – you seize them with confidence because you know you're worthy of success.
- **Gratitude and visualisation:** In this phase, you practise gratitude for the financial abundance that's already flowing to you. You visualise money coming into your life, not as a distant dream but as something that's already happening. This visualisation helps align your energy with wealth and opens you up to receive more.

Magnetic money – Phase 4: The evolution

The evolution phase in money is about shifting and evolving your financial mindset and habits. As you grow and expand, your relationship with money will change. This phase is about letting go of old patterns, upgrading your money habits and stepping into new levels of wealth.

- **Letting go of scarcity mindset:** As you evolve, you shed the scarcity mindset that once may have defined your relationship with money. You stop worrying about 'not having enough', and instead focus on the abundance that's available to you. This phase is about evolving into a mindset where money flows easily and effortlessly.
- **Upgrading your money habits:** Evolution in money also means upgrading your financial habits. You start making smarter decisions – investing in yourself, saving wisely and spending intentionally. You no longer waste money or fear making financial moves because you're grounded in an abundant mindset.
- **Facing challenges with grace:** Even in the realm of money, challenges will arise. In this phase, you learn to handle financial setbacks – whether it's unexpected expenses or market fluctuations – with grace and confidence. You trust that money will continue to flow, even in the face of obstacles.

Magnetic money – Phase 5: Magnetic aura

In Phase 5: Magnetic Aura, you reach a state in which money flows to you effortlessly. You're no longer stressed about finances because you've aligned your energy with abundance. At this stage, your relationship with money is healthy, prosperous and magnetic.

- **Effortless financial abundance:** Money flows to you because you're in a state of gratitude, alignment and abundance. You don't chase money anymore; it comes to you naturally because you've done the inner work to become magnetic to wealth. You're no longer operating from scarcity or fear.

- **Opportunities for wealth expansion:** In this phase, financial opportunities seem to appear out of nowhere, whether in the form of a lucrative deal, a business opportunity or a raise. Your magnetic energy attracts wealth in unexpected ways, and you're always open to receiving it.
- **Generosity and flow:** In this phase, you understand that the more you give, the more you receive. You're generous with your money because you know that it's always flowing back to you. You're in a constant cycle of giving, receiving and expanding your financial influence.

Magnetic money is about aligning with an energy of abundance, shifting from scarcity to gratitude and creating a healthy, prosperous relationship with money. Through the five phases of magnetism, you move from mastering your money beliefs to defining your financial values, embodying wealth, evolving your financial habits and reaching a state in which money flows effortlessly. In this state, you no longer chase money – money comes to you, and you attract wealth through your alignment, gratitude and energy.

THE POWER OF MAGNETISM IN ALL AREAS OF LIFE

Magnetism isn't just some feel-good concept – it's a force. A real, powerful force that, once you tap into it, changes everything. It's not just about personal growth; it's about shifting the energy in every area of your life. When you step into your magnetism, it doesn't just affect you – it creates a ripple that touches everyone around you. Your family. Your friends. Your colleagues. Even people you don't know yet. That's how big this is.

Money is a tool,
not the end goal.
Defining your money
values helps you connect
your financial goals
with your bigger
purpose in life.

The truth is, magnetism spreads. It's contagious. The way you show up, the energy you bring – it impacts the world around you. And when you evolve, guess what? The people in your orbit evolve too. Your magnetism elevates your life and everyone else's. You become the person who inspires others to grow, to rise and to step into their own power. But it starts with you.

The more you commit to this work, the stronger your energy gets. And when you keep doing the work, something shifts. You stop chasing. You stop hustling for things that should already be yours. Instead, you attract. Opportunities, money, success – they all start flowing to you because your energy pulls them in. That's the magic of magnetism.

But remember – this isn't a one-and-done thing. Magnetism is a lifelong practice. The deeper you go with the five phases, the more your life expands. Here's the kicker: it's not just about you. You've got the power to change lives. You've got the power to inspire, uplift and influence every single person you encounter. That's the real power of magnetism. When you embrace it fully, you don't just transform your life – you transform your entire world.

12

SIGNS THAT YOU'RE ON THE RIGHT TRACK

RIGHT TRACK
RIGHT TRACK

You've come this far, and that means you're already stepping into your magnetism. And you know that this journey isn't just about reading words on a page – it's about owning everything that *Becoming Magnetic* has laid out for you. If you've been applying these principles – really doing the work – you'll see yourself already moving in the right direction. When you fully commit to this process, you'll start seeing your magnetism take root in *all* areas of your life.

But let me remind you to prepare for something – this journey won't always feel easy.

When you truly decide to show up as the most potent, powerful and authentic version of yourself, things can get challenging. As you've seen, stepping into your magnetism requires internal work that some people won't understand, especially those who've known you long before you began this transformation. It's not all smooth sailing, and that's something you need to get ready for as you continue this journey.

TURBULENCE WARNING

I've always hated flying, and there was one flight from Sydney to Melbourne I remember well. It was pouring rain, and I was already dreading the take-off. It was dark, and the storm felt intense. Right before we left the ground, the pilot came on and calmly explained that it was going to be a rough take-off due to the weather, but that once we hit cruising altitude, we'd be above the storm and things would smooth out. (Don't we all love a communicative pilot?)

Now, I didn't feel any less nervous, but knowing what was coming and being told to expect turbulence actually helped me stay calm. It made me feel like *there's nothing wrong here, this is a part of the process.* It's the uncertainty that often makes things worse. I share this because stepping into your magnetism can be a bit like that flight: there's going to be turbulence. Things might feel rough at times, but that doesn't mean you're off course. It means you're right where you need to be, rising above the storm.

You've already committed to this work, and that's a big deal. But, as you keep going, you'll notice some things will feel harder before they get easier. This isn't a sign that you're failing; it's a sign that you're evolving. Challenges are often the best indicators that you're on the right track. You're growing, expanding and becoming magnetic – and yes, that can disrupt old patterns, relationships and ways of being.

But how do you know you're making progress? How can you tell that you're truly stepping into this new, magnetic version of yourself? While there's no meter to measure your magnetism, there are clear signs that show you're on the right path. Just as signs on the road guide you to your destination, there are signals in life that tell you you're aligning with your highest self.

In this final chapter, we'll go through those signs. Some of them might not look or feel like 'progress' at first glance, but trust me, they are. These signs will help you see the shifts happening within and around you as your magnetism grows. When things get challenging, when the turbulence hits, you'll be able to recognise that it's all part of the process – and that you're exactly where you need to be. Now it's time to land this plane.

Magnetism isn't about becoming someone new; it's about solidifying and crystallising what's already there, deep inside you.

YOU HAVE A STRONG SENSE OF SELF

One of the first signs that you're stepping into your magnetism is a stronger sense of self. Magnetism isn't about becoming someone new; it's about solidifying and crystallising what's already there, deep inside you. The work you've done – whether it's removing limiting beliefs, ditching the negative self-talk or facing uncomfortable truths – begins to strengthen your foundation. You'll notice that the pieces of yourself that felt shaky or uncertain now start to feel unshakable.

At first, the changes might feel subtle. You may not wake up one day suddenly transformed, but over time, you'll see the shifts. Maybe it's how you react in situations that would have previously thrown you off. Maybe it's how you start saying 'no' without apologising. Or maybe it's that you find yourself less affected by the opinions of others. These are the markers of a stronger self – a self that isn't bending to please others or reacting out of insecurity.

You're starting to recognise who you really are, and more importantly, who you aren't. That's the beauty of magnetism. It strips away the unnecessary, the false narratives, the masks we wear to fit in. What remains is the core of who you are – your essence. And that essence is solid, powerful and magnetic.

When you take yourself out of your comfort zone, this stronger sense of self becomes undeniable. It's in those moments when you stretch yourself – whether it's taking a risk, speaking up or stepping into new territory – that you start to realise what you're truly made of. You find new inner resources you didn't even know you had, because they've never been tested before. That's where the real growth happens. You dig deep, and you discover the strength, resilience and confidence that have been waiting for you all along.

You'll also notice that you stop second-guessing yourself so much. The constant internal debate – *Am I good enough? Will they like me?* – fades. Instead, you start trusting yourself more. You start moving with purpose, not hesitation. People-pleasing starts to dissolve, and you realise that you don't have to twist yourself into knots to make others happy. You are a piece of art and you're creating a masterpiece from your life – *and* you get to create yourself time and time again.

Reality check

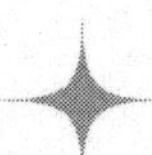

Here's the good news: this shift, this stronger sense of self, is proof that you're on the right track. If you've noticed yourself standing taller, feeling more secure or caring less about external validation, you're exactly where you need to be. It may not always feel easy, but the discomfort is a sign that you're growing. So, when those moments come when you feel tested or stretched, embrace them. They're not setbacks. They're signs of progress. You're building a version of yourself that is solid, resilient and magnetic, and that's something no one can take away from you. Keep going: this is just the beginning.

YOU PROTECT YOUR ENERGY AND SPACE

As you become more magnetic, your awareness of the energy exchange between yourself and others sharpens. You start to realise that not everyone deserves access to your energy. Your magnetism is always 'on' and every interaction – whether in person, over the phone, on social media or simply being in the same room – creates an energetic exchange. The stronger magnet always influences the weaker one, and this isn't about charisma or volume; it's about who's grounded, aligned and in control of their energy.

When you step into your magnetism, you begin to protect your energy with intention. You stop tolerating low-frequency interactions like gossip, negativity or drama. You realise that every person you let into your space can either elevate or drain you, and you're not willing to allow others to dilute your frequency. You understand that you become like the people you surround yourself with, not just through their words, but through their silent energy. This is why magnetic people are selective. They're careful with who they let in because they know their energy is precious, and they've worked hard to cultivate it.

It's not just about avoiding 'negative' people – it's about aligning with those who amplify your magnetism. You've stopped giving your time and energy to people or situations that pull you away from your purpose. You protect your space, choosing instead to surround yourself with those who vibrate at a high frequency and are in alignment with where you're going.

Reality check

If you find yourself being more intentional about who gets access to your energy, that's a clear sign you're on the right track. You're not being selfish – you're being wise. Protecting your space doesn't mean isolating yourself; it means preserving the energy you've worked hard to cultivate. You're elevating your life, and that means not everyone is going to come along for the ride. Keep guarding your energy. It's what will allow you to continue growing, thriving and staying in your magic.

YOUR CIRCLE WILL GET SMALLER

As you grow into your magnetism, one thing is inevitable – your circle will get smaller. This isn't a sign of loss, but of refinement. As you elevate your energy and step into your true power, you naturally become more discerning about who you allow into your inner circle. You start to see that not everyone is meant to stay, and that's perfectly fine.

The reality is, **not everyone will evolve with you**. As you level up, some friendships and relationships will feel misaligned, and they will begin to fade. You'll notice that the people who truly matter – the ones who celebrate your wins, stand by you in hard times and accept you as you are – will become more apparent. The rest? They may naturally fall away, and that's a good thing.

Quality over quantity is the mantra here. We often get caught up in the idea that we need to have a huge social circle to be validated but the truth is, the size of your circle doesn't matter. You need meaningful connections that support your growth and align with your values. The reality is that it's a privilege to have even three, four or five truly deep friendships. Most of us are lucky if we have one or two real friends who will ride or die with us through every season of life.

You'll find that the deeper you go into your magnetism, the more selective you'll become. The connections that survive this refinement process will be stronger, more authentic and more fulfilling.

This shift is not about shutting people out; it's about honouring your evolution. As your circle gets smaller, it will also become more powerful, because the people who remain are the ones who truly resonate with your journey. You no longer need to hold on to relationships out of habit, guilt or fear of being alone. You're ready to embrace the depth that comes with fewer, but far more meaningful, connections.

Reality check

If your circle is shrinking, don't see it as a loss – see it as growth. You're refining who has access to you, and that's a massive win. A smaller circle doesn't mean you're lacking; it means you're aligning with people who truly get you. Keep trusting the process. As your magnetism increases, so will the quality of the relationships in

your life. The right people will stick around, and the ones who aren't meant to stay will fall away. That's how you know you're levelling up.

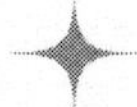

YOU SEE CHALLENGES AS LESSONS AND WELCOME THE GROWTH

When hard things happen now, you don't break. You know that no matter how difficult the challenge seems in the moment, you can handle it – just like you've handled everything before. Your resilience is your power. More than that, you've come to understand that every challenge is happening *for* you, not *to* you. There's always a lesson or a gift hidden in the hardship.

Now, don't get me wrong – when life throws something painful your way, you don't slap on a fake smile or try to use positive thinking to find your way out of it. You allow yourself to feel the emotions and deal with what comes. But once the storm passes, once you've had time to breathe, ground yourself and reflect, you see it with fresh eyes. You know that challenge is a teacher. You work through obstacles with a different lens now – one that sees growth as inevitable.

The result? You no longer crumble under the weight of difficulty. You're not defined by your hardships. You deal with them, heal from them and allow them to make you stronger. Every challenge becomes an opportunity to grow, and you've learnt to expect that hard things will come, but they no longer have the power to break you; now they MAKE you who you are.

Reality check

If you're finding yourself facing challenges with more grace, knowing deep down that each one holds a lesson, congratulations – you're on the right path. The world isn't always smooth sailing, but your resilience and perspective have shifted. You don't run from challenges; you meet them head on and trust that they're here to grow you. If this sounds like where you're at, you're more magnetic than you think.

YOU'RE TUNED INTO YOUR INTUITION

One of the clearest signs that you're stepping into your magnetism is when you start making decisions based on intuition rather than logic alone. Sure, you check the facts, weigh up the pros and cons, but at the end of the day, you lead with how your gut feels about it. You've built a deep sense of trust in yourself, and that inner guidance system – your intuition – becomes your compass.

When you're magnetic, you don't ignore those subtle gut feelings. You know they're there for a reason. Intuition isn't some airy-fairy concept; it's a powerful force that allows you to navigate the world in alignment with who you truly are. It's the voice that nudges you when something feels off, or lights up when something is exactly right for you. And when you've done the work to build self-confidence, that voice becomes loud and clear.

The stronger your magnetism, the more you trust your gut to lead you in the right direction. This doesn't mean you throw logic out the window – there's room for both. Magnetic people have learnt that, ultimately, their internal guidance system knows what's best. You're not second-guessing yourself anymore. You're tuned in, and you trust the decisions you make because *you trust yourself*.

This kind of decision-making is a game-changer. Instead of being influenced by external opinions or getting caught up in overthinking, you simply check in with yourself and ask, *How does this feel?* You know that your gut is the most reliable guide because it's rooted in your own energy, experience and self-awareness. The more you use it, the stronger it gets.

There's a sense of ease that comes with trusting your intuition. You're no longer paralysed by indecision or overly dependent on external validation. You've built a strong foundation of self-confidence, and that trust in yourself translates into action. When you listen to your gut, you're acting from a place of alignment, not fear or doubt. And that's where your power lies.

Reality check

If you're making decisions based on intuition and trusting your gut more than ever, you're on the right track. This is a sign of self-confidence and deep alignment. You've built trust with yourself, and that's not something everyone can say. Keep tuning into your inner guidance system – it's always going to lead you where you need to go. Trust that the more you listen to your gut, the more magnetic you'll become, because you're acting in alignment with your true self. Stay connected to that inner voice – it's your superpower.

YOU REPEL SOME PEOPLE

As you become more magnetic, you'll start both attracting and repelling people, and that's a powerful sign of growth. When you're standing in your power, people will naturally be drawn to you – but not everyone will be good for your energy. Some people will want to soak up your magnetism like it's fuel, but you need to be discerning about who gets access to your space. Letting go of the need to be liked by everyone is a crucial part of this process.

Many women feel uncomfortable with the idea of repelling people, but let me explain why this is something to celebrate. When someone is repelled by you, it's because you're standing fully in your authenticity. You're not for everyone, and you're not meant to be. The women I work with often feel pressure to be liked by everyone and to keep everyone happy, but here's the truth: you're not here to be one-size-fits-all vanilla. You're here to be your own unique flavour. The more you step into your magnetism, the more you'll find that those who don't align with you will naturally fall away – and that's exactly what you want.

Magnetism is about aligning with your internal joy. When you stop wasting energy on people who aren't right for you, you'll have more time to focus on what truly fulfils you. Be confident in who you are. Let those who resonate with your energy stay, and release the rest.

Reality check

Now, think about how you feel about the word 'repel'. Were you raised to believe you should be kind to everyone, liked by everyone and never make waves? Have you been taught to seek approval and validation from others? Do you get upset when someone criticises you? If so, this process may feel uncomfortable at first. But let me tell you, to truly attract the life you want, you're going to repel some people, and that's not just okay – it's necessary.

When the critics come, *you are doing it right!*

When the haters come, *you are doing it right!*

When the judgement comes, *you are doing it right!*

When you ruffle some feathers, *you are doing it right!*

When people talk about you behind your back, *you are doing it right!*

When they say, 'who does she think she is', *you are doing it right!*

Do not get discouraged, my friend: this is you doing it right.

YOU BECOME UNREALISTIC

When you fully step into your magnetism, you start attracting and accomplishing things that seem impossible to others. To some, you might even look delusional. Your point of attraction becomes so strong that it feels like everything you put your mind and energy to manifests into reality. You're not just wishing for it – you're pulling your future self into the now, acting as if what you desire is already done and you're taking real, tangible steps to make it happen.

Here is where you become a magician of the material world. You're working with the universe, the laws of attraction and your own energetic power, but you're also firmly grounded in action. You're mixing the 'woo' of manifesting with the real work required to bring those dreams into existence. To some people, you might look downright unrealistic, but that's their limitation, not yours. You're no longer bound by what others think is possible.

You're not just sitting around visualising – you're moving with intention, making decisions as if the future you want is already yours. You have a winner's mindset, and you believe – truly believe – that anything is possible for you. You refuse to listen to the naysayers, the people who want to limit your vision because they're stuck in their own limitations. You know deep down that there are no limits to what you can create, and you prove it every day by taking bold action.

This level of magnetism is powerful. You're not waiting for permission or validation – you're making things happen. And yes, you may seem unrealistic to those who don't get it, but you're okay with that. You're operating on a different frequency, where the impossible becomes possible. You see things others can't, and because of that, you accomplish what others won't.

And let me tell you something – even if you don't realise it yet, people are watching you. If you've got kids, they're seeing how you show up, how you dream big, how you chase the unthinkable. That's the next-level impact right there. You're not just changing your life – you're teaching those around you, especially the younger generation, that anything is possible. You're showing them what can happen when you refuse to be limited by fear, doubt or the opinions of others.

Reality check

If people are starting to call you unrealistic, take it as a compliment. It means you're on the right track. The truth is, the most magnetic people are the ones who see beyond what others think is possible.

You're not here to play small or stay inside someone else's box. You're here to break barriers and achieve what seems unthinkable. Keep mixing that manifesting power with real, grounded action, and watch as you continue to pull your future toward you. Don't let the opinions of others slow you down. Their limits don't apply to you. Stay focused, keep dreaming big and keep showing up as the magnetic, unstoppable force you are.

OTHER PEOPLE'S OPINIONS STOP MATTERING SO MUCH

One of the most liberating changes you'll notice when you step into your magnetism is that other people's opinions start to matter less. I don't just mean in a 'brush it off' kind of way – I mean truly, deeply, you stop caring what others think. You stop bending over backward to please everyone around you, and you certainly stop taking every comment or criticism personally.

This shift can happen in subtle or even extreme ways. You might start noticing that the people who are the most critical are often the ones who are the most bitter or hurt themselves. These people are often projecting their own insecurities onto you, mirroring their fears, self-doubt or pain in the form of judgement. So it literally has nothing to do with you; it's all their stuff. Their opinions say more about them than they ever do about you (this knowledge is a gift you received after doing loads of inner work). It's important to remember, they're usually not people you'd take advice from anyway – so why let their opinions weigh you down? They're not living your life, they're not in your shoes and they don't have to deal with the consequences of your decisions. You do.

What other people think of you is honestly none of your business.

For me, one of the biggest breakthroughs came when I realised that I'm the one hanging out with me every day. My opinion of myself has

You're operating on a different frequency, where the impossible becomes possible. You see things others can't, and because of that, you accomplish what others won't.

a far bigger impact on my life than anyone else's ever could. So why let the opinions of others dictate how I feel about myself? It's not their job to validate me or give me permission to live my life. It's mine.

This kind of liberation is true freedom. Once you start letting go of other people's opinions, it's like a weight has been lifted off your shoulders. One of the clearest signs that your magnetism is growing is when you stop giving a damn about what others think and start caring more about what you think.

You're not here to conquer the hearts of the world – no one can do that. As Byron Katie says, 'I'm a generous person. I allow people to think whatever they want about me.'

Reality check

If you find yourself caring less about what the world thinks and more about what you think, you're on the right track. If the opinions of keyboard warriors and random critics don't faze you anymore, but you still care about what your closest loved ones think, then you know you're on the right path. You've got your priorities straight, and your energy is focused where it should be – on building your life, your way.

YOU SET BOUNDARIES WITH TOXIC OR UNHEALTHY FAMILY MEMBERS

As we've learnt, magnetism isn't just about attracting the right people into your life – it's also about protecting your energy from the wrong ones, even when those people are family. This is an area I've become notorious for upholding because I know firsthand how crucial it is to set and maintain boundaries that honour your needs, as well as the wellbeing of your children, partner or household. Family relationships can be complicated, and while family can be a source of love and support, some can also be the source of significant stress and emotional drain.

Setting boundaries with family is one of the most powerful things you can do to protect your magnetism. Many of us feel a sense of obligation or guilt when it comes to family, thinking that because someone shares our blood, we owe them unlimited access to our time, energy or emotional space. But let me tell you – there is nothing magnetic about allowing toxic or unhealthy family members to have unrestricted access to your life.

I've experienced this personally with my own mother. While I love her deeply and we have a connection, I've also had to set some of my toughest boundaries with her. Without them, I would lose my joy, my energy, and often find myself knocked off course. I had to learn that just because someone is family that doesn't mean they get a free pass to disrupt my peace. Upholding boundaries is an act of self-love and self-respect, and it's necessary for protecting your energy.

Setting boundaries with family can be one of the hardest things to do because there's this ingrained sense of duty and expectation, or even cultural guilt. But hear me when I say: you don't owe anyone unlimited access to your life, especially if it leaves you feeling drained, angry or resentful. Boundaries are not just suggestions; they are lines you draw to protect your emotional, mental and physical wellbeing. And once those boundaries are set, they must be upheld with consequences – because without consequences, a boundary is just a preference.

This can look like saying 'no' to family holiday traditions that you've always felt obligated to attend, even though every time you leave feeling drained, triggered or even re-traumatised. It could mean distancing yourself from a family member who always criticises your choices, belittles your dreams or brings negativity into your space. Boundaries with family are about protecting yourself and creating space for the relationships that nurture you, not deplete you.

Reality check

If you've started setting and upholding boundaries with toxic or unhealthy family members, you're doing exactly what you need to protect your energy and preserve your magnetism. Don't feel guilty for prioritising your peace over someone else's expectations. Boundaries are essential, not just in relationships with strangers or acquaintances, but especially with family. By setting these limits, you're honouring yourself, and that's how you keep your vibe strong. Remember, it's not about cutting people out – it's about protecting what matters most: your energy, your wellbeing, your peace and your happiness. Keep standing firm. You deserve to feel safe and respected, no matter who the other person is.

YOU EMBRACE DISCOMFORT

One of the clearest signs that you're stepping into your magnetism is when you start embracing discomfort. Let's be real – whenever you step into new terrain, one of the first things you'll feel is discomfort. It's different from your usual. The energy is unfamiliar, and it shakes up your routine. That shaky, unsure feeling is completely normal, and it's actually a great sign. Why? Because discomfort means growth.

Think about it like starting a new job. No matter how great the job is, the first few weeks always feel awkward. You don't know the systems, the people or the culture. You ask a lot of questions because you're navigating new territory. It's the same when you start working with magnetism: it's new, and it's stretching you in ways you haven't been stretched before.

When you feel out of your comfort zone, that's exactly where you need to be. The growth zone isn't cosy or familiar. It's challenging, and that's the point. When you begin to hone in on your magnetism, things will feel uncomfortable. Magnets are powerful, and they attract and repel people, places and situations with force. Sometimes it happens so fast that you feel like you've been hit with a tidal wave of change. Opportunities, invitations and connections can come flooding in; if you're not ready for this, it can feel disorienting.

The truth is, as exciting as it is to manifest at lightning speed, it can also feel overwhelming. You might even question if you're ready for all the things you've been calling in. That's completely normal too. Discomfort is a natural part of the process when your life starts aligning with your magnetism. But here's the thing – discomfort means you're growing. If you stay too comfortable, nothing changes.

There's actually a sweet spot for discomfort, and that's where real growth happens. It's like a deep stretch – not so extreme that you feel like you're going to snap, but enough of a stretch that you're challenging yourself to expand. Too little discomfort means no growth, but the right amount pushes you forward without overwhelming you. That's where the magic happens.

When I did my TEDx Talk, it was a HUGE stretch for me. I spent years manifesting it, talking about it and visualising it, but when it finally happened, I still felt completely out of my comfort zone. There were moments when I doubted myself, questioned my ability to deliver, and felt like I was on very shaky ground. I am pretty sure my mouth has never felt so dry as it did when I finally delivered my talk on stage. But you know what? That discomfort was exactly what I needed to grow into the person who could stand on that stage and absolutely own it.

When you work with magnetism, you're going to feel discomfort. You're going to be stretched beyond what you thought was possible. This is a sign you're on the right track. As your magnetism increases, so does your capacity to handle discomfort. Confidence isn't created in your comfort zone. A sign you're on the right track is when you become more comfortable with being uncomfortable and your bandwidth for growth expands.

The internal changes you're making reflect the external changes happening in your life. When you stop making decisions out of fear and start using magnetism to manifest what you truly want, your comfort zone shifts. You start living boldly, daring to go for big dreams and expanding your willingness to take risks. It's a whole new way of living, and with it comes incredible results.

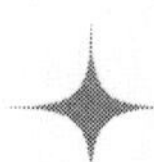

Reality check

Feeling uncomfortable? Good. That means you're growing. When you start embracing discomfort as part of the process, you're on the right track. If you're feeling stretched, challenged or even a little shaky, don't back down. Discomfort is a sign that you're stepping into new territory, and that's where real transformation happens. So, when the discomfort shows up, lean into it. It's proof that you're expanding, growing and becoming more magnetic by the day. Keep going – you're doing it right.

YOU NOTICE MORE SYNCHRONICITIES

When you increase your magnetism, you might start to notice something magical happening: synchronicities. These are meaningful coincidences that feel like the universe is orchestrating things just for you. It's like the puzzle pieces of your inner world and the outer world suddenly click together in ways you couldn't plan or predict. This is the universe conspiring in your favour; when you're magnetic, these moments happen more often.

Dr Carl Jung, the Swiss psychiatrist who introduced the idea of synchronicity, described it as the meaningful collision of the inner and outer worlds. He believed that things can happen in our external reality that perfectly align with what's going on internally, outside the laws of probability. It's that feeling you get when everything seems to be falling into place in ways that feel almost too perfect to be random.

One of Jung's most famous examples comes from his work with a highly rational, difficult patient. She wasn't making progress in therapy, and Jung knew she needed something unexpected, something that would break through the mental barriers she had built up. One day, she was recounting a dream in which she was given a piece of jewellery in the form of a golden scarab beetle. Just as she was sharing this, Jung heard a tapping at the window. When he opened it, he found a scarab beetle outside – an incredibly rare occurrence in that climate. Jung picked it up and handed it to the woman, saying, 'Here is your scarab.' That moment shattered her rigid, rational mind and became the breakthrough they needed. It was a synchronistic moment that completely shifted her reality.

But here's the thing: synchronicities aren't just for people like Jung or his patients. They happen to all of us, and when you're working with magnetism, you'll notice these events showing up more frequently. The universe responds to your energy, and as you strengthen your magnetic field, you'll start to see these meaningful coincidences unfolding around you. It's like you're finally tuned into a higher frequency, and everything starts aligning in ways you couldn't predict.

You'll become more aware of the subtle interplay between your intuition and the world around you. Those little nudges from the universe? They're not random. They're signs that you're on the right path, and the more you pay attention, the more you'll notice them.

I've had so many moments in my life where synchronicities led me to exactly where I needed to be. When I'm fully tuned in, aligned with my inner self and working with the forces of magnetism, these coincidences show up to guide me. And I know they will for you too.

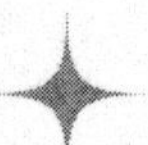

Reality check

If you're noticing more synchronicities – whether it's the perfect opportunity showing up out of nowhere, or a random event that aligns perfectly with what you've been thinking or feeling – take it as a sign. These moments aren't just coincidences; they're confirmations from the universe that you're on the right track. The more magnetic you become, the more you'll experience these synchronicities. Don't brush them off. Pay attention. They're the universe's way of showing you that you're aligned with your purpose and your power. Keep trusting the process, because the signs are all around you.

YOU EMBRACE AND CELEBRATE YOUR EVOLUTION

As you step into your magnetism, one thing becomes crystal clear: you are constantly evolving. Who you are today is not who you were six months ago, let alone ten years ago. Life is about growth, change and continual evolution. Every new experience, challenge and success shapes you into a newer version of yourself. The opinions people once had of you? They don't define you. Your evolution does.

You are not static. You're not a fixed, neatly defined version of yourself that the world can label and categorise. We evolve daily, whether we realise it or not. Think about it: your body is constantly changing. Your skin regenerates, your bones rebuild and your cells are replaced. Why would your mind, emotions or psyche stay the same? They don't. And thank goodness for that.

We were born to change, to adapt, to grow. That's who we are at our core. But here's the challenge – society wants us to stay the same. It wants us to be easy to understand, easy to define. People get comfortable with a version of you that they think they know. They want to put you in a box, slap a label on it and say, 'This is who you are.' But the reality? They're clinging to a ghost. They're holding onto a version of you that no longer exists.

You are not the same person who navigated last year's challenges or even yesterday's conversations. Every single day, life throws experiences

When you're anchored in the reality that you're always evolving, you realise that the opinions of others don't matter.

at us – some big, some small – that shape and mould us. The 'you' of yesterday is already history, and the 'you' of tomorrow? She's a mystery, even to yourself. That's the beauty of evolution.

So, when someone tries to box you in to a past version of yourself, remember: they're judging a single frame of the epic movie that is your life. It's like trying to understand the ocean by looking at one wave. They don't see the depth, the currents, the storms or the calm beneath the surface. Getting caught up in what other people think of you? It's a waste of time. They're clinging to a version of you that's long gone.

Your journey of evolution is yours alone. It's marked by victories, challenges, triumphs and transformations. Along the way, you'll shed countless versions of yourself – some with love; some with relief. Each one is a chapter in your story, but none of them is the finale. The beauty of your evolution is that it's never-ending. There's no finish line, no place where you 'arrive' and are done growing.

In embracing this, you unlock a profound freedom – the freedom to be unapologetically yourself, to explore your passions and to live without the weight of external judgement. When you're anchored in the reality that you're always evolving, you realise that the opinions of others don't matter. They're fleeting. Temporary. As insignificant as a passing shadow.

Magnetic people don't shy away from change; they embrace it. They let evolution guide them, shape them and carry them forward on their journey. They understand that change is not something to fear – it's something to celebrate. It's through this constant evolution that you grow, learn and become the fullest, most vibrant version of yourself.

The next time you find yourself worrying about what others think, remind yourself: they're judging someone who no longer exists.

You've already moved forward, transforming with every breath, every challenge and every dream. Your evolution is your power. It's what sets you apart, and it's what makes you magnetic.

Your evolution isn't just personal – it's your legacy. It's the mark you leave on the world, a testament to your journey of continuous self-discovery. So, keep evolving, keep changing – and let the world marvel at your transformation. You are the embodiment of constant growth, and that is a power few people will ever understand.

Reality check

If you're embracing your evolution and no longer holding on to past versions of yourself, you're exactly where you need to be. When you stop worrying about who you were and start celebrating who you're becoming, you're on the right track. Evolution is the key to your magnetism – it's what keeps you moving forward, breaking boundaries and growing into your fullest potential. Let the past stay in the past. You're not finished yet. You're evolving, and becoming a new version of yourself every day.

YOU DESERVE THE MAGNETISM YOU DESIRE

This journey isn't easy, but you didn't sign up for 'easy'. You signed up to be magnetic. And in order to do that, you have to cut loose anything that's holding you back from stepping into the woman you're meant to be. This is some of the most important work you'll ever do. It's the work that creates a life that is joyful, fulfilled and aligned. A life that's worth living – one where every day feels intentional, purposeful and real.

I can tell you firsthand, after living through hardship and trauma, and overcoming the odds, that the life of your dreams is absolutely 100 per cent available to you. But it's not going to fall into your lap.

You have to fight for it. You have to work for it. And you have to become the woman who is ready to live it. That's the key.

What you want – the confidence, the alignment, the purpose, the magnetism – it's not some distant dream. It's real, and it's meant for you. If you desire it, if it's in your heart, it's already on its way to you. The only thing standing between you and that life is becoming the version of yourself who is ready to claim it. That's where the work lies.

This isn't about waiting for permission, waiting for the right moment or hoping everything falls into place. It's about stepping into the woman who lives that magnetic life, right now. It's about making decisions, setting boundaries and showing up fully as her – every day. Because when you start to do that, the universe responds. Things begin to align, opportunities open up and you become a magnet for the life you've always wanted.

There's no better way to live than aligned, purposeful, confident, authentic and magnetic. I've seen it time and time again – not just in my own life, but in the lives of countless women I've worked with. The ones who commit to this work, who choose to show up as their most magnetic selves, are the ones who create lives they never thought possible. They're the ones who look back and say, 'It was worth every single challenge, every setback and every uncomfortable moment.'

So, as you continue on this journey, remember that magnetism is a choice. It's a commitment to show up fully as yourself, to let go of what no longer serves you and to trust that you deserve everything you desire. And let me be clear – you do deserve it. If you have the desire for more in your heart, it's because you were meant to have it. You don't need to shrink, hide or settle for less. You need to become the woman who knows, without a doubt, that her dreams are within reach, and the woman who steps into that truth every single day.

This is the life you've been waiting for, but more importantly:

It's the life that's been waiting for *you*.

Now it's time to ***be*** **MAGNETIC.**

THE MAGNETIC MANIFESTO: WORDS TO LIVE BY

When you're living in alignment with your true self, you naturally lift others up with your high-frequency vibes and positivity.

You've committed to the work. You've walked through the fire, faced the challenges and emerged stronger, more aligned and more magnetic than ever.

Now, it's time to claim everything that comes with that.

This manifesto is your declaration, a statement of who you are and what you stand for. It's a reminder that your magnetic power isn't just a phase or a fleeting moment – it's a way of living, a way of being.

This manifesto is your promise to yourself, a daily affirmation of the energy you're committed to radiating. It's not just words on a page – it's the embodiment of everything you've learnt, lived and cultivated on this journey.

This is your moment to step fully into the powerful, magnetic force that you are.

Own it.

Live it.

Breathe it.

And watch as the world around you aligns with the energy you've worked so hard to create.

THE MAGNETIC MANIFESTO

Full presence

I am showing up fully, knowing that how I do anything is how I do everything. Consistency in my energy is key across all areas of my life.

Values over goals

I pursue values, not just goals. I live by my virtues, and I don't chase after empty milestones that don't align with who I am or what I want.

Radical authenticity

I keep it real. Authenticity is non-negotiable – I'm not faking it, and I refuse to pretend. Who you see is who I am, always.

Radical responsibility

I own my actions, my energy, my words and my results. No excuses, no blaming others or myself. Radical responsibility is my compass, and I hold myself accountable to it, no matter what.

Magnetism is a lifestyle

I understand that magnetism is not a final destination. It's a way of being, an energy I carry with me daily. There's no place to 'arrive' at – it's who I am.

Meaningful connection

I seek deep and fulfilling connections with others. Magnetism thrives in co-creation with others, and I prioritise meaningful connections that align with my energy.

Energy management

I cultivate and protect my energy. I do what makes me feel good, ensuring that my energy is clean, flowing and free of leaks. I'm intentional about the energy I bring into every space.

Unapologetic self-expression

I am unapologetically myself, fully embracing who I am. I refuse to let the opinions of others dictate how I move through the world. #FWOT (f*** what others think).

Mindful company

I am selective about the company I keep. Not everyone gets access to my energy, and I guard my space with intention and care.

Claiming your space

I take up space. I show up, I stand up and I speak up – there is no shrinking here.

Committed to growth

I do the work. Growth is a priority, and I'm always evolving, learning and levelling up in every area of my life.

Humility is power

I remain humble. Humility is my superpower, and I balance self-awareness with emotional intelligence, keeping myself grounded in truth.

I am powerful. I am limitless. I am magnetic.

Magnetism isn't something you do; it's something you *are*.

And when you live by this ethos, you become an unstoppable force, attracting what you want and repelling what you don't.

BONUS SECTION: PRACTISING MAGNETISM

ELEVEN SECRETS TO ALIGNMENT, ENERGY AND MORE MAGNETISM

MORE MAGNETISM
MORE MAGNETISM

As we close *Becoming Magnetic*, I'd like to share some of my personal practices I do in order to keep myself in alignment and in my magnetism. I think of these as my personal manifesto and way of life, and I hope they support you on your journey to becoming magnetic.

I LIVE AN ALIGNED LIFE – LIKE, FOR REAL

LIVE and practise your values. Living an aligned life means being true to your values, not just when it's convenient, but also – especially – when no one is watching. This is where true integrity in your magnetism is born. These are the microskills I use:

- **Identifying my core values:** I take time to identify, reflect on and write my values down. Then I take a life inventory to ensure my actions, behaviours and long-term goals align with these values. This helps me pinpoint any changes that need to be made. See Chapter 6.
- **Self-reflection:** I like to spend time in reflection and remember what matters most to me. I write these things down and review them regularly. See Chapter 5.

I LOVE MY LIFE

This is a crucial component of living a magnetic life. I mean it: I love my damn life, I am happy and grateful and purposeful on a daily basis, and yes, even when sh*t sucks, I will (in time) find the gift in it. This state of contentment and joy comes from within and is literally the opposite of a scarcity mindset. When you genuinely enjoy your life, you exude a magnetic vibe and an energy of abundance.

- **Cultivate your own joy:** Find activities, hobbies and routines that bring you genuine happiness. Engage in activities that excite and energise you. Whether it's spending time with loved ones, pursuing a passion or simply enjoying being present in the small moments, prioritise joy in your life.

I MAKE TIME FOR EXERCISE AND MOVEMENT

This is one of the secrets to how I have so much energy. Exercise and movement are my fundamental go-tos. When I move my body, I have so much energy. I am happier and my day is so much better. Movement is life, and it provides me so many benefits. I literally work out now because it makes me a happier person. We are designed to move, and staying fluid and mobile is crucial. Regular exercise not only improves physical health but also boosts mental wellbeing by releasing endorphins and happy hormones. Movement keeps you flexible, agile and resilient, which are key attributes of a magnetic person.

- **Small steps:** If you're not used to exercising, or you're recovering from illness or injury, remember that something is better than nothing. A gentle five- or ten-minute walk or workout every day builds the habit, and as you get stronger and fitter, you can challenge yourself to do more.
- **Find something you enjoy:** Moving your body stops being a chore when it's something you like. Experiment with different things and see what you enjoy. If you hate running, for example, don't force yourself to run because you think you 'should'. Gentle yoga, going for a walk or putting on some music and dancing in the living room are just as good!

I HAVE GREAT RELATIONSHIPS

The older I get the more decisive I am with whom I allow into my inner circle and personal space. Surrounding yourself with positive, supportive people is vital. Great relationships are a source of joy, strength and inspiration. They create a cycle of good energy that enhances your magnetism. Building and maintaining these relationships requires effort, empathy and a willingness to invest time in others. Be selective about who you allow into your inner circle, ensuring they uplift and support you.

- **Quality over quantity:** Focus on building deep, meaningful relationships rather than trying to maintain numerous superficial connections. A few genuine friends are far more valuable than a large network of acquaintances.
- **Energy exchange:** Be mindful of the energy exchange in your relationships. Spend time with people who energise and inspire you, and distance yourself from those who drain your energy or bring negativity into your life.

I SPEND TIME ON THINGS THAT MAKE ME HAPPY

I love to engage in activities that bring me joy and fulfilment. Whether it's a hobby, spending time with loved ones or pursuing a passion, these activities recharge my spirit and enhance my magnetism. Doing what you love fills you with positive energy that radiates outward, making you more attractive to others.

- **Prioritise activities you love:** Make time for the hobbies and activities that bring you joy, whether that's travelling, pottery classes, yoga or op-shopping. Doing what you love regularly enhances your happiness and sense of fulfilment.
- **Engage with like-minded people:** Participate in activities that allow you to connect with others who share your interests.

Building a community around your hobbies can lead to new friendships and a deeper sense of belonging.

I BELIEVE IN ABUNDANT ENERGY

I believe that everything I want is coming. I don't know when or how exactly, but I BELIEVE it is on the way. I just do. I have felt this since I was a little girl and I focus my energy on what I desire (not on what I don't have). I'm abundant in the way I give to others, and generosity creates more generosity. When I meet someone I metaphorically give them an A+ in my class; I start them with the highest grade possible – they have to work their way down to D or F. Some people have trust issues or don't see the good in anyone, and you feel as if you have to break through a brick wall to get to them, meaning you have to PROVE your worth: that exhausts me. I am giving and open and abundant – and when I operate like this, I get this energy back in spades.

- **Believe that everything you want is coming your way:** Operating from a place of abundance means giving generously and expecting positive outcomes.
- **Start each interaction with an open heart and assume the best in others:** This mindset creates a reciprocal flow of positive energy, enhancing your magnetic presence.

I DO WORK THAT LIGHTS ME UP

For me, finding work that excites and inspires has been a game changer. If I'm not passionate about what I'm doing, it drains my energy and blocks my magnetism. I've learnt that I can't hate my work and expect to thrive – my environment and energy are too interconnected for that. So, I've made it a priority to either shift my approach to the work I do or seek out projects that genuinely ignite something in me.

When I'm passionate, it shows, and this enthusiasm naturally attracts opportunities and people who resonate with my vibe.

- **Take a good look at your work:** Is it giving you what you need? If it's not, what can you change? Can you ask for different projects, take classes, volunteer?
- **Look at your finances:** If you need to make radical changes in your work, it's a good idea to ensure you have an 'emergency fund' saved so you have a bit more freedom to manoeuvre.

I AM PRESENT WITH MY KIDS

Being fully present with your children (if you have them) can be one of the most fulfilling (and sometimes – let's be real – challenging) experiences in life. I have never been happier than when I look into their eyes. For a while there, at the start of building my business, I struggled to be present. My husband and I made arrangements so I could lean into work and he could support them, but as soon as I realised that time was ticking and the things all parents with older kids tell you are true (they grow so fast) I started to prioritise PRESENCE. I'm still a boss: I get on my phone, work from home at times, do emails, but when I am with them, I am *with* them, and I feel as though I have pressed the slo-mo button on time. Presence has been the best thing I could give myself, as they are the greatest gifts from the universe. They keep me young. They are so funny; they have interesting questions, stories and perspectives; they go deep and they challenge us on so many levels. Children and my love for them definitely impacts how magnetic I am. This presence not only strengthens your bond but also enhances your overall magnetism. The joy and love you share with your kids and your family becomes a source of powerful, positive energy they carry into their lives and future.

- **Put your phone away:** Be as present with your kids as you are with others.
- **Help your kids co-regulate their emotions:** When they're upset, don't try to talk them out of it. Use the active-listening skills we learnt about in Chapter 7.

I PRACTISE GRATITUDE DAILY

And I mean daily. I have rewired my brain to see the good in EVERYTHING. Every night when I go to bed, I take a moment to breathe my life in, to be grateful for all of it – each moment, my children, my husband, my clients, my life, the friends I have, my health, my business. All of it matters, and every night I go to bed with a gratitude attack, my heart fills with oxytocin and I feel deep love for my life and for who I have become. I have this deep exhale, internal smile, OMG-pinch-me type of emotion come over me at night, and it's so nice to feel this, to cultivate this. I think it feels like the opposite of fear. It's so amazing and electric – and I have that feeling before bed each night. I feel alive, purposeful, tuned in and enthusiastic about life.

- **Cultivate a daily gratitude practice:** Keeping a gratitude journal is a great way to do this. Focus on the positives in your life, no matter how small. Gratitude shifts your perspective, making you more optimistic and resilient, and magnetically attracts good things into your life. Focus on what IS working well, on what you DO want, on where you are going. When you step into gratitude, it's the energy of manifestation – you are grateful for all the goodness that's on its way to you.
- **Tell someone why you are grateful for them:** They will love to hear it!

I PRIORITISE GOAL SETTING AND PLANNING

This is a must for me, as I want to live with purpose and intention. At the end of every year, Hamish and I do a very deep intention-setting and goal-setting full-day workshop together, where we map out the year to come. We meet regularly as a couple, as a family and as business partners with our team, constantly checking in on where we are headed, if we're on track or if we need to readjust. We also do a ten-year plan every three to five years to map out things well in advance. This allows us to set long-term goals and visions for the future that align with our core values, which help with knowing what we want to manifest, attract and magnetise. Setting clear goals and planning your future helps you make it real.

- **Long-term plans:** Try journalling a ten-year plan, then breaking it down into smaller steps. What's your five-year plan? What's your plan for the year ahead?
- **Regularly review and adjust:** That way, your goals stay aligned with your vision. This proactive approach keeps you focused and motivated, enhancing your magnetic presence. Goal-setting is not just about achieving milestones but about creating a life map.

BOUNDARIES

Repeat after me: a boundary is not a preference. I once interviewed someone on my podcast who said this to me, and OMG, it was a game-changer. The reality is that boundaries are 100 per cent necessary for every single one of us to have.

- **Remember, boundaries are for you, not the other person.** You can't control how others behave, but you can control how you respond. If they won't respect your boundary, walk away.

- **Some people will take your boundaries personally and that's okay.** Let them have their response, but don't get pulled into trying to make them feel better.

These are the steps I live by. They have supported me over the years to become discerning, to know who I am and to notice what's best for ME. They may not all resonate with you, but I want you to find the ones that do, and I want you to see how you CAN become magnetic. By incorporating these practices into your daily life, you can step into your full power, without apology. This IS available for you right now. No, it won't happen overnight, but it *will* happen, and the more you commit to tangible actions, the closer to your magnetic power you will become. Each step will enhance your confidence, build deeper connections and support you to radiate positive, empowered energy. Becoming magnetic is a journey, and it's already in you. Practise these skills consistently, and over time, you will transform into the highest version of yourself.

RESOURCES AND NEXT STEPS

You know that you are enough, exactly as you are. You attract effortlessly because you're aligned with who you truly are and what you deserve.

If you've enjoyed *Becoming Magnetic* and want to dive deeper into this journey, I invite you to explore more ways to work with me and continue your transformation. Head to becomingmagnetic.com.au for free resources, programs and additional learning tools designed to help you step further into your magnetism. Whether you're looking for more insights, interactive courses or personalised coaching, you'll find it all there.

For those of you who have purchased *Becoming Magnetic*, you'll also get access to *Becoming Magnetic: The Private Podcast*! This exclusive podcast series dives even deeper into the concepts from the book, giving you actionable steps and insights to ignite your magnetism right away. Head to becomingmagnetic.com.au and enter your order number, and the podcast will come to you via email along with *The Ultimate Magnetism Playbook* free download!

For live events, workshops and opportunities to work with me directly, please visit thequeenofconfidence.com. It's the perfect place to connect with a community of women on the same path to owning their space and stepping into their power.

Let's connect on socials! Follow me across all the socials to receive daily doses of confidence, empowerment and real talk. And be sure to tag me when sharing your biggest insights from *Becoming Magnetic*:

@thequeenofconfidence
The Queen of Confidence
Erika Cramer
The Queen of Confidence Channel
and check out my podcast *The Confidence Chronicles*
on all major platforms!

This journey doesn't stop here. Let's keep doing the work – together.

TO GET IMMEDIATE SUPPORT WITH MENTAL WELLBEING

For adults

Lifeline, 13 11 14, lifeline.org.au. Anyone across Australia experiencing a personal crisis or thinking about suicide can call Lifeline.

Suicide Call Back Service, 1300 659 467, suicidecallbackservice.org.au. A free nationwide service providing 24/7 phone and online counselling to people affected by suicide.

Beyond Blue, 1300 22 4636, beyondblue.org.au. Mental health support services for anxiety, depression and suicide. You can visit the site for general information and advice, call the helpline or chat with a counsellor online. NewAccess (currently only available in New South Wales and Queensland) is a confidential, guided six-session mental health coaching program for anyone feeling stressed or overwhelmed about everyday life issues. It is free of charge and no GP referral is required. Visit beyondblue.org.au/get-support/newaccess-mental-health-coaching

Relationships Australia, 1300 364 277, relationships.org.au. Relationship support services for individuals, families and communities.

MensLine Australia, 1300 78 99 78, mensline.org.au. Relationship advice and mental health support for men.

Healthdirect, healthdirect.gov.au/mental-health-where-to-get-help. Government website with advice on where and how to get help and advice about mental health.

For young people

Kids Helpline, 1800 551 800, kidshelpline.com.au. Free support and talking through problems on any topic for people aged 5–25. Everything discussed is private and confidential – and you can remain anonymous.

headspace, 1800 650 890, headspace.org.au. A site for young people looking for information about mental ill-health, and for people who want advice on supporting young people struggling with their mental health.

ReachOut, au.reachout.com. A safe place to chat anonymously, get judgement-free support and build the resilience to manage challenges now and in the future.

TO WATCH

The Shadow Effect, written by Debbie Ford, directed by Scott Cervine, 2009, thefordinstitute.com/the-shadow-effect-movie/

Finding Joe, written and directed by Patrick Takaya Solomon, 2011

The Shift, Dr Wayne Dyer, discover.hayhouse.com/theshift-movie/

Inside Out (parts 1 and 2) – great for kids!

my TEDx talk on *Radical Responsibility*, youtube.com/watch?v=L3RENEfxVEc

Cuddy, Amy, *Your Body Language Shapes Who You Are*, TedX talk, ed.ted.com/lessons/your-body-language-shapes-who-you-are-amy-cuddy

Knowles, Beyoncé, 'The first time I felt something else come into me!', *BET Presents Beyoncé*, 4 April 2011, www.youtube.com/watch?app=desktop&v=BtTlFW9_sTI

TO LISTEN

Winfrey, Oprah and Eckhart Tolle, *A New Earth: Awakening to Your Life's Purpose*, podcast, OWN, www.oprah.com/own-podcasts/a-new-earth-awakening-to-your-lifes-purpose-chapter-1_3

This is a chapter-by-chapter breakdown series, with Q&As all about the book.

Check out my alter she-go playlist on Spotify:

My podcast *The Confidence Chronicles* is all about empowering women to create self-confidence, to step up and go for what they truly desire. Here's a selection of episodes on some of the topics covered in *Becoming Magnetic*:

Speaking up

This is a five-minute coaching session for right before you need to have a difficult conversation. 'Play me when you need to have a difficult conversation':

In this episode I invite you to confidently approach conflict and give you some tips on how to do so. 'Confidently dealing with conflict':

How are you expected to experience true growth and change without communication? This episode will help you to achieve the clarity that only comes from real talk. 'Life-changing conversations you're missing out on':

Friendships

As we change and shift so will friendships, and sometimes we have to let some friends go. This episode will equip you with actions steps and insights to help you navigate friendships when things get tricky. 'When friendships get tricky':

Picking up other people's energies

If you're sensitive to other people's energies, this podcast will supply the tools to thrive even when spending time with energy vampires. 'Picking up other people's energies':

Helping your kids be more confident

If you want to become more present and attuned to your children's needs, this episode is for you. 'Helping your kids be more confident':

Helping your kids through anxiety and worry

Magnetic parenting includes developing the ability to support our children when they are going through tough times. 'Helping your kids through anxiety and worry':

The circles of truth exercise (see Chapter 5)

In this episode I share one of the most transformative exercises I have ever done to get unstuck, for you to follow and apply in your own life: 'The exercise that changed everything for me':

Reframing impostor syndrome

In this episode I offer support so you can normalise feeling scared, doubtful and uncertain while pursuing your goals. 'Reframing impostor syndrome':

Magnetic business

My four hundredth episode (!) and one packed with advice on achieving success in your career. 'How to become the queen B of you industry':

Magnetic money

If you have struggled with your money mindset or negative money stories in the past, this episode will be a game changer. 'The number one money mindset hack that changed my life':

Moving through an identity shift

As we learn, grow, evolve and gain wisdom, who we know ourselves to be will come into question, and that can be a lot to deal with. 'Who am I? How to deal with an identity shift':

TO BROWSE

Gary Vaynerchuk, garyvaynerchuk.com/attention

MarthaBeck, marthabeck.com

Unlimited Dr Joe Dispenza, drjoedispenza.com/dr-joes-blog/tuning-in-with-your-heart-creating-your-future

TO READ

Cramer, Erika, *Confidence Feels Like Sh*t*, Dean Publishing, Mount Macedon, 2020.

Campbell, Joseph, *The Hero with a Thousand Faces*, New World Library, Novato, CA, 2012.

Carnegie, Dale, *How to Win Friends and Influence People*, Pocket Books, New York, NY, 1998.

Dispenza, Joe, *Breaking the Habit of Being Yourself: How to Lose Your Mind and Create a New One*, Hay House, Sydney, 2012.

Dyer, Wayne, *Happiness is The Way*, Hay House, Carlsbad, CA, 2020.

Dyer, Wayne, *Change Your Thoughts, Change Your Life*, Hay House, Carlsbad, CA, 2007.

Herman, Todd, *The Alter Ego Effect: The Power of Secret Identities to Change Your Life*, Harper Business, New York, 2019.

Katie, Byron, with Stephen Mitchell, *Loving What Is: How Four Questions Can Change Your Life*, Rider, London, 2002.

Murdock, Maureen, *The Heroine's Journey*, Shambhala Publications, Boulder, CO, 2010.

Singer, Michael A., *The Untethered Soul*, New Harbinger Productions, Oakland, CA, 2007.

Tolle, Eckhart, *A New Earth: Awakening to Your Life's Purpose*, Michael Joseph, London, 2018.

TO FIND THE IN-DEPTH RESEARCH

Adam, Hajo, and Adam D. Galinsky, 'Enclothed Cognition', Journal of Experimental Psychology, vol. 48, no. 4, July 2012, pp. 918–25, www.sciencedirect.com/science/article/abs/pii/S0022103112000200?via%3Dihub

Burleson, K.O and G.E. Schwartz, 'Cardiac torsion and electromagnetic fields: the cardiac bioinformation hypothesis', *Med Hypotheses*, vol 64, 2005, pubmed.ncbi.nlm.nih.gov/15823696/

Clough, Sharice, and Melissa C. Duff, 'The Role of Gesture in Communication and Cognition: Implications for Understanding and Treating Neurogenic Communication Disorders', *Frontiers in Human Neuroscience*, vol. 14, August 2020, www.frontiersin.org/journals/human-neuroscience/articles/10.3389/fnhum.2020.00323/full

Cohen, D., 'Magnetic fields around the torso: production by electrical activity of the human heart', *Science*, vol 5, May 1967, pubmed.ncbi.nlm.nih.gov/6023659/

Gustafson, Craig, 'Bruce Lipton, PhD: The jump from cell culture to consciousness', *Integrative Medicine: A Clinician's Journal*, vol 16, December 2017, pmc.ncbi.nlm.nih.gov/articles/PMC6438088/

HeartMath Institute, *Science of the Human Heart:An Overview of Research Conducted by the HeartMath Institute*, n.d., www.heartmath.org/research/

May, Kate Torgovnick, 'Some Examples of How Power Posing Can Actually Boost Your Confidence', *TEDBlog*, 1 October 2012, blog.ted.com/10-examples-of-how-power-posing-can-work-to-boost-your-confidence

National Marriage Project, 'Reports', n.d., nationalmarriageproject.org/reports

Paulise, Luciana,'75% of Women Executives Experience Imposter Syndrome in the Workplace', 3 August 2023, www.forbes.com/sites/lucianapaulise/2023/03/08/75-of-women-executives-experience-imposter-syndrome-in-the-workplace/

Roth, Bradley., 'Biomagnetism: The First Sixty Years', *Sensors*, vol 23, 23 Apr 2023, pmc.ncbi.nlm.nih.gov/articles/PMC10181075/

Stanford WELL for Life, med.stanford.edu/wellforlife/research/stanford-well-for-life.html

Strader, Samantha, '3 Workplace Trends and Takeaways from Gallup's 2023 Report', 25 July 2023, *Padilla*, padillaco.com/insights/3-workplace-trends-and-takeaways-from-gallups-2023-report/

Walter, Linda, 'Hypnotherapy and its Benefits for Autoimmune Disease', *Psychology Today*, 21 June 2017, www.psychologytoday.com/au/blog/life-without-anxiety/201706/hypnotherapy-and-its-benefits-autoimmune-disease

Whitford, Danielle Owen, 'The Power of Poses', Pioneera, pioneera.com/content/blog/power-poses

ACKNOWLEDGEMENTS

Wow. Writing a book takes a village, but writing a *second* book? That takes an entire community showing up with even more love, support and dedication. This one took every ounce of me to write. My first, *Confidence Feels Like Sh*t*, was born during the wild days of the 2020 pandemic – actually the perfect circumstances for writing. But *Becoming Magnetic*? This journey was something else entirely. From signing the contract in December 2023 to submitting my first draft, so much happened in between. It was my biggest year in business, with more travel than ever and the added challenge of caring for my sick mom back home in the States. This book came with me everywhere, and there were many late nights, early mornings and days surrounded by the love and chaos of my young family. I wrote down some parts, spoke others and edited on countless airplanes. And there's no way I could have done ANY of this without the incredible team and support system around me.

To my husband, Hamish, my rock, my in-house editor, my everything – thank you for protecting my energy, my time and my space. You held down the fort with our two boys, our team and our clients, making it possible for me to bring this book to life. Your unwavering dedication to our vision, mission and impact means the world to me. I could never thank you enough for how much you have helped me become the woman I am. Thank you for your encouragement, patience, brilliance and love. You know your wife is a bit loca but WE DID IT, BABE!

To my boys – thank you for showing your mother so much love and encouragement. I know there were many days, nights and weekends with mami at the computer in the kitchen. Both of you were so gracious, curious and proud of me. You've shown me how important the work in this book truly is and I couldn't be prouder of the magnetic and confident boys you are. May you continue to stand in your authentic power. I am so happy I get to be your mom. I love you both dearly.

To Nicki, Jacqui and my TQOC team. Ha! Never a freaking dull moment, hey? Thank you for supporting me to get this book, the content and collateral out into the world. The designs, the graphics, the magnetic merch – none of it could have come to life as it has without you. Thank you for caring about this book just as much as I do.

To the amazing Nina, thank you for trusting us and walking into our retreat with the readiness to heal and release the things that no longer served you. Thank you for doing the work and being the example of what is possible for so many women out there. Your dedication to the inner work and pushing through your discomfort is not only inspiring but it will also be life-changing for so many who read your story in this book.

To my clients past and present, your relentless drive and commitment to growth have been my reason for writing. I am honoured to be part of your journey. Your bravery and resilience keep me going.

To my sisters, my homegirls, the beautiful women in my life who guided and supported me through the writing of *Becoming Magnetic*, 'thank you' doesn't cut it. Your support served me more than you'll ever know.

To my online community and podcast listeners, thank you for following me, for tuning into my show, for messaging me, emailing me and allowing me into your world. I know there are so many people pulling for your attention online and the fact that you choose to follow and connect with me is an unbelievable honour. I hope you know how much it means to me. Thank you very much.

Penguin Random House Australia team, you are phenomenal! Izzy, your insight and dedication made this book what it is. Clive, you've been there for every question and concern, and I'm beyond grateful. To Kit, Lily, Madi, Isabelle, Veronica and the entire Penguin crew, THANK YOU. Your care and attention to detail made this book shine.

And I'm going to thank me for believing in me. I am proud of myself for moving through some of the hardest personal and professional challenges while writing *Becoming Magnetic*. This book taught me about resilience, about celebrating wins and about asking for help, even when I thought I didn't need it.

Finally, thank YOU, the one reading this. Whether you've been on this journey with me or you're just discovering my work, thank you for trusting me to guide you through this real, raw and sometimes uncomfortable AF journey to becoming magnetic. You are the reason I do what I do. Please promise me you'll give this work a go. Dive deep into self-mastery and commit to evolving into the masterpiece that is YOU.

And when you're ready, reach out. Tell me all about the incredible things you create, the manifestations you bring to life and the impact this journey has on you and on those you love.

Thank you, from the bottom of my heart.

Here's to you becoming MAGNETIC.

Powered by
Penguin